Understanding Assessment

Understanding Assessment provides a timely discussion of the debates concerning assessment in schools and colleges. The book provides an overview of assessment and adopts a pragmatic approach in recognising the value of different forms and purposes of evaluation. The book looks at the 'examinations industry', the technicalities of external examining and the financial implications of assessment. The authors then make a strong case for formative classroom assessment, arguing that in the current system external testing is over emphasised. They explore both external and internal classroom assessment, which they characterise as conflicting cultures of assessment in education. In a detailed case study of teacher assessment they show how these two cultures can be reconciled.

David Lambert is Reader in Education at the University of London Institute of Education. He previously taught in secondary comprehensive schools and is currently involved in teacher education at PGCE and Masters levels. His main research interests are in the fields of assessment, values education and text books.

David Lines is currently a Lecturer in Education, also at the Institute of Education. He has worked as a Chief Examiner for two examination boards. He is a Subject Leader (Business and Education) in the PGCE programme and he is an Associate of the International Centre for Research on Assessment.

Key Issues in Teaching and Learning
Series Editor: Alex Moore

Key Issues in Teaching and Learning is aimed at student teachers, teacher trainers and inservice teachers. Each book focusses on the central issues around a particular topic supported by examples of good practice with suggestions for further reading. These accessible books will help students and teachers to explore and understand critical issues in ways that are challenging, that invite reappraisals of current practices and that provide appropriate links between theory and practice.

Teaching and Learning: Pedagogy, Curriculum and Culture
Alex Moore

Reading Educational Research and Policy
David Scott

Understanding Assessment: Purposes, Perceptions, Practice
David Lambert and David Lines

Understanding Schools and Schooling
Clyde Chitty

Understanding Assessment

Purposes, Perceptions, Practice

David Lambert and David Lines

London and New York

First published 2000 by RoutledgeFalmer
11 New Fetter Lane, London EC4P 4EE

Simultaneously published in the USA and Canada
by RoutledgeFalmer
29 West 35th Street, New York, NY 10001

RoutledgeFalmer is an imprint of the Taylor & Francis Group

© 2000 David Lambert and David Lines

Typeset in Goudy by
Florence Production Ltd, Stoodleigh, Devon

Printed and bound in Great Britain by
TJ International Ltd, Padstow, Cornwall

British Library Cataloguing in Publication Data
A catalogue record for this book is available from the British Library

Library of Congress Cataloging in Publication Data
A catalogue record for this book has been requested

ISBN 0–7507–0992–8

Contents

Figures

Series Editor's Preface

THE KEY ISSUES IN TEACHING AND LEARNING SERIES

Understanding Assessment: Purposes, Perceptions, Practice is one of five titles in the series *Key Issues in Teaching and Learning*, each written by an acknowledged expert or experts in their field. Other volumes explore issues of *Teaching and Learning*, *Understanding Schools and Schooling*, and *Reading Educational Research and Policy*. The books are intended primarily for beginner and newly or recently qualified teachers, but will also be of interest to more experienced teachers attending MA or Professional Development Courses or simply interested in revisiting issues of theory and practice within an ever-changing educational context. *Understanding Assessment* will also prove an invaluable reference book for a wide range of professional and lay readers involved in compulsory education, including school governors and school inspectors.

TEACHING AND THEORISING

There is currently no shortage of books about teaching, offering what must sometimes seem a bewildering choice. Many of these books fall into the 'how-to' category, offering practical tips and advice for teachers on a range of matters such as planning for students' learning, managing classroom behaviour, and marking and assessing students' work. Such books have proved very successful over the years, providing beginner-teachers in particular with much of the support and reassurance they need to help them through their early experiences of classroom life, as well as offering useful advice on how to make teaching maximally effective. Increasingly, such books focus on sets of teacher competences – more recently linked to sets of standards – laid down, in the UK, by the Office for Standards in Education (OFSTED) and the Teacher Training Agency (TTA) (see, for instance, OFSTED and TTA 1996). Other books have focused on the teacher's need to be reflective and reflexive (e.g. Schon 1983, 1987; Valli 1992; Elliott 1993; Loughran 1996). These books may still be described as 'advice books', but the advice is of a different kind, tending to encourage the teacher to think more about human relationships in the teaching–learning situation and on the ways in which teaching styles connect to models of learning and learning development.

More predominantly theoretical books about teaching for teachers are perhaps in shorter supply, and those that do exist often address issues in decontextualised ways or in very general terms that do not immediately speak to classroom practitioners or take account of their particular academic backgrounds. These is, furthermore, evidence that, partly through time constraints, some of the most profound works on sociological educational theory are very little read or discussed on teacher training courses (Moore and Edwards 2000), while the work of developmental psychologists, which used to feature very prominently on PGCE and BAEd courses, has become increasingly marginalised through a growing emphasis on issues of practical discipline, lesson planning, and meeting National Curriculum requirements.

Understanding Assessment, like the other books in this series, seeks to address this imbalance by exploring with teachers a wide range of relevant educational *theory*, rooting this in classroom experience in a way that encourages interrogation and debate, and presenting it in a language that is immediately accessible. These books do not ignore or seek to devalue current trends in educational practice and policy. Rather, they strive to provide readers with the knowledge and skills they will need in order to address and respond to these and other educational discourses in critical, well-informed ways that will enhance both their teaching and their job satisfaction.

With this aim in mind, *Understanding Assessment* – as the title implies – does not tell readers exactly how they should assess; nor does it seek to provide its readers with pre-packaged, ready-made theory. Rather, it seeks to present issues, questions and dilemmas *about* assessment processes and practices, to which it invites teachers and student teachers to formulate their own responses through guided activities, through discussions with colleagues, through further reading, and, most importantly, through refining their own educational theory in terms of what articulates best with or most effectively challenges their existing philosophies and practice.

Structure and content of the book

The book falls broadly into four parts, comprising:

- an introductory overview of assessment and an introduction to *key concepts* (Chapters 1 and 2);
- a section dealing with various aspects of *external assessment* (Chapters 3 to 6);
- a section that looks at issues of *classroom assessment* (Chapters 7 to 9); and
- a concluding section (Chapters 10 and 11) which summarises the book's central arguments and illustrates how teachers can reconcile what the authors call the 'two cultures' of assessment (external, summative assessment and classroom-based, formative assessment) through their own informed, professional practice.

Each chapter starts with a helpful summary, while lists of key points, suggestions for further reading, and ideas for further consideration are provided at appropriate points throughout the text. While the readings and activities can be undertaken independently, they are designed so that they can also be completed collaboratively, providing the basis for small-group discussions on BAEd, PGCE, MA and Professional Development courses for teachers. As with other volumes in the *Key Issues in Teaching and Learning* series, boxes have been used in the body of the text to highlight particularly important points or useful summaries.

A PRAGMATIC APPROACH TO ASSESSMENT ISSUES AND PRACTICES

As the authors recognise, assessment is a contentious issue, often leading to intense and not always helpful debates in which protagonists may find it difficult to move from entrenched and polarised positions. Without abandoning their own ideological positionings, Lines and Lambert manage to adopt an approach to their topic that is both pragmatic and critical, and that enables them to engage sensitively and constructively with the sorts of 'real world' concerns and dilemmas faced by practising teachers. This involves the authors taking us on an informative and illuminating journey through a fascinating and sometimes discomforting terrain that includes:

- thought-provoking considerations of the differences between – and rationales behind – formative and summative assessment;
- critical explorations of what is sometimes referred to as 'the examinations industry'; and
- elaborations of the possible effects of formative and summative assessment on students' work and attitudes *and* on teachers' practice.

In summary, *Understanding Assessment* provides an invaluable introduction to thinking about current issues in educational assessment and in formulating informed and principled critiques of dominant discourses in this important area of teachers' work. It is also, however, an invaluable tool for helping us – however experienced or inexperienced we may think we are – to interrogate, to make sense of and to modify our own assessment practices within a properly understood context of what is possible and what is desirable.

REFERENCES

Elliott, J. (1993) 'The relationship between "understanding" and "developing" teachers' thinking' in J. Elliott (ed.) *Reconstructing Teacher Education*, London: Falmer Press.
Loughran, J. (1996) *Developing Reflective Practice: Learning About Teaching and Learning Through Modelling*, London: Falmer Press.

Moore, A. and Edwards, G. (2000) 'Compliance, Resistance and Pragmatism in Pedagogic Identities' paper presented at the Annual Conference of the American Educational Research Association, New Orleans, 24–28 April 2000.

OFSTED/TTA (Office for Standards in Education/Teacher Training Agency) (1996) *Framework for the Assessment of Quality and Standards in Initial Teacher Training 1996/7*, London: OFSTED.

Schon, D. A. (1983) *The Reflective Practitioner: How the Professionals Think in Action*, New York: Basic Books.

Schon, D. A. (1987) *Educating the Reflective Practitioner*, San Francisco: Jossey-Bass.

Valli, L. (ed.) (1992) *Reflective Teacher Education*, New York: State University of New York Press.

1 Assessment in Education: Making Connections

INTRODUCTION: AN OVERVIEW OF ASSESSMENT

The first two chapters together form an introduction to the book as a whole. Although we lay down a number of definitions of key terms that underpin the book, just as important, in our view, is our theme 'making connections'. By this we want to promote from the start an understanding that the field of assessment in education is large, complex and, most importantly, interconnected. This is an ambitious aim for an introduction. Some readers may wish to return to it after delving into the main text in order to 'cherry-pick' its contents to meet their immediate questions or concerns – be they about marking, teacher assessment, GNVQs, GCSE or another specific topic within the large field we wish to consider. Whether the first two chapters are read now, or left until later, we hope that they serve as a useful guide to the territory we refer to as assessment in education.

WHAT IS ASSESSMENT?

It is important to realise that this book is not designed solely to be a practical manual. For one thing this would be a hopeless task for a single book, for in the secondary phase of education (the focus of this book), all practice, including assessment practice, is heavily contextualised by the subject discipline: practical advice needs to be subject-specific. Except when providing particular examples, or as in the case of Chapter 10 where we present a case study, this book approaches assessment generically – and therefore mainly on the level of principle. It is written primarily for teachers in training and with the training standards in mind (DfEE Circular 4/98), though we hope it will be of interest to all teachers engaged in continuing professional development (CPD). We believe that making sense of the standards and developing professionally depends on the capacity among trainees to think clearly about assessment and to make connections between this and their wider function as teachers.

Just a cursory glance at the DfEE standards shows that statements made under 'C' (monitoring and assessment) connect with others under 'A' (subject knowledge) and 'B' (planning, preparation and classroom operations). We cannot discuss assessment sensibly without making connections with other aspects of teaching and learning. Thus, we find in Chapters 7–9, for example, reference made to theories of learning: any discussion of learning needs to include consideration of the role of assessment in its promotion (or otherwise), and any discussion of assessment needs to take account of the kind of learning we wish to promote.

Making connections such as this, between assessment and learning, encourages a holistic approach to the analysis of assessment in education and its impact. Thus, on a number of occasions in this book you will read phrases like:

- assessment is a fact of life for teachers, part of what teachers do;
- it is an organic part of teaching and learning; and
- using assessment evidence is part of the planning process.

There is nothing 'difficult' about such viewpoints on assessment; indeed they may have the ring of self-evident truth about them. However, it is our experience that assessment often appears to be taken as an issue separate from the creative processes of teaching and learning. After all, examinations are taken at the end of courses or modules, and marking is often taken home, to be done in the evening or weekend. Of course, these examples of assessment are 'part of' education, but they sometimes appear to be a separate part – epitomised perhaps by the 'dark suits' of the awarding bodies and the apparently inert and dry appearance of the mark book. It is not often we find a teacher who claims to like marking. It is more common to find marking, and assessment in general, treated as a kind of necessary evil, or chore to be undertaken as quickly and as efficiently (and painlessly) as possible.

We hope that this book will make a contribution to changing such a state of affairs. It sets out to do this by engaging the reader in a critical analysis of assessment in education. In undertaking this we have provided a great deal of information on assessment procedures and processes, so that the critique you may carry away with you is both informed and, we hope, sophisticated. We do not think that everything in the assessment garden is rosy, nor that all the recent reforms of assessment are in the interests of pupils and their teachers. But what we hope to avoid in this book is arriving too quickly at a clear cut position in relation to assessment debates.

For instance, although we advocate a better balance between external tests or examinations and internal classroom assessment, we do not fall into the trap of polarising our discussion. Whilst our analysis emphasises claims made by researchers that too much 'high-stakes' (i.e. the outcomes really matter, deciding for example the future educational or job opportunities) external assessment can distort teaching and learning in school, we never conclude that testing children is therefore necessarily 'bad'. Many years ago the '11+' examination was done away with (though this policy was success-fully resisted in several locations) as part of the drive to introduce compre-hensive schooling in the 1960s and early 1970s. This examination, designed to aid the selection of children for grammar schools, was simply abolished: no more selection, no more tests. With the advantage of retrospect, we can now see that this simple equation was not sensible. A generation later, we now have national tests at 7, 11 and 14 years – we think there may be too many, and with the publication of results since the mid-1990s, they carry a high stake – born partly out of genuine, widespread and urgent concern about educational standards. The absence of a national framework even to discuss educational standards probably allowed teaching and learning to 'drift' in a fog of inconclusive claims and counterclaims about its effectiveness. We now have a situation in which the government of the day can establish national targets for the proportion of children attaining 'level four' at age 11 years: that is, we now have a national framework which can focus national debate on educa-tional expectations.

The establishment of 'level four' is a convenient point at which to note another of our broad goals in writing this book: to identify significant trends in the 'technology' of assessment. By this we do not mean computers! We use the term to conjure up a picture of teachers and examiners enabled in their task by drawing from a range of instruments and approaches found in their professional tool-bag. Long gone are the days when assessment was seen as unproblematic, and essentially just a matter of dreaming up a few questions to ask the pupils. The language of 'level four' is understood by many to be a real advance, certainly on the days of the 11+. To see why, we need to refer to a couple of fundamental ideas in the world of assessment:

- the difference between ranking and grading. The former is relatively easy and was the main function of the 11+. Collect in the pupils' responses to a few questions and rank order them in terms of quality: the top 20 per cent could go to grammar school. Grading is harder, because it requires the marker (or rater) to judge each piece of work according to its value – which is more than merely saying whether it is 'better' or 'worse' than somebody else's;
- the difference between norm referencing and criteria referencing. One of the limitations of the 11+ was that, no matter how reliable (see page 11) it was, it could not say much about the achievements of the children who sat it. It was good for ranking purposes, but less useful for grading; it was essentially norm referenced. Modern testing design pays far more attention to the criteria which are believed to best describe various levels of attainment.

Key distinctions such as these are woven into the book, and they underpin much of the 'technology' of assessment.

Having briefly described, with some examples, what we believe to be the purpose of this book and our goals in writing it, we are still in need of an initial definition. What is assessment in education? The summary below, when read in conjunction with the previous paragraphs, should make sense. It amply suggests the scale of the discussion ahead! The following section of this chapter goes on to outline how we set out to tackle this.

SUMMARY

Assessment is:
'the processs of gathering, interpreting, recording and using information about pupils' responses to educational tasks.'

Assessment involves:
- more formal contexts and procedures including written, timed tests marked under strict conditions; and
- less formal settings including reading pupils' work and listening to what they have to say.

'Thus assessment encompasses responses to regular work as well as to specially devised tasks.'

Assessment requires:
- teachers to make judgements about pupils' responses measured against some standard of expectation. This is either (or a combination of):
  - norm referenced (set by the average performance of the group); or
  - criterion referenced (set by predetermined and explicit knowledge, understanding or skills).

The purposes of assessment are:
- to provide feedback to teachers and pupils about progress in order to support future learning: *the formative role*;
- to provide information about the level of pupils' achievements at points during and at the end of school: *the summative role*;
- to provide the means for selecting by qualification: *the certification role*;
- to contribute to the information on which judgements are made concerning the effectiveness or quality of individuals and institutions in the system as a whole: *the evaluation role.*

TWO CULTURES OF ASSESSMENT

We have divided the book into two main parts, Chapters 3–6 (External assessment) and 7–9 (Classroom assessment). We do so because we perceive such a distinction is a crucial one to understand. Indeed we go as far as to claim in Chapters 10 and 11 that so profoundly different are the two that we can usefully think in terms of two 'cultures' of assessment. In broad terms these are characterised by the evocative phrases 'assessment *of* education' and 'assessment *for* education', which capture the vital difference in function. The former is often described as primarily summative assessment, taking place at the end of a course of study and being concerned with 'summing up' what has been learned – facts, principles and generalisations, applications and skills. The latter is often termed formative assessment, taking place during the course of study and concerned more with spelling out what has been learned, what is being learned and what the next learning steps may be: mistakes are valued because they can give clues to where there may be learning blocks.

External summative assessment has secured a prominent role in the education system in England and Wales, some of the reasons for which we explore in Chapter 3. Its main functions are to contribute to accountability systems on a number of levels (including measuring the effectiveness of individual teachers), and to enable selection (for example, of 16 year olds for the most appropriate pathway of post-16 study or 18 year olds for employment, further education or higher education). It therefore needs to be sure of its own fairness and reliability. As we shall see, much of the contents of Chapters 3–6 address in various ways the processes and procedures that allow awarding bodies (the former examination 'boards') to claim that they can ensure fairness and reliability. At the same time, we shall note that people and agencies that consume the products of external summative assessment need simple, readily comparable aggregate scores of candidates' performances. This system depends on our accepting a basic assumption that the assessment of learning can be measured, or at least adequately approximated, by way of an examination or test instrument. Even if we can agree to accept this assumption we need to face further complexities: for example, the assessment of learning may be accurate as well as fair and reliable, but none of this says anything about the value of what has been learned. In an article concerning schooling for the future, one journalist wrote recently:

> we will certainly have completely to reconsider the notion of 'qualifications'. When I worked as an executive at the BBC, interviewing hundreds of job applicants every year, I stopped looking at the formal qualifications on their CVs. They told me virtually nothing that I needed to know about the person sitting in front of me, and they certainly didn't argue anything useful about the quality of their ideas. That I could discover only by asking the right questions.
>
> (Aaronovitch 1999)

Interestingly, Aaronovitch was not arguing against tests *per se*. Indeed, his headline nicely captures the tension in the case he was attempting to make: 'We need old Gradgrind back in our schools – at least for now'. In his own words:

> So here we have a paradox. In the short term we must put up with a bit of command education, so as to put the basics in place . . . but over the longer period any residue of Gradgrindism, of a longing to go back to regimentation in education, must . . . be expunged.
>
> (*ibid.*)

Thus, he describes a tension between 'machine-fed learning versus creativity', two contrasting approaches to education (and assessment) quite closely related to that which describes the basic structure of this book: external assessment, predominantly summative, versus classroom assessment, which is predominantly formative. Unlike many commentators he resists the temptation to come down, simplistically, on one side or the other: both have a role and a part to play in producing talented individuals who are capable and confident about learning. In a similar vein we argue that preparing for external summative assessment is an essential part of the work teachers do (in Chapters 7–9 of this book), even though we are aware and critical of the impact the examinations industry can have on teachers and pupils if allowed to dominate. But we also argue (in Chapters 10 and 11) that formative assessment, which taps into individual progress and achievement in a manner that encourages creativity in the classroom, should occupy a central place in the classroom.

In many ways the two cultures of assessment are *determined* by their different purposes. As we shall see, writers on such matters have concluded often that a single assessment system cannot possibly serve purposes as divergent as summative and formative assessment at the same time. We broadly agree (which is why we have organised this book into two distinctive areas). On the other hand, we also agree that teachers have no choice but to grapple with and be part of these two cultures: they need to be part of both. To manage this, we believe a good grounding in the principles that underpin assessment in education is essential. To provide such a thing is one of the goals of this book. We will be asking you to examine your perceptions of assessment, particularly with regard to its purposes, and encourage you to adopt practices that are principled.

The next chapter outlines in more detail three of the basic concepts referred to throughout our discussions: validity, reliability and fitness for purpose together with an introductory discussion about the vexed issue that lies at the heart of any attempt at assessment, how to judge fairly (or ascribe value to) individuals' performances.

2 Key Concepts in Assessment

INTRODUCTION

Ultimately, the idea behind all assessment is to discover something about the person being tested. It may be new, useful information, such as when a potential employer looks at an examination grade, or it may have a retrospective feel, such as when a teacher sets a test as a way of confirming that learning has taken place. Importantly, it may also give the person being tested information, about their achievement in maths, for example, which may or may not be something they already knew or suspected. Whatever the precise use or circumstances, it is vital that what the test says about that individual is correct; what Black (1998: 37) calls 'confidence in the result'. In technical terms this means that the test must be both valid and reliable.

Because both validity and reliability are different concepts we shall initially deal with them separately, but their interconnectedness is important to recognise and understand, so we will draw them together at the end of the section.

VALIDITY

An assessment task is said to be valid when it tests what it sets out to test, though as we shall see later, this is neither as simple as it may sound, nor does it tell the whole story. As Wood says, 'validity is a huge topic, witness Messick's 90-page chapter in the 3rd edition of *Educational Measurement* (Messick 1989)' (Wood 1991: 146). Clearly such detail is inappropriate here, but it is necessary to explain, albeit briefly, the traditional view of validity and then move on to Messick's notion of it as a unitary concept.

The traditional view

Stobart and Gipps (1997) identify four types of validity: *predictive, concurrent, construct* and *content*. Generally their names offer strong clues as to their concern.

First then, *predictive validity*. As one might expect, this measures the extent to which the score on one type of test enables someone to predict a performance later on. So, for example, the major accounting firms generally regard A-levels as good predictors of the intellectual skills required to become a trainee within the profession, and of course universities use the same device to sift applicants. The problem with using these exams in this way is that only those who *pass* A-levels are considered by the Institute of Chartered Accountants or by universities, so there is no way of comparing their performance with those who do not (Geddes 1995; Stobart and Gipps 1997). Furthermore, as Wood points out, the influence of A-levels on degree performance necessarily diminishes as the course progresses (1991: 151).

Concurrent validity is the second type of validity. As its name suggests, this is a measure of the accuracy of two tests that purport to measure the same thing. However, both tests must be independently valid as well; having a high correlation between two tests can mean nothing if one or other is not.

Construct validity is the notion that for a test to be *valid* it has to test those attributes it is supposed to. Psychologists call these attributes, or underlying skills, 'constructs', because they are a construction about the nature of human behaviour. So, if we wanted to test 'reading' we would want to examine all the underlying skills involved, such as reading both aloud and silently, with accuracy, fluency and perhaps with verve if it is to an audience, understanding the content, recognising the difference between reading poetry and prose, and so on. In practice, however, tests tend to concentrate on comprehension alone, because that is the easiest thing to test. So someone interpreting a 'reading score' would need to know what aspects of reading had been tested before they could interpret them and perhaps draw some comparisons between schools and certainly between different nationalities (Gipps 1994).

The fourth type, *content validity* is, as one might expect, concerned with the content being tested. In the context of an external examination, Wood neatly defines it as 'a function of the success with which the board translates what the syllabus says into an operational examination' (1991: 148). Testing whether an examination does do this is difficult, as we shall see in Chapter 4, because categorising the content of an examination paper into one or other skill domain is always open to interpretation.

There are other types of validity. For instance, concurrent and predictive validity are often combined to give *criterion validity* 'because they both relate to predicting performance on some criterion, either at the same time or in the future' (Stobart and Gipps 1997: 41). Wood (citing McClung 1978) mentions *curricular validity* and *instructional validity*. The first links what is taught in school with what is examined (in the case of external examinations). 'Since the connecting rod between the two is the syllabus, and schools and teachers are supposed to follow the syllabus, and the board is supposed to set questions on it, curricular validity ought to be assured', writes Wood (1991: 147), but the number of caveats in that one sentence indicates that such assumptions may not always be correct.

Instructional validity, unsurprisingly, looks at the instruction provided in advance of the tests. Here the problem is that both exam boards and schools provide such instruction, and while in England and Wales the former have been offering more and more help in this area (as we shall discover in Chapters 3–6), it is still up to teachers in classrooms to translate, decipher and augment this information for students. As a result, the extent of instructional validity cannot be guaranteed.

From the above it might seem that complexity is piled on complexity, and indeed there are other measures of validity that have been defined that we have not mentioned here (see, for instance, Black 1998: 43). Nevertheless, one aspect of Messick's (1989) paper that cannot be left out, if only because of its importance to our argument in the rest of the book, is validity as a *unitary concept*.

Unitary validity

The notion of unitary validity rests on what inferences and actions are drawn from the tests. So, no matter how well constructed a test, no matter how *valid* it is in terms of the criteria mentioned above, *if the results are not used appropriately it will not be valid*. Stobart and Gipps cite the examples of 'a maths test to select students for a Fine Art course or a music test to select engineers' (1997: 42) to illustrate this; the point being that making an engineer sit a music test will tell you nothing about his skills as an engineer (though as the Summary Box shows, such decisions are not always as clear-cut). They go further, 'it is the *use* of test results that determines validity. The importance of this for teachers is that, in using test results, validity is an issue of professional responsibility rather than merely the concern of test developers' (*ibid.*).

In 1999 the Teacher Training Agency in England and Wales announced that it would be setting maths tests for all teachers in training on courses that had begun just a month earlier. This caused some controversy, not least on the grounds that because it was announced *after* people had started the year, there was a feeling that the ground rules had been changed *ex post*. There was also a debate that relates to 'unitary validity'. The National Association for the Teaching of English (NATE) were reported in the *TES* (28.1.2000) as believing that 'the new maths tests to be taken by all new teachers this summer are unfair. It (NATE) says they could deprive the profession of excellent English teachers who are not able mathematicians' (p. 1). The debate also raised the issue of the validity of GCSE mathematics (or equivalent), that all trainees have to possess: was that qualification no longer sufficient proof of the numerical abilities of candidates for the profession?

It is also important to recognise that the unitary concept does not only concern itself with predictive validity, what Black (1998: 44 and 54) calls the 'forward aspect', it is also to do with the backward aspect, namely the learning process that resulted in the test score. So, as Black puts it:

> The inferences that might be drawn from a test result fall into two main categories. One type of inference might look forward to the future performance of a student in new learning programmes or in remedial work on the previous programme. The other might look back at the previous learning programme and so lead to changes to improve test results for future students.
>
> (*Ibid.*: 44)

Conclusion

Validity is thus far more than the simple (perhaps simplistic) statement that a test should test what it sets out to test. But in addition to having a complex structure, it is also difficult to research. As Wood (1991) puts it:

> Validity is ultimately more important than reliability but any attempt at validation depends crucially on the reliability of the observations. If these cannot be trusted, then a misleading judgement concerning validity is likely to be reached. That must be why validity has been so much less explicated than reliability.
>
> (p. 147)

If we take the unitary view of validity as the *use* of test results, then we begin to question the assumptions lying behind the heavy reliance on data from external examinations that has developed in England and Wales over the past few years. By asking examinations to do more and more, not just in terms of the ways they are used to evaluate the performance of individuals, but also as a means of judging departments, schools, local educational authorities and so on, the precise purpose of each one becomes less and less clear, and thus less valid. This 'confusion of purpose' will be a theme to which we will frequently return throughout the book.

In summary, validity:

- is complex and hard to research;
- is more than a statement that a test should test what it sets out to test;
- traditionally consisted of four forms: *predictive, concurrent, construct* and *content*;
- is now recognised as being a unitary concept, with a backward as well as a forward use; and
- is ultimately, probably more important than reliability.

RELIABILITY

As we noted above, reliability has been researched more thoroughly than validity, probably because it is easier to undertake (Wood 1991: 132; Black 1998: 53). Like validity, it consists of a number of sub-sets with complicated-sounding names, resting beneath the fairly straightforward notion that if we test someone then the test will be reliable if the result is exactly the same across all occasions, tasks, observations and settings.

There are two elements that may cause an error in this process, one is the candidate and the other is the assessor or marker; both of these will be dealt with in more detail in Chapter 4. It is apparent, however, that we can never have identical candidates on two occasions, because even the same person will change. As a result:

> we use other measures as a proxy for this: *test-retest reliability*, which is based on gaining the same marks if the test is repeated; *mark-remark* reliability which looks at the agreement between markers; and, *parallel forms/split-half reliability* in which similar tests give similar marks.
> (Stobart and Gipps 1997: 42. Emphasis in original.)

Such technicalities usually fall within the domain of test developers and assessment researchers, and within the context of external examinations; they are not techniques with which practising teachers often concern themselves. Nevertheless, it is important for teachers to recognise the need for reliability, which Wiliam (1992) calls *dependability*. He cites *disclosure* and *fidelity* as important for such dependability. Disclosure investigates the extent to which a student gets a question right or wrong depending on the nature of the question itself (it is a well tried technique of teachers to re-phrase a question so as to encourage a positive response) and fidelity looks at the way the evidence is, or is not recorded. Fidelity can be lost in three ways: either because the teacher does not observe it, or because it is incorrectly observed, or because, despite observing it correctly, it is not recorded (Stobart and Gipps 1997: 43).

To summarise, reliability:

- has been researched more than validity;
- can be tested using test-retest, mark-remark and split-half measures; and
- in the classroom assessment is dependable when disclosure and fidelity are present.

The interrelationship between validity and reliability

As has already been stated, when it comes to making a judgement about which of validity or reliability is the more important in assessment terms, validity 'wins'; after all if a test does not tell us anything useful and usable about the individual being examined, what is the point in doing it? Despite this pre-eminence, validity has been less well researched and even, in Wood's words, 'neglected' by the examination boards (Wood 1991: 151). Furthermore, this position has not changed since; in fact it may have got worse. As Black argues in the context of the National Curriculum, it at least had an 'initial concern for validity' but this changed 'to obsession with manageability and, more recently, to concern with reliability' (Black 1996: 94).

It is apparent that both validity and reliability are interconnected. Black (1998) explains this connectedness and we will quote him at some length:

> A test giving scores which are reproducible over a wide variety of conditions (i.e. a reliable test) would nevertheless be of no value if the attainment that it measures is irrelevant to (say) the learning being explored, or if that attainment is too narrow an aspect of the whole to be of any significance (i.e. an invalid test). A set of test items which clearly reflect the aims of a course and can be seen to evoke the type of performance that the course aims to promote (i.e. a valid test) is of little value if it turns out that examiners cannot agree on how to mark the outcome, or if a different set of apparently comparable items would produce very different scores with the same pupils on a different occasion (i.e. an unreliable test). If it turned out that there was no correlation between a test score and the future attainment that it was designed to predict, then it could be that either or both of the reliability and the validity of the test were defective.
>
> (pp. 48–49)

The extent to which validity *depends* on reliability will alter according to circumstances. In the case of high stakes external examinations, reliability is an essential prior condition to validity because the decision cannot be changed very quickly. For example, if university entrance depends on A-level grades, it is vital that the marking and grade awarding processes are reliable in a technical sense (or at least *believed* to be so), because if they are not the entire system will collapse, as both candidates and users sense that on a different occasion or with a different marker the result would be substantially different.

However, ensuring a high level of reliability is very expensive because, as we shall see in Chapter 4, at just a basic level, scripts have to be marked, remarked, checked against other markers and so on, and even then in, say, an essay paper, different examiners could (legitimately) argue for two different marks for the same work. This complexity explains the pressure for multiple choice tests (and the main reason for their popularity in the USA until quite recently). Because of their high reliability at relatively low cost, multiple choice tests have obvious attractions. But they are often not *valid* – they cannot test certain domains and are not necessarily good predictors. Therefore, given limited resources, an external examination will often contain different types of papers, as a compromise or trade-off between reliability and validity.

Within classrooms, where decisions can be reversed relatively easily and quickly, the need for reliability is not paramount, though it cannot be ignored. Take the case where a student does well on a test and the teacher decides to move on to the next topic as a result. If the same level of reliability was needed as in an external examination, the test would have to be re-sat, perhaps be marked by someone else, results averaged and so on before such a decision could be reached. This is clearly impractical. In these circumstances, validity is the key for diagnostic purposes (Wiliam and Black 1996; Harlen and James 1997; Black 1998).

In summary,

- validity and reliability are interconnected;
- the extent to which validity depends on reliability will alter according to circumstances;
- external examinations have to be reliable; classroom assessments less so; and
- different types of examination papers offer different levels of reliability and validity and so an examination often consists of a number of papers as a compromise between the two.

FOR FURTHER THINKING

In the same edition of *The Times Educational Supplement* (28 January 2000) as quoted in the box on p. 9, there was an article written by Patricia Rowen, a former editor of the paper. She argued (though without using the term) that a mathematics test for new entrants to the teaching profession was perfectly valid on the grounds that 'Even music and art teachers – perhaps especially music and art teachers – need to be at home with numbers to do their jobs. It would be hard to function efficiently as a teacher if you couldn't pass this very basic test' (p. 17).

1. What is your view of the necessary minimum educational qualifications that all teachers should possess?
2. Given that GCSE mathematics is a requirement for teacher-training, what does the imposition of a mathematics test for those in training say about the GCSE examination?

FITNESS FOR PURPOSE

Throughout this book there will be many references to the Task Group on Assessment and Testing (TGAT) report (DES/WO 1988), which was set up to provide the assessment framework for the National Curriculum. It is not appropriate here to examine the events of the time in detail, though as a piece of educational history it is fascinating to read of the tensions between those with what might be termed a 'political' agenda, others jockeying for power and influence over education, and even factions within the teaching profession itself. For interested readers, Daugherty's *Review of Policy, 1987–1994* will provide such detail (see Further reading). Suffice to say that the TGAT report was highly influential and put the terms *formative* and *summative*, amongst others, 'into common circulation and defined them' (Harlen and James, 1997: 366).

Paragraph 23 of the TGAT report described the two terms as follows:

–   formative, so that the positive achievements of a pupil may be recognised and discussed and the appropriate next step be planned
–   summative, for the recording of the overall achievement of a pupil in a systematic way

(DES/WO 1988: para 23)

This means, in plain language derived from the root of each word, that formative assessment is concerned with the way the student develops, or *forms*, whilst summative is a *summation* of what that student has achieved over the length of a course of study.

The TGAT report made it plain that the two were not essentially different, and that it would be possible to build up a summative picture 'by aggregating, in a structured way, the separate results of a set of assessments designed to serve formative purposes' (*ibid*.: para. 25). But Harlen and James argue that this has led to confusion, and they quote examples where teachers have failed to recognise the need for *reliability* in summative assessment, preferring instead to rely on classroom validity (Harlen *et al*. 1995: 5; Gipps *et al*. 1995; Harlen and James, 1997: 367). In other words, and to emphasise again the point made on p. 13, because the loop between student performance and feedback is so short, and the impact of an unreliable formative assessment relatively small, such unreliability doesn't matter as much as when the assessment is summative; in contrast, high-stakes summative external examinations *have* to be as reliable as possible, since there is no immediate recourse, and published results are used extensively for predictive purposes.

It is therefore important to clarify the purpose of the assessment. Formative assessment is undertaken by teachers using criteria that may well extend beyond subject knowledge to include the amount of effort (apparently) put into the work, the student's past performance, the need to encourage and so on; in other words it will depend on the context of the work as much as the content. The assessment will thus be *criterion referenced* (see p. 17) but also *pupil referenced* (or *ipsative*). The latter is important because it places the student at the centre of the assessment activity and provides *diagnostic* information on the progress (or otherwise) of the individual. Again it is worth stressing that simply because something is teacher assessed does not automatically make it formative; indeed we will argue that one danger with modularisation at Advanced and AS levels is that increasing use will be made of past papers, so that the assessment regime will become a series of mini-examinations, all essentially summative in nature.

None of these issues and arguments is new. Teachers have always made formative judgements of their pupils, but we will make the case that such judgements, indeed the whole use and application of formative assessment measures have to be approached in a far more structured way than they often have been in the past, and that a theoretical understanding of the process can help underpin more effective classroom practice.

External examinations and summative assessment

Since the majority of external examinations are sat at the end of a course (for this reason they are often called *terminal* examinations), the assumption is often made that they are all summative. In their very nature of course, the vast majority are, but coursework, which is tested externally, can also perform a formative function. Many teachers will have experienced the motivational benefits derived by students from investigations, as well as the development of important, wider 'key skills', such as decision making and working with others.

One of the innovations of GCSE was the introduction of syllabuses, in subjects such as English, which were assessed exclusively by teacher-marked, board moderated coursework. Despite the heavy marking loads this imposed, such courses were popular, largely because of their formative benefits, although there was also a summative 'pay-off' through higher grades than traditional written terminal examinations (teachers also gained through professional development). Indeed, it was these higher grades that excited controversy and, in the end, resulted in a limit being set on coursework in all external examinations.

JUDGING PERFORMANCE

Assessment involves teachers, and others, making judgements about students' performance – in tests, examinations or in the classroom. To do this they need a mechanism or way of 'referencing' the judgement. Broadly there are two ways of referencing assessment – using norms and criteria. In practice the two approaches are usually used in combination.

Norm referencing

'Norm referenced' is a term used to describe a system of assessment that judges the performance of an individual within a group against the whole group's performance. If the sample is large enough, it will form a bell-shaped curve with the same mean and standard deviation as the whole population (see Figure

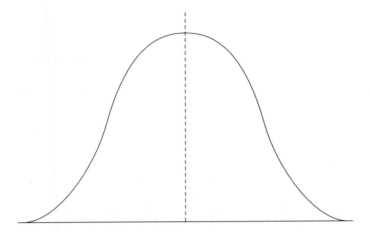

Figure 2.1 The normal distribution: a bell-shaped curve

2.1). However, if it is not, it may either be skewed, or have a different mean. If either of these is true, and only a certain proportion of the sample are allowed to 'pass' each test, then it is possible to perform exactly the same on two different testing occasions, pass on one but fail on the other. This apparent 'unfairness' has resulted in a greater emphasis on 'criterion referencing' (see p. 17).

To repeat, the degree to which a population exhibits 'skewness' depends on its size; the larger the sample the more it will statistically conform to the whole. This explains why using norm referenced judgements in a single class, or perhaps in a single school, is dangerous. Although the information from a test will tell us the rank order of the students, it will not be possible to make any statement about how their performance compares with the rest of the population. Yet teachers do use norm referencing alongside criteria and ipsative referencing: the *best* performance in a test sets a standard. The teacher can say, 'If X can now understand and can do it, then so should the rest of the class'. There is nothing wrong with that as long as it is used for diagnostic purposes, such as 'Was X's score far beyond the rest of the class? In which case why?' 'Did I teach in a particular style that suited certain individuals and not others?' and so on.

In the case of external examinations with large entries it is statistically probable that each year-group will exhibit the same characteristics, which is why, as we shall discover in Chapter 4, awarding bodies use the previous year's performance as a starting point for the award of this year's grades. Nevertheless, it is important to note that certain examinations attract different students so that, for instance, you should not expect the grade profile of a subject like Latin, for instance, to have the same one as business studies.

Criterion referencing

Criterion referencing is the principle of defining what is required *before* a test is sat, and then judging individuals against those criteria. This means that regardless of the performance of the sample, those who deserve to pass will do so. In a classroom setting, defining the criteria is fairly straightforward since the scheme of work will provide the evidence required, at least in terms of subject content, though as we have already stated there may be other factors that the teacher may wish to take into account when assessing individuals.

Examples of successful criterion referenced externally judged tests are often taken from vocational areas (though strictly speaking these are 'competence tests' − a special form of criterion tests: see Chapter 5 for more details). So, for instance, in order to be awarded a swimming certificate, the criteria will be that you have to swim a certain distance within a certain time. You might be the last swimmer out of the group that starts, but that is irrelevant if you do it in the time. Similarly, the driving test defines certain actions that have to be carried out competently; if you do so you will pass, regardless of how many people before you on that day also passed.

The difficulty faced by this apparently straightforward idea is that defining *precisely* what is required is very difficult. If we return to the driving test, the criterion for a successful hill start is that the vehicle does not roll backwards. But what would constitute an A-grade hill start as opposed to a C-grade one? Trying to define such detail is challenging indeed. As Wolf puts it,

> The more serious and rigorous the attempts to specify the domains being assessed, the narrower the domain itself becomes, without, in fact, becoming fully transparent. The attempt to map out free-standing content and standards leads, again and again, to a never-ending spiral of specifications.
>
> (Wolf 1995a: 55)

The National Curriculum was the first time that a serious attempt was made in England and Wales to describe the criteria required for assessing different subjects (see Chapter 5). The theoretical arguments for criterion referencing were persuasive, but their practical application was beset with difficulties, as overseas experience had already shown (Daugherty 1995: 178). Describing attainment in science exemplifies the problem that the subject working parties faced. The first set of proposals from the Science Working Group contained no fewer than 354 statements of attainment grouped into ten levels in each of twenty-two separate attainment targets. Clearly this was unmanageable, and eventually resulted in a teacher boycott and a revision of the National Curriculum following the Dearing Review (1993).

Manageability

Manageability simply means that the assessment task must not take excessive administrative time so that the costs, in the widest sense, do not outweigh the benefits. One of the early problems with the National Curriculum was that it required teachers to spend a great deal of time confirming 'achievement' by means of boxes that had to be 'ticked'. This gave rise to increasing discontent amongst the profession, the boycotting of certain Key Stage Tests and ultimately the setting up of the Dearing Review (1993), which was established with a brief to reduce, amongst other things, the extent of teacher involvement in managing National Curriculum assessment. Manageability is one of the never-ending tensions in assessment.

Transparency

In the context of examinations the word *transparency* is used to describe the extent to which all the participants, teachers, parents, governors and the candidates themselves know what is required of them, know the system by which they will have their work assessed and the ways the marks are awarded. Until fairly recently, external examinations were something of a 'secret garden', where only those on the inside really knew all that was required; indeed finding out such information was often the prime reason why teachers became examiners. Over time such a situation was recognised as being unfair, and, dating from the introduction of GCSEs in the late 1980s, examination boards, now called awarding bodies, have increasingly recognised the need for transparency, as we shall discover in more detail in Chapter 4.

It is not just in external testing that transparency is needed, however. Marking a piece of homework requires thought and reflection in advance so that a mark of, say, 'eight out of ten' is given based on criteria that both teacher and student recognise (Brant *et al.* 2000). In addition, consideration of the impact such a mark might have must also be taken into account (see Chapter 9).

EQUITY AND BIAS

Transparency also relates to notions of equity, because if an individual or group knows what examiners are looking for and others do not, the latter will be disadvantaged. However, equity extends beyond transparency, as we shall discover below and in Chapters 3–6.

It is possible that questions set in a test or an examination will favour a particular sex, class or culture. For instance, it has been suggested that the introduction of coursework in GCSEs favoured girls (Black 1998) especially if it was at the expense of multiple choice questions, which tend to favour boys (Gipps and Murphy 1994); Latin polysyllables may favour middle class children and will almost certainly disadvantage second-language learners (Pollit *et al.* 1985); and cultural bias can have a potentially devastating effect, as was witnessed some years ago in California where a multiple choice test was used to allocate children into classes for the 'educable mentally retarded'. There, a case was found against the California education authorities (*Larry P v Riles*, 1979) on the grounds that the tests were racially and culturally biased and had a discriminatory impact upon black people, which resulted in the 'permanent placement of black children into educationally dead-end, isolated and stigmatised classes' (Evans and Waite 1981 quoted in Gipps and Murphy 1994).

Unfortunately, as in so many aspects of assessment theory, the apparently straightforward notion of equity is far more complex than might at first appear. For example, there may be a confusion over cause and effect, such as in the reported differences in IQ between black children and white children (even accepting the validity of such tests). It has been shown that once social circumstances are taken into account, these differences disappear (Macintosh 1986). Instead, as Wood (1991) puts it, 'Social circumstances or class overrides the power of race, and certainly gender, to determine life chances' (p. 167). Indeed, as we shall see in Chapter 6, recent developments in schools' value added analysis have attempted to allow for social and economic circumstances by taking into account the proportion of children having free school meals. Black (1996) takes a slightly different tack, arguing 'whether or not these differences [IQ scores between black and white children and those from different economic circumstances] are due to test bias or reflect real differences with other origins − for example in denial of educational opportunities − is not easy to determine' (p. 51).

Ensuring equity by the avoidance of bias is not easy. Technically there are two types of bias, one *item content bias* and the other *statistical item bias* or *differential item functioning*. The first refers to the possibility of a group, say males or females, detecting perceived bias in the questions; the second is a statistical measure of differences in the performance of two groups who are equally good at the attainment being tested. But even attempting to reduce such bias is fraught, because it may be that by eliminating perceived bias the point of the test is lost. So, if the test is designed to determine verbal reasoning, at which girls are generally better, any attempt to alter the make-up of the test by, say, including questions known to favour boys will give a 'false' result (Gipps and Murphy 1994).

At the end of their book entitled *A Fair Test?* Gipps and Murphy declare that 'there is no such thing as a fair test, nor could there be: the situation is too complex and the notion too simplistic' (p. 273). Nevertheless, the fact that bias is difficult to avoid is not a reason for not trying to do so. Stobart and Gipps, in a section entitled 'Towards Fairness and Equity', suggest a number of areas where action can be taken:

> It is likely that a wide-ranging review of curriculum and syllabus
> content, teacher attitude to boys and girls and minority ethnic groups,
> assessment mode and item format is required . . . if we wish to make

assessment as fair as possible. Although this is a major task, it is one which needs to be addressed, given the growing importance of standards, national assessment and public examinations.

(p. 64)

It is significant that the authors see equity as a wider issue than that concerned with testing, since they emphasise 'curriculum' and 'teacher attitude' as much as syllabus content. Transparency and equality of access must, they argue, apply to courses and subjects as much as they do to external summative examinations, especially in the context of increasing numbers of high-stakes testing occasions and results against which students, schools and teachers are judged. Almost certainly, to the young person denied access to education for whatever reason: social, environmental or economic, assessment theories are little more than an irrelevance, and we would hope that this wider picture will be borne in mind, as we now move to the detail of that theory in Chapters 3–9.

SUMMARY

- Formative assessment is undertaken so that the positive achievements of a pupil may be recognised and discussed and the appropriate next step be planned.
- Summative assessment is designed to record the overall achievement of a pupil in a systematic way.
- Clarity of purpose is essential when determining whether an assessment task is formative or summative.
- Examinations have to be administratively manageable.
- Transparency is the idea that all involved in an examination process have equal access to and knowledge of the processes involved.
- Bias can take three forms: *item content bias*, *statistical item bias* or *differential item functioning*.
- Fairness and equity apply to the curriculum and courses of study as much as to examinations.

FOR FURTHER READING

Daugherty's *National Curriculum Assessment: a Review of Policy 1987–1994* was written in 1995. It takes a critical view of the early steps of establishing the National Curriculum assessment framework. It is authoritative and describes in some detail the difficulties faced at a *policy* level.

We shall be referring to Stobart and Gipps' *Assessment. A Teacher's Guide to the Issues* quite frequently throughout this book. It too is authoritative but also concise and readable.

3 The Examinations Industry: Foundations and Controversies

EXTERNAL ASSESSMENT

General Introduction

Chapters 3–6 consist of two parts. Chapter 3 is technical, in the sense that it attempts to equip the reader with the details of the ways external examinations are organised and run. For many years such information has been something of a 'secret garden' open only to those professionally involved in the process, and whilst there has been a considerable opening up recently, it remains something of a mystery to many teachers. The chapter will show the lengths to which the examination boards, now called 'awarding bodies' go, in order to ensure reliability and, to a lesser extent, validity. Nevertheless, and this is the link with Chapters 4–6, it will be argued that such efforts, though well intended, can only ever be partially successful, though for a government intent on increasing centralisation the perception of an ever dependable 'gold standard' is vital.

Chapters 4–6 develop our larger argument: namely that in England and Wales there has developed something of an obsession with external, largely summative examinations, so that students are overburdened with this form of assessment at the expense of other, more creative ones. We will suggest that this is largely the result of a confusion over purpose, which in turn relates to the more recent notion of validity that we explored in Chapter 2, as well as a particular view of teachers and their professional standing in society.

Introduction to Chapter 3

This chapter briefly describes the historical background to external assessment, revealing its roots in ancient China, and then going on to explain its importance within the educational system of England and Wales. The story shows that the process was underpinned by commendable aims and objectives, because it was designed, in nineteenth-century Britain, as a means of encouraging greater equality and accessibility to higher education and to the professions. This meant, however, that it was necessarily predicated on the notion of pass and fail, acting as a hurdle or barrier to

*entry. The universities played a major role in the emerging system, espe-
cially since they formed the examination boards, now called awarding
bodies, that are so important today in running what has become an 'examination industry'. This industry is crucial, given governments that have
increasingly engaged in centralising both the academic and vocational curricula, because summative, high-stakes assessment has been seen as a way
of measuring overall teaching standards as well as student achievement.
The chapter will conclude that the emphasis on such measures is mis-
placed, because it confuses the need for an aggregated view on policy
with the needs of individual students, whose progress can and should be
assessed using a variety of less stressful but equally informative methods.*

A NOTE ON TERMS

As we explained in Chapter 1, summative assessment is not the same as an
external examination; nor is an external examination necessarily or exclusively
summative. Nevertheless, the kind of high-stakes external examinations that
prevail in England and Wales are often conflated with summative assessment
by the teaching profession, parents and the media and indeed are so predominantly summative that we might appear to use the two terms synonymously.
We are careful, however. When the two are the same we apply them in this
way for the sake of our wider argument about the use and application of
external examinations. But underlying this is the hope that readers will come
to recognise and understand the differences, and more importantly question
those who make policy decisions as if they were identical.

EXTERNAL ASSESSMENT: AN ANCIENT ART

The origins of external assessment go back a long way. For a thousand years
examinations were used in China as a means of selecting people from all walks of
life to enter the civil service. The aim was praiseworthy and one probably common to all such systems of assessment: namely to enable the most talented, regardless of their background, to reach positions of power and influence. The reality
was somewhat different, however, for over time the Chinese entrance exam
became increasingly a test of memory, focusing on a factual content that had less
and less to do with the knowledge and skills required to organise and run the
country. By testing attributes that were not consistent with the skills required by
those who passed it, the examinations therefore became less *valid*, eventually producing a civil service in China more and more divorced from the realities of the
state and the lives of the people for whom it was established to serve (Hanson
1993; Black 1998). Such a trend is not untypical, however; because it is easier to
test some attributes than others, these are the ones that tend to be tested. Another
tendency is for examinations to atrophy: syllabuses are usually written and tests
set by those who have previously succeeded in passing them. Such individuals
will have a natural tendency to value those aspects that they themselves were
good at, rather than those they found more difficult.

EXAMINATIONS IN ENGLAND AND WALES: THE BACKGROUND

Until the nineteenth century, entry to universities and the professions in England and Wales largely depended on patronage and family connections, reinforced by a system of oral examinations that necessarily supported 'like-minded' individuals from similar backgrounds (Black 1998). Together this system resulted in the dominance of an elite few, which was neither fair nor efficient. The move towards written entrance examinations, which happened progressively throughout the nineteenth century, can therefore be seen as a manifestation of the growing power and influence of the middle classes, who

DO EXAMINATIONS OFFER EQUAL ACCESS OR BUILD BARRIERS?

Cambridge University has traditionally set its own entrance examinations, in order to supplement the information A-levels provide. It does so, partly to subdivide groups of students who have already displayed high levels of achievement and partly because the University believes its courses require special skills that A-levels do not necessarily reveal. Such specialised examinations, however, tend to favour certain groups of students, especially those from independent schools who, working in small classes with specialist staff, can be 'taught to the test' in a way denied most other schools. The result is that in 1996, for instance, fewer than 50 per cent of students admitted to Cambridge were from state schools compared to 61 per cent across all universities. In August 1999 the University announced that it was planning to drop its entrance exams in favour of the Government's new 'world-class test', but only on the condition that the test was as 'rigorous' as the one devised internally (*Times Educational Supplement* 20 August 1999: 1).

Three points are raised by this:

- It is clear that the national examinations framework is not providing equal access for all, since an additional hurdle favours certain groups.
- It is equally apparent that Cambridge University is aware that its unique entrance exam is not doing the job intended for it, because it believes it is missing out on talented individuals who are going to other institutions around the country.
- The fact that Cambridge retains its right to set tests reveals the tension that has been evident in the examination system for many years: namely the one between organisations competing to provide assessment instruments – in this case the universities still jealously guarding their 'independence' – and governments, intent not only on ensuring fairness for all, but also exerting control over a system that it largely funds.

for reasons of equity alone argued for equal access to the professions and higher education. Their logic could not be denied, but in any case there was also a practical imperative: quite simply the demand for an educated and trained workforce relevant to modern needs exceeded the numbers that could be supplied from traditional sources.

Nevertheless, the introduction of examinations in themselves did not open the way for the whole population to compete. After all, 50 per cent of the population was automatically excluded because of their sex, another significant segment because of their religion, whilst a further tranche were more subtly, but nonetheless just as effectively, kept out by their economic circumstances. However, entrance examinations were a considerable step forward and may be seen as an indicator of a developing industrial society.

The introduction of examinations as a means of selecting candidates established a number of structures, which to a large extent remain in force today, more than one hundred years later. Their underlying aim, of course, remains the same, namely to provide the opportunity for people from all walks of life to achieve their potential (see box on p. 23). Nevertheless, the ways of achieving that aim have been controversial and have always created tensions, some of which we shall examine below.

THE ROLE OF GOVERNMENT IN NATIONAL TESTS

As shown below the history of external assessment in England and Wales reveals a tension between the 'private' sector as represented by the universities and the awarding bodies, and government, with the former fighting what appears to be a rearguard action to retain independence and the latter arguing that it has a right to exert control and influence over an area that is so crucial to long-term economic growth and societal change, and in which it has a large financial and electoral stake.

The historical battle between the state and the universities continues to this day. Consider the following article taken from the *Guardian* in December 1999.

A-level points switch row

David Blunkett, the education secretary, was last night on a collision course with universities over their plans to change the A-level system used to award points to candidates seeking admission for undergraduate degrees.

He warned the Universities and Colleges Admissions Service (Ucas) that a proposal agreed by its board yesterday would devalue the achievements of the best A-level candidates. . . . Mr Blunkett would be calling in the interested parties to find 'a more sensible way forward'.

> But Tony Higgins, chief executive of Ucas, said it would press ahead . . .
> 'We have taken the decision to introduce a new points tariff. Ucas owns
> the tariff and our decision will stand.'
> Mr Higgins was supported by John Dunford, general secretary of the
> Secondary Heads Association. 'It is not up to the government to tell the
> university community how to organise its admission criteria.'
> (*Guardian* Saturday 11 December 1999, p. 1)

It is possible to trace the tension revealed in the box back over the past one hundred and fifty years, in a way that helps to explain much of the debate over curriculum and testing, which continues to this day. Given the underlying *laissez faire* philosophy of the nineteenth century, it is perhaps unsurprising that institutions, especially the older universities, regarded education as their sole concern and a subject which had nothing, or very little to do with governments (Green *et al.* 1999). Education was, after all, overwhelmingly organised and run within the private sector, with independent schools supplying virtually all the candidates to higher education whilst the state, at the start of the century anyway, was uninvolved with educating the masses. As the century unfolded, however, two trends developed that increased the tension between the universities and governments.

The first was the introduction of examinations by the universities. In 1838 the University of London set a matriculation examination, an innovation that was rapidly followed by Oxford and Cambridge, who started to set their own entrance exams. It can therefore be seen that from a very early stage the universities acquired an expertise in setting and marking papers, upon which they based their argument that they were the only bodies competent to know what standards were and should be. But it was equally clear that such tests were effectively setting wider national, even international standards, and this meant that over time the involvement of government was inevitable.

The second trend was the direct involvement of the state in education. As the nineteenth century passed, governments found themselves with the responsibility for running an ever more complex industrialised economy, as well as an expanding empire. From around 1870 it was also apparent that Britain was falling behind her main rivals, especially Germany and the USA and one reason for this, it was believed, was that both of them had at least embryonic forms of mass education. Thus, in 1880 schooling was made compulsory in England and Wales and in 1891 it was made free. Nevertheless, schools were not placed under the control of county and borough councils until 1902 and, as remains the case today, independent, fee-paying ones continued to exist alongside.

The corollary of the state being increasingly engaged in paying for the education of the masses was its verification of educational standards, not only through the inspectorate but also more indirectly through its influence over examinations. Early on, therefore, there was a proposal to establish a single Examinations Council, but the leading public schools, concerned about state 'interference', encouraged the universities of Oxford and Cambridge to establish what became the Oxford and Cambridge Examinations Board, building on the experience of examinations that the latter had developed over the years. In a real sense this marks the birth of what we here call the 'examinations industry', based around a rather bizarre organisational structure of semi-autonomous examination boards, now called 'awarding bodies'. They, like their early patrons the ancient universities, defend their independence whilst at the same time recognising the state's right to influence and perhaps even interfere in their increasingly commercial activities.

This tension, between independence and centralised control, has thus been evident for at least one hundred years and over that period the state has played an increasingly influential role. The process continues to this day, but its pace has quickened in the last twenty years and especially since the introduction of the National Curriculum in 1988 (Graham 1993; Tattershall 1994; Davis 1999). The formation of successive government quangos charged with influencing, some might say controlling, curriculum and assessment has once again raised the question of whether there should be a single examination board (see p. 29–34). This debate has been fuelled by the controversy over examination 'standards', with increasing evidence of teachers switching boards on the grounds that some examinations and even syllabuses within the same board are 'easier' than others (see the box below).

SYLLABUS SWITCHING: A RESPONSE TO EXTERNAL PRESSURES?

In 1998 researchers at Staffordshire University examined the rate at which teachers switched syllabuses between boards in two A-level subjects, Economics and Business Studies. They used a stratified randomised systematic one-in-three sample of University and College Admission System (UCAS) centres to discover the pattern of syllabus switching, and then used telephone interview surveys to investigate reasons for switching in greater depth (p. 49). The percentage of centres changing syllabuses in each year was found to be as follows:

Year	85	86	87	88	89	90	91
%	2	1	2	3	2	6	5

Year	92	93	94	95	96	97
%	9	7	14	19	15	2

From the data they concluded that:

> the rate of syllabus switching increased after 1993, coincident with the publication of school examination league tables. . . . Between 1990 and 1993, at a time when the debate on school standards was escalating, the proportion changing their syllabuses doubled to around 7%. Following the introduction of examination league tables in 1993 there was a further doubling in the rate of syllabus switching, with between 14 and 19% of schools changing their syllabus each year between 1994 and 1996 – roughly 1 in 6 of centres. . . . 1997 marked a return to relative stability, though this was probably due to the hiatus caused by uncertainty over whether the Dearing Review of 16–19 qualifications [Dearing 1996] was likely to be implemented.
>
> (pp. 56–57)

They identified three main 'pull' factors that prompted teachers to change syllabuses, one of which was that 'The new course would attract more students and at the same time improve grades' (p. 7).

(Staffordshire University Business School 1998)

RATIONALISING THE EXAMINATION INDUSTRY

Self evidently examinations are important, not only to the lives of the young people who sit them, but also to the country as a whole (Sutherland 1996). They are, however, expensive. In 1999 it was estimated that GCSEs alone cost £90 million to organise and run, whilst entry fees constitute a high proportion of any school or college's budget. The 'examinations industry' is by any measure large scale.

From the data in Figure 3.1 it is clear that small examinations are more expensive per candidate than large ones and so it makes economic sense to rationalise boards and syllabuses in order to benefit from economies of scale. In recent years, therefore, governments have been pressing for amalgamations, but in any case competitive forces were, by the middle 1990s, causing changes: some boards were effectively insolvent, whilst their original sponsors, the universities, were either unable or unwilling to support them as loss making enterprises, which they had done in the past.

Amalgamations were in part a response to an historical legacy. Over time some strange and somewhat illogical combinations had developed that needed to be rationalised. Thus, whilst there was a University of Cambridge Local Examinations Board (UCLES) and a University of Oxford Delegacy of Local Examinations (UODLE) there was also an Oxford and Cambridge Schools Examination Board (OCSEB). Inevitably each one only had a small and, over time, diminishing market share. Rather than face the embarrassment of a

In 1995 the *direct costs* (see note below) of a multiple choice test were estimated as follows:

	500 cands.	2,500 cands.	10,000 cands.
Chief examiner	£250	£250	£250
Setting paper	£205	£205	£205
Revising paper	£515	£515	£515
Marking	£250	£1,250	£5,000
Awarding	£333	£333	£333
Cost/candidate	£3.11	£1.02	£0.63

In contrast, short answer tests were:

Cost/candidate	£13.59	£4.88	£3.18

and an A-level type examination but with scenario/case-study type questions and problems were:

Cost/candidate	£17.98	£8.38	£6.52

Figure 3.1 The financial cost of examinations

Source: Centre for Curriculum and Assessment Studies, University of Bristol and the International Centre for Research on Assessment, University of London (1995: 44–47)

Notes:
1. These were all *direct* costs, in other words only those associated directly with the exam itself. It therefore did not include the salaries of exam board officials, the costs of running the board's offices and other additional expenses such as marketing, public relations and so on. As might be expected, economies of scale mean that large entry subjects have lower direct cost than small ones.
2. Since this research was undertaken most boards now pay chief examiners a responsibility allowance that takes into account the size of the entry, but the effect on unit costs of this change is minimal.

financially insolvent examination board, the three agreed to a merger, which resulted in the Oxford and Cambridge Examinations and Assessment Council (OCEAC). This, however, was short-lived, because the government was applying increasing pressure to reduce the number of boards (and syllabuses).

The aim of rationalisation was also true in vocational areas, where the three main vocational awarding bodies existed alongside 'myriad' smaller ones (Wolf 1995b: 14). The three were, the Business Technician Education Council (BTEC), the Royal Society of Arts (RSA) and City and Guilds. It seemed logical therefore that, following various other reforms, these awarding bodies should join forces with three examination boards. OCEAC was therefore re-configured with RSA to form 'OCR', the name standing for Oxford, Cambridge and RSA; BTEC joined with London Examinations to form EDEXCEL, whilst the AEB teamed up with their long-time rival the Northern Examinations and Assessment Board (NEAB) and the City and Guilds to form the Assessment and Qualifications Alliance (AQA). Finally, their generic names were changed in order to reflect their wider briefs; they are now all called 'awarding bodies'.

Commentators were quick to point out the 'convenience' of having three awarding bodies which combined nicely with the major examination boards (Lloyd 1999). It suggested a pragmatic solution rather than a clearly thought-through, rational strategy taking into account market shares, profitability and so on. On the other hand the industry is not simply commercial; it operates in a 'quasi-market' because it provides a vital service to the country with the state acting as the funder buying services from a variety of providers such as the awarding bodies who do not simply seek to maximise their profits (Le Grand 1991; Hurd *et al.* 1997). That being the case, why have *three* awarding bodies; why not go the whole way and have only one? Such a situation is not uncommon in other parts of the world, so what are the arguments, for and against?

A single awarding body: arguments in favour

Proponents for a single body argue that first, it holds out the possibility of greater consistency. At the moment it is sometimes suggested that a grade in the same subject from two examination boards, is not necessarily equivalent. It is therefore possible for a candidate to 'fail' a subject with one board but 'pass' with another. Certainly schools and teachers tend to believe there is some truth in this because as schools and teachers have been made more publicly accountable there is evidence of increasing 'syllabus switching' (see the box on p. 26).

Second, a single awarding body could ensure that standards are maintained. At the moment if schools and teachers perceive one to be 'easier' than another, there is an incentive to switch to that one. The danger then is that because they are to a certain extent commercial organisations, awarding bodies may be tempted to attract customers by making all their examinations easier, and so a form of Gresham's Law comes into effect, with the bad (i.e. easier examinations) driving out the good (i.e. the harder, or more rigorous ones. See box (p. 30) and Bishop (1995) for a similar effect in US High School course selection).

Third, examinations are so important, goes the argument, that they should be exclusively in the hands of government through a single organisation. After all, the state pays for the education of the vast majority of its citizens, and indeed for their examination entry fees as well. Why should private organisation profit from what is essentially a central service? Furthermore, since other Key Stages in the National Curriculum are not tested through different awarding bodies, why should they be at Key Stages 4 and 5?

AWARDING BODIES: OLIGOPOLIES IN ACTION

An oligopolistic market is one with a few very large producers. As any econ-omist knows, such an industry possesses certain characteristics. First the few producers cannot compete on price, because any price fall by one will be instantly matched by the others and so everyone will lose out. In contrast, any price rise by one will not be matched by the others with the result that market share will disappear completely for the more expensive producer. Second, there is almost no product differentiation, because with so few producers any innovation will be instantly copied. Third, what competition there is comes through marketing. Indeed, oligopolistic firms *believe* they are madly competing because they spend so much on advertising, and of course they have at least to match the expenditure of their rivals.

So how does this correspond to the examinations industry? Well, awarding bodies do not compete on price – each syllabus costs more or less the same at each level; even 'uneconomic' syllabuses are subsidised, though for how long that will be so remains to be seen. The product is more or less homogeneous because each syllabus is subject to control by a govern-ment watchdog, QCA, which specifies core elements and will only approve syllabuses containing them. So how do awarding bodies compete? As we have seen in the theoretical model, the answer is through marketing. They send large volumes of information to schools, regardless of whether each one is an existing centre or not; they compete to provide better INSET with chief examiners offering technical advice that will 'improve grades' and so on. This is all expensive, naturally, and can only be justified if it attracts more customers. It is therefore inevitable that the awarding bodies will be tempted to win more market share in any way they can, even to the point, perhaps, of making papers easier.

As the analysis in the box shows, it seems as though competition is wasting resources. Thus each of the awarding bodies now sends expensively produced marketing brochures to *all* schools, regardless of whether they are existing centres or not. They have to do this to protect their market share as much as trying to expand it. All of this would be unnecessary with one body. Additionally, examinations contain both fixed and variable cost elements. Fixed costs include the fees paid for setting the papers, computer systems for processing the data and so on. These costs would hardly change if the exam-inations were two or three times as big (see the box on p. 28). A chief examiner will be paid more or less the same fee for writing an exam paper, regardless of whether 2,000 or 20,000 candidates sit it, and the same goes for printing the papers – once set up the marginal cost is very low indeed. One might also argue that the expensive systems that currently exist in order to ensure the maintenance of standards, including government watchdogs such as QCA would also be unnecessary, and so cost savings could be made there as well.

In addition, a single awarding body would make small entry subjects viable, whereas they are currently under threat. This is once again an argument based around the fixed and variable costs of an examination. Since awarding bodies currently charge more or less the same fee per candidate regardless of whether 2,000 or 20,000 enter, it is possible, indeed likely that the fixed costs (which are approximately the same for both) will eat up all the revenue earned from the small entry subject. Indeed, because this is often the case, examination boards have traditionally cross-subsidised these subjects from the profits they make on the large ones, but there is no guarantee that such *largesse* will continue given an increasingly competitive environment. The alternative, to charge higher fees for minority subjects, has so far been rejected on the grounds of equity. However, the argument is made that if there was only one awarding body and it was controlled by the government, such cross-subsidisation would continue because the state would recognise the educational imperative of keeping such subjects in the curriculum, and would therefore continue to offer them, regardless of the cost.

Finally, it is suggested that a single, what might be termed *nationalised* awarding body might act as a constraining element on politicians, who are at times keen to interfere with examination systems almost at a whim, without recognising the costs and complexities involved. Lloyd quotes a number of occasions in the 1990s when politicians made decisions apparently 'off the cuff', which resulted in large-scale and expensive revisions of papers simply because there was a lack of recognition of the time and expense such changes require:

> The restriction on coursework assessment to 20% of the whole
> . . . was announced by the then Prime Minister at a dinner not
> specifically concerned with education, and when syllabuses to which
> it had to apply had already been drafted. The requirement to allocate
> 5% of the marks for GCSE to spelling, punctuation and grammar
> . . . was introduced in 1992 after the examination papers and mark
> schemes to which it applied had been printed. In 1993 new A-level
> syllabuses had to be written, in which there was a widespread desire
> for modular schemes to be introduced; however the rules to govern
> such schemes were unknown because SEAC as it then was (the
> present QCA), was unable to agree upon them.
>
> (Lloyd, 1999: 7)

Briefly, then, the arguments in favour of a single awarding body are that it would ensure:

- greater consistency;
- a maintenance of standards;
- that exam fees remain within the public sector;

- that all the Key Stages are treated the same;
- the survival of small entry subjects; and
- more considered judgements by politicians when making statements about examinations.

A single awarding body: arguments against

The arguments against a single awarding body are as follows. First, it would eliminate choice. The fact that schools and teachers can switch from one awarding body to another means that each has to remain up-to-date and offer a good service. The danger of competition resulting in a lowering of standards is countered by the existence of checks and balances. For instance, QCA and OFSTED send teams out to compare marking and awarding procedures; comparative statistical analysis is undertaken, both by the awarding bodies themselves and by outside agencies such as universities; and these, when combined with publicity, especially when results are announced, promote consistency. In addition, the awarding bodies recognise their responsibilities, as well as the potential threat to their existence, and in recent years have become more open. The latest example of this is an experimental programme to send annotated scripts back to candidates, so that they and their teachers, can see where they have gone wrong (or got things right).

Many people believe a single awarding body would discourage curriculum innovation. Organisations such as the Nuffield Foundation have a history of curriculum development, sometimes introducing syllabuses that were relatively unpopular at first but which proved to be signposts for the future, and ones that the rest of the boards have eventually followed. The danger with having only one awarding body is that such innovation might be stifled. Indeed, there are indications that by reducing the number of syllabuses awarding bodies are allowed to offer, such a situation is already developing (Lines 1999). This is because an 'experimental' syllabus, if it cannot sit alongside an existing one with the same name, is an even greater risk than before, even assuming it is 'allowed through' by the QCA.

Tattersall (1994: 295) argues that 'a single board would be no guarantee of absolute comparability since the examination system relies on imperfect words to express assessment criteria and imperfect human beings to interpret those criteria and make judgements about attainment'. In other words, there is no reason why the imperfections of the current system would be addressed, much less solved, by a single awarding body. Lloyd (1999) argues in a similar vein to Tattersall, though perhaps less esoterically. The mechanics of running a single examination in some of the subjects would, he argues, simply make standardisation impossible. As we shall see in Chapters 7–9, at the moment every effort is made to ensure that all examiners become what might be termed 'clones' of the chief examiner, so that a script marked by anyone on the team will receive the same mark. This is difficult, even when there are relatively few scripts requiring a fairly small examining team, but if the numbers went into the hundreds of thousands of scripts, requiring huge examining teams, then the task would be almost impossible. Whether this inconsistency would be any greater, or less, than exists at present between the same-named subject being marked by different awarding bodies is, of course, open to debate, but the awarding bodies themselves argue that it would be.

Finally, a single awarding body would almost certainly be run by the government or its closely controlled agency. In effect this would mean examinations would be nationalised. Whilst there are many theoretical arguments in favour of nationalised industries, the current perception is that in practice they usually fail to deliver them. In addition this would mean yet more centralisation in education, which some oppose as a matter of principle.

In summary the arguments against a single awarding body are:

- it would eliminate choice;
- it might stifle curriculum development and innovation;
- it would no more guarantee consistency than exists under the present system;
- in practice ensuring consistency in a huge national examination would be impossible; and
- nationalised industries have a poor record in terms of efficiency.

A single awarding body: a conclusion

We have argued that the 'examinations industry' is an odd hybrid, in that it is dominated by a small number of large scale producers who do not seek necessarily to maximise profits. Within this 'quasi-market' the state acts not only as the sole customer, in the sense that it pays for the majority of the services provided, but also as 'referee', because it appoints quangos, currently QCA, to oversee the activities of the awarding bodies. For a long time the system worked, partly because the universities acted not only as ultimate paymasters to the examination boards, but also as guarantors of standards. It was also the case that governments were less interventionist.

The 'safety fence' of the universities has now largely disappeared, with the result that awarding bodies are being forced to compete ever more strongly in ways that, we have suggested, are not efficient and which may in the long run have an impact upon standards. It could be that a single awarding body is the logical outcome of this historic pattern, but we would resist such a move, mainly on the ground of its likely impact upon curriculum innovation and change. A single body would have autocratic powers and, like the Chinese example we quoted at the start of the chapter, would almost certainly retreat into a defence of the status quo. It is also likely, given the evidence of other state monopolies, that inefficient working practices would creep in, with little that schools, teachers or students could do to respond. But this is also part of our larger argument about the excessive and pervasive influence of examinations in and on our classrooms. Indeed Davis (1999) argues that through control of the curriculum, the inspection process and 'payment by results', built around league tables and examination grades, teachers are already in effect being told *how* to teach. Should governments gain absolute control of the examination process, the circle would be complete.

A CONSPIRACY THEORIST'S DREAM

If you believe in dark conspiracies dreamed up behind closed doors in Whitehall (and we don't), it is easy to conjure up a plan that would ultimately result in a single, nationalised awarding body. We have already seen in the box on p. 30 that in bringing the examination boards together, the government effectively created an oligopoly. Given the theoretical model, the effect was entirely predictable: the awarding bodies, unable to compete on product or price, are forced to gain market share and income by other means. The following article illustrates this.

Exam boards paid to approve textbooks

> Examination boards are under investigation over secretive deals with publishers in which they give their seal of approval to certain school textbooks, sometimes in return for a fee.
>
> In the past year, the three main exam boards – in fierce competition with each other for candidates to follow their GCSE and A-level syllabuses – have developed close commercial relationships with some educational publishers.
>
> They sometimes enter exclusive deals with one publisher, saying the book is approved or 'the official text-book'. Others endorse the books of several publishers for different subjects. And in some cases, boards charge a 'royalty' fee per book sold.
>
> (Rosie Waterhouse, *The Independent on Sunday* 28 November 1999: 15)

Now, returning to the conspiracy theory: if the three awarding bodies were seen to be less than perfectly ethical, what better reason could there be for the state to intervene and create a single, nationalised awarding body?

FOR FURTHER THINKING

We have tried to put both sides of the debate over a single board as fairly as possible, but we have suggested that the balance of the argument just favours the continuation of more than one awarding body.

1. What is your position in this debate?
2. Bearing in mind the shortcoming of an oligopolistic model, is there any way the examinations industry could be made more competitive, so that market share is fought over in different, more efficient ways than by marketing or other slightly questionable activities such as endorsing textbooks?

TENSIONS BETWEEN THE 'ACADEMIC' AND 'VOCATIONAL' PATHWAYS

One feature familiar to observers of the examination system in England and Wales today, is the existence of vocational qualifications sitting alongside what are commonly known as 'academic' ones. The creation of these different 'pathways' or 'tracks'[1] have their roots in the nineteenth century, when professional bodies created qualifications that sat outside mainstream education. Thus, training to become a chartered accountant, a lawyer or a doctor necessarily involved highly practical components that could neither be taught nor examined through the classroom/summative examination route alone, yet it also contained strong theoretical elements. This duality caused tensions between those who regarded the training as essentially vocational and others who regarded it as academic (Geddes 1995). The result was a division, which remains to this day, but it is one that many educationalists, as well as politicians, are now trying to close. Indeed, had this book been written ten years ago, and possibly even five, it is quite likely that vocational awards would have received little or no attention at all. The introduction of GNVQs have changed that, as they now occupy large parts of the whole curriculum in schools and colleges. No teacher or aspiring teacher can ignore them.

A BRIEF HISTORY OF VOCATIONAL QUALIFICATIONS

The history of vocational qualifications shows a similar pattern to the one described above in academic fields, in that over time changing social and economic circumstances forced attitudes and previously held assumptions about training to change. Even by the middle of the twentieth century the industrial landscape had altered markedly from that of one hundred years earlier, bringing with it the need for new skills and therefore different types of preparation for work. This change was particularly true of apprenticeships, the traditional form of training for those who, for whatever reason, were unable to gain academic qualifications but who were nevertheless gifted.

Progressively, and increasingly up to the 1980s, the number of industrial apprenticeships available to school leavers declined. Perhaps the most important reason for this was that they were largely based in the traditional, 'heavy' industries that have been for many years in serious, often terminal decline. This contraction not only resulted in a limited number of training opportunities, but also indicated that, even after serving a long period on poor wages, once qualified there would be no guarantee of a lifetime's employment. At the same time, growing industries tended to be in the service sector where flexibility was the key; the nascent information revolution required different skills, often ones unrelated to age or experience.

There were also more short-run reasons for the decline. First, the high wage settlements of the 1970s were said to have discouraged employers from taking on apprentices and finally, especially in the 1980s, periods of recession brought about by restructuring, as well as a determination to break the cost-push, demand-pull inflationary spiral, together resulted in heavy youth unemployment and a lack of training opportunities (Wolf 1995a; Green *et al.* 1999). Whilst unemployment remained high, it was argued, there would be little pressure on wages and that in turn would prevent costs and prices rising.

Nevertheless, whilst industrial apprenticeships declined, the need to qualify people in other vocational areas did not diminish, and so the proliferation of awarding bodies continued. Indeed, it was not until the 1964 Industrial Training Act that any attempt was made to reduce the number, and even this move was criticised for being too restricted and bureaucratic (DoE 1972). The underlying principle for training appeared to be what Unwin calls 'voluntarism and self-help', which, she says, continues to this day (Unwin, 1997: 77). It may also be a reflection of a somewhat ambiguous attitude towards vocational training itself. On the one hand such training is generally held in low regard, unlike other countries such as Germany (Green *et al.* 1999); Wolf calls this, 'the old English prejudice that there are only two tracks: academic and other' (1995b: 12). On the other hand, and apparently without any sense of contradiction or irony, vocational qualifications are seen as the only valid entry to the best-paid and arguably most prestigious professions: medicine, law and accountancy (Smithers 1998), though it is instructive to note that all three maintain their own assessment regime, which they jealously guard against what they regard as government 'interference'.

Thus, in the same way as the universities and government have vied for pre-eminence in the field of academic qualifications over the past one hundred and fifty years, so awarding bodies and the government have jockeyed for position in the vocational arena. The case of the accountancy profession is a typical example.

TENSIONS IN VOCATIONAL TRAINING – A CASE EXAMPLE

The Institute of Chartered Accountants of England and Wales (ICAEW) received its Royal charter in 1880, which gave it the right to set the standards to which all members of the chartered institute would have to comply. Like the ancient universities, the ICAEW was an august body, which argued that it was the only institution that could properly determine whether or not a person was suitably qualified to become an accountant. Understandably, much of the training involved was purely vocational. By becoming 'articled' to a firm, trainees demonstrated that they could practise, but in addition they also had to follow a curriculum leading to examinations. Up to 1945 this curriculum extended well beyond accountancy to include optional subjects such as Latin, Greek, geography, geology, history and a modern foreign language. This was because in those days most articled accountants left school aged fifteen or younger without any formal qualifications, and so the profession offered a wider education than simply that concerned with book-keeping. There was, therefore, a strange ambivalence about the role of the ICAEW, in that it was offering what could only be described as 'mainstream' education alongside a purely vocational one. This dual role was not lost on governments, and when in 1949 the Carr-Saunders report suggested that accountancy training should take place in commercial and technical colleges, the spectre of state control prompted stiff resistance, in which the ICAEW was at the forefront (Geddes 1995). It is significant that the government backed off and both training and the examinations remained the sole responsibility of the profession, as they still do today.

However, tensions between the two parties remain. Partly this is the result of an increasing cynicism towards self-regulation in general. Whether it be in accounting, the law, medicine or the police, self-regulation, in which examinations play an important part, is subject to considerable and increasing criticism, and it may be that the systems established in the nineteenth century have had their day. There is also the feeling that whatever the strengths of the argument that only the profession knows in detail what is appropriate to join its ranks, there is always the suggestion that entrance examinations are simply a way of controlling the labour supply, in order to maintain job security and salary levels for those 'allowed in'.

Then there exists the danger of duplication and inefficiency. Thus, for the vast majority of candidates, training to be a chartered accountant requires an intense period of examinations even *after* obtaining a degree. Indeed, academic accountants in universities are seen as a different breed from practising ones and have only a marginal input into the training process (Geddes 1995). The state is therefore supporting a university education leading to an accounting degree that is almost disregarded by the profession, whereas in many countries it is seen as the obvious and logical way to gain the necessary qualifications to practise.

Finally, it is hard to write *valid* written examinations for vocational subjects, because as we indicated at the beginning of this chapter (p. 22) it is always simpler and cheaper to test those things that are easy to test, regardless of their relevance. This is a criticism which has been levelled at accountancy examinations, for instance (Hoskin and Geddes 1997), and which is reminiscent of the situation that developed in the Chinese civil service. The qualification exams still emphasise the rote learning of accounting principles and practices and the manipulation of figures and yet today's accountants are increasingly required to demonstrate wider business skills such as decision making, team working, ICT competence and so on. Such a narrow approach would be bad enough in itself, but because of the increasing pace of change in the business world, even the basic principles are often rendered out of date within a very short time because of legislative changes; the examination has therefore tested inappropriate skills and emphasised knowledge retention of only partial relevance to the practising professional.

In referring to such professions as accounting, medicine and the law we are necessarily concentrating on the most prestigious vocational qualifications, but it must be remembered that there are literally hundreds of others that are built around a form of summative assessment, though most are work-based and emphasise the ability to demonstrate 'competence' in a number of tasks. Like the professions, these standards grew up over time to meet the needs of the trades or industries concerned. However, their underlying assumption was that an individual, once trained, would stay in the same line of employment for the rest of their working life. This assumption has been and is increasingly subject to challenge, which carries the danger that people will question the value of training altogether; an attitude that can only be countered by offering qualifications with a universal currency, which, like academic ones, can be taken from job to job. By the mid-1980s it was apparent to the government that some form of standardisation in vocational qualifications was needed, and so in its 1991 White Paper, the then Conservative government attempted to bring all the vocational qualifications under a single banner, that of National Vocational Qualifications (NVQs). At the same time it introduced a new and significant qualification, General National Vocational Qualifications (GNVQs).

THE 1991 WHITE PAPER, EDUCATION AND TRAINING FOR THE TWENTY-FIRST CENTURY

The 1991 White Paper was important in a number of respects, not least in the creation of different 'tracks' or 'pathways' for post-16 students to follow. The first of these tracks was what is still called the 'academic', despite efforts to re-name it; the second the vocational and the third, a new qualification, GNVQs. At the same time as these tracks were established, two government quangos were set up to oversee their development. One, the School Curriculum and Assessment Authority (SCAA) had responsibility for the National Curriculum, GCSEs and A-levels, and the second, the National Council for Vocational Qualifications (NCVQ), overlooked vocational qualifications, including GNVQs. Some commentators have argued that the aim of having three tracks was to avoid any dilution of A-level standards, because less able students would be able to pursue other qualifications whilst still staying on at school – something which the government was keen to encourage (Hodgson and Spours 1997; Young 1997).

From their creation in 1991, SCAA and NCVQ were independent, though liaison was often close. In 1998 they were brought together under a single authority called the Qualifications and Curriculum Authority (QCA). This represented a significant change, and an attempt to rationalise all qualifications. This task has proved to be a difficult one, however, because the history of academic and vocational qualifications is, as we have seen, quite different, and that in turn has resulted in assessment regimes that are also quite distinct. Nevertheless, the existence of a single body does represent a further step along the path of government influence over, and control of assessment. In some ways this has been an underlying theme of the whole chapter and so we will finish by exploring the issue of centralisation in more depth.

EXTERNAL ASSESSMENT, CENTRALISATION AND THE CURRICULUM

The formation of QCA, the quasi–autonomous educational agency of the Department for Education and Employment (itself a marriage of separate 'education' and 'employment' departments), is the latest symbol of the historic progression we have explored throughout this chapter, namely increasing central government involvement in, and control of all aspects of education and training. The precise manifestations of this policy are to some extent cloaked by incremental decisions concerning the organisation of external, largely summative examinations. These policies, such as defining subject cores, insisting on syllabus approval and so on, all appear relatively insignificant and to possess an internal logic of their own, but when added together they result in a significant shift in emphasis. We would argue that when they are combined with a raft of other policies designed to make schools more accountable and local education authorities less influential, the impact has far reaching consequences on the curriculum that few have so far identified.

In detail, there are a number of features that lead to this conclusion. The first is within schools themselves, where each one has been given more autonomy, largely at the expense of local authorities. This is important at a policy level because LEAs were often large enough to resist central government directives – indeed that was one of the main reasons why governments wanted to reduce their powers in the first place (Thatcher 1993; Baker quoted in Davies, 1999). Now individual schools are not strong enough to do so, especially since alongside independence, accountability has also increased, not only through 'league tables' but also with tighter employment contracts and proposals on performance-related pay (Green et al. 1999). The question of how accountability should be measured is a thorny one (see Chapter 6), although to some politicians it appears relatively simple: external examination results are seen as perfectly accurate, fair and efficient (Black 1998) and so that is the yardstick against which schools and teachers should have to perform. The result is an emphasis in classrooms on 'teaching to the test' to the detriment, not only of formative assessment but of curriculum innovation and development generally (Stobart and Gipps 1997; Davis 1999c).

'RAISING STANDARDS'

The current education secretary, David Blunkett, has decided to judge his own performance against examination results. He says he will resign if fewer than 75 per cent of Year 6 children have not reached level four or better in mathematics and 80 per cent of them in English by the year 2002. Davis, cites this as a mistaken belief that it is 'raising standards'. Raising standards, he says 'is not a synonym for improving examination performance' (Davis 1999: 2). More subtle, of course, is the message that the education secretary is sending to schools and the public: that if such tests are an appropriate measure of his performance then they must be equally so for the profession generally.

It is important to recognise that in reducing the power and influence of LEAs, the education sector has lost what was often a fertile ground for curriculum and assessment innovation. LEAs were able to gather like-minded teachers together relatively cheaply, usually prompted by a forward thinking adviser (now often and significantly re-named an 'inspector'), not only to foster development in the subject, but also to enrich the professionalism of the teachers involved. Furthermore, such local initiatives could be supported by Mode 3 examinations, i.e. ones designed, set and marked locally but moderated by an examination board to ensure respectability and credibility. Whilst it is wrong to say such local initiatives have entirely stopped, there are few that are funded and supported by LEAs (Tattersall 1994).

The box on p. 34 speculated on a strategic pattern that may be discernable at a policy level. If the ultimate aim is to raise standards by making schools more accountable, and if the only way to measure effectiveness is through external examinations then the options are clear. First, remove the influence of local education authorities, second, produce and publish league tables, third, impose a rigid inspection regime and fourth, get a tight grip on the examinations industry. All of these policies have been effected over the past decade or so. Of course everyone supports the idea of raising standards, but using examinations as a central weapon to achieve it is dangerous, because as Stobart and Gipps point out with reference to an earlier experiment to introduce payments by results based on exam performance, in 1862:

What this historical episode clearly shows is that using assessment to raise standards may have unintentional consequences. . . . Not only did the scheme eventually collapse under its own bureaucratic weight, it also produced some of the worst examples of 'teaching to the test'

(Stobart and Gipps 1997: 4)

FOR FURTHER THINKING

In many European countries, most notably in Europe's most successful economy of the second half of the twentieth century, Germany, vocational training is perceived to be as demanding and worthwhile as the academic route.

1.   What is it about vocational qualifications that makes them seem somehow inferior in Britain? Is this a peculiarly British, perhaps even English trait that is inextricably bound up with the country's historical development?
2.   How might we change attitudes in the UK, and what would be the implications of such changes in our schools?

FURTHER READING

For those interested in a more detailed discussion of language testing see Chapter 19 in R. Wood (1991) *Assessment and Testing*. This book will also provide a rich source for readings on many aspects of examinations.

Andrew Davis has produced a brief pamphlet called *Educational Assessment: a Critique of Current Policy* (1999) which is quite brief and easy to read. It is controversial and represents an all out attack on the current system. In some ways it is a more accessible version of his full length book, entitled *The Limits of Educational Assessment* (1998b).

NOTE

1 Whether they are called 'pathways' or 'tracks', Hodgson and Spours (1997) argue, is important. 'Pathways' suggests the possibility of movement from one to the other, 'tracks' does not. The word 'track' is correct, they say, because the system is assigned to prevent 'leakage' from the vocational to the academic, something which Young (1997) suggests was reinforced by the Dearing 16–19 Review (1996).

4 Examination Technologies

This chapter traces the development of GCSEs, A-levels and National Curriculum tests, as well as GNVQs and vocational qualifications. It provides details on the processes involved in external examinations and shows the extent to which the system is designed to ensure fairness towards candidates and a valid test of performance and aptitude. Thus, aspects of what might be termed the 'technology' of formal assessment are discussed. These include specified aims, assessment objectives, relationships with objectives and examination components, levels of performance and mark schemes. The chapter tracks the process of setting and marking papers and shows that despite the aim of improving both reliability and validity, neither can be achieved with absolute certainty all of the time. This conclusion casts some doubt on the notion of the examination 'gold standard'. The final section offers a further critique of the role of government in the process.

A NOTE ON TERMS

One of the differences between what are often termed an 'academic' and a 'vocational' subject is that the former was described by means of a 'syllabus' and the latter by a 'specification'. In order to achieve the aim of harmonising qualifications wherever possible, it was decided that from 2000 onwards the word *specification* will be used by both. That being so, we have adopted the same policy, except where we describe historical events.

SETTING EXAMINATIONS

In this section we shall examine the process by which papers for external examinations are set. In the last few years strenuous efforts have been made by the awarding bodies, with prompting from the government's *regulatory bodies* in charge of assessment (now QCA), to standardise these processes and the names and functions of those involved in the setting and marking of examinations. Alongside these changes, and no doubt connected to them, has been the acceptance by the awarding bodies of a greater degree of account-ability to schools, teachers, candidates and the public generally.

In this section we will detail the names and functions of those *directly* involved in an examination, but any exam will normally consist of a number of *components*, which may include course work as well as written papers. It should be borne in mind that awarding bodies are now large scale businesses and so have a complex management structure that exists to help run them. This management tier is only indirectly involved in the examining process, though it makes all the strategic decisions. As organisations the awarding bodies are unique, not least because their full-time employees are vastly outnumbered by seasonal, part-time homeworkers who have little or no say in the running of the business and virtually no employment rights (see Lloyd 1999: 9–12).

The Chair of Examiners

This person is a subject expert and generally someone with a great deal of experience of examinations. The role is designed to ensure consistency of stan-dards between specifications, where an examination board has two or more with the same name. Such a situation may arise through the introduction of a curriculum development project's specification, or as a result of a modular specification sitting alongside what are commonly called 'linear' ones (i.e. those with a synoptic examination taken at the end of the course). Thus EDEXCEL offered Nuffield Economics and Business A-level in 1996, but it already had separate syllabuses in both economics and business studies. There it was neces-sary for the Chair of Examiners, in this case an academic economist, to ensure that the papers within each specification, and also across syllabuses, appeared to be equally challenging. His job also involved chairing the awarding meet-ings and setting grade boundaries, so that an A grade, a C grade or whatever, represented an equivalent standard, regardless of specification. Finally the chair will be required to submit a report on the examination as a whole.

The chief examiner (CE)

In many respects the chief examiner is the most important person in the whole examining process. He or she sets at least one component of the overall examination, draws up the mark-scheme, liaises with the reviser, the principal examiner(s) and the Chair of Examiners. In setting the paper and in overseeing the entire examination the CE will not only have to ensure that the entire specification is covered over a number of years and that each exam covers a satisfactory range within the specification, but also that it covers the assessment objectives, and gives satisfactory weight to each. The CE will also have to monitor each component to ensure that each is equally demanding.

The chief examiner will run the Standardisation Meeting (see p. 46) and make judgements on answers that candidates make and the performance of the team of examiners. She or he will advise the awarding committee on grade boundaries and will write a report on the work of candidates after the exam is finished. The CE will also re-mark scripts where there has been an appeal, and may write individual reports where candidates request them. Increasingly the CE is required to front INSET meetings and 'post-mortems' on the last set of papers.

Clearly the role of chief examiner is a vital one, not just in purely practical terms, but also because it is effectively exerting influence on the specification and to a certain extent the teaching that takes place in schools. It should be remembered that just as in the legal arena where there is 'statute law' that is laid down by parliament, there is also 'case law', which results from decisions made by judges when applying the statutes in court, so in examinations there is a specification (statutory law), but then there are the examinations themselves (case law), which may well 'move' the specification somewhat, as the chief examiner attempts to keep it up-to-date. Any teacher new to a particular subject must therefore read both the specification and recent examinations, as well as attending INSET sessions. Finally, and as we saw in the last chapter somewhat controversially, many chief examiners also write textbooks; it would be a confident or foolhardy teacher who did not purchase at least one copy!

Of course, the chief examiner's power is by no means absolute; he or she will have to respond to a number of individuals and to committees before the examination is sat, and then to teachers and candidates afterwards. Generally chief examiners are appointed for five-year terms, but this is reviewed annually, and it is not unusual for the contract not to be renewed if the examination has proved highly controversial. Indeed some chief examiners feel somewhat exposed – praise for good papers is rarely expressed, and when it is the awarding body and the subject committee often take as much credit as they do, but when the opposite happens, it is the chief examiner who bears the brunt of the criticism, even to the extent of being dismissed. Nevertheless, it is an exciting and challenging role and one that in some senses reflects the pinnacle of subject expertise.

Over the years the responsibilities and commitments of the chief examiner have grown alongside the examinations industry. Modular examinations sat on a number of occasions throughout the academic year, the high number of re-marks, the requirement to provide INSET, adhere to codes of practice, write reports, update reading lists and so on mean that the job has become virtually full-time. Where once it was a post that a practising teacher or university lecturer could fill, its demands, especially in large entry subjects have now made this more difficult, with the result that many chief examiners are now either part-time or retired. It is possible, therefore, to foresee a time when chief examiners are offered secondments from their school or college, or even become employees of the awarding bodies themselves. This would at least improve their conditions of employment, which are at the moment, poor.

The principal examiner

This person has a similar role to the chief examiner, except that he or she only takes responsibility for one component rather than the entire examination. Very often the principal examiner will become the chief after the latter has served their term of office.

The reviser

The role of the reviser, as the name suggests, is to examine drafts of exam papers set by the chief and principal examiners. He or she will be looking for a consistent coverage of the specification and in particular will want to ensure that the paper does not deviate too far from those of previous years. It is a great temptation for chief examiners to get 'too clever' as the years roll by because they know that they have asked questions on particular areas of the specification before and they will want to avoid repetition; sometimes they achieve this by making the questions more obscure and thus more difficult. It is the reviser's job to remind the setters that for most candidates this will be the first and only time they will sit the paper, and asking mainstream, apparently 'easy' questions is as fair, perhaps fairer, than asking ones that only the high grade candidates will be able to answer well (see pp. 63–65 for what makes an examination 'hard' or 'easy').

The reviser and the paper setters will work quite closely together, but in an iterative way. It is not good for the paper if the reviser becomes a 'rubber stamp' because there will be times when, for the sake of the candidates, he or she simply has to disagree with the chief examiner, in which case the dispute will have to be settled by the subject committee.

The assessor

The assessor works through the paper as if he or she were a candidate. This is a means of checking for ambiguities and any errors in the printing or preparation of the paper. Importantly, timing is checked, both in terms of the overall requirement and also in terms of individual questions, so that the mark allocations reflect the time taken to answer them. The assessor will then check the provisional mark scheme to ensure that it matches the paper. This aspect of pre-testing is taken still further with multiple choice papers, where certain centres sit 'mock' exams. The answers are analysed statistically – which, given that they are machine marked is relatively easy and cheap – and ambiguous questions re-written or eliminated. It is also possible to discover which questions are hard and which easy, and so an actual paper can be set using the question 'bank' with a profile of difficulty known in advance. The lack of such pre-testing was one of the problems with the early GNVQ tests, which quickly developed a poor reputation amongst schools and colleges (Capey 1995).

The standardisation meeting

One principle of examining is to ensure maximum reliability, i.e. that as much as is humanly possible, if an identical script is marked by different examiners, the mark will be the same. The ideal is that all the examiners think and act as the chief or principal intends; that they are, in effect, 'clones'. Of course this is not possible (and in other ways undesirable), and examiners are therefore under considerable pressure at least to mark consistently, because an erratic marker is the most difficult to deal with. So, about five or six days after the examination, a standardisation meeting is held. A small number of scripts will have been photocopied immediately after the examination has ended and sent to all the examiners. As far as possible they will have been selected (usually on the advice of the teacher responsible for preparing the candidates) to cover the mark range.

At the moderation meeting the chief and principal examiners will go through the exam paper, and then the photocopied scripts. By this time the assistant examiners will also have had a chance to look at their own allocation and will raise points that require clarification. This can be controversial and discussion can become heated, but ultimately it is important for the chief examiner to make a decision, even if some of the examiners don't agree with it! The crucial factor is that when the same issue comes up again when the examiners are marking their own scripts that they know what to do and whether or not to award marks.

There are always some points that only arise after the standardisation meeting, in which case the chief examiner makes a decision, and then passes that decision down to the team leaders who in turn inform their assistant examiners. This process has necessarily to be both quick and precise because it may require examiners to go back over scripts already marked, to ensure that the decision applies to all candidates. It is at this stage that the mark scheme, which up to this point has been called 'provisional' becomes a fully working document, and it is the chief examiner's job, with the help of the awarding body's officer, to compose a 'clean copy' for circulation.

THE STANDARDISATION MEETING: A PERSONAL MEMOIR

I was once a chief examiner responsible for a paper that consisted entirely of essays, which are known to be amongst the most difficult to standardise. As Wood puts it, 'It might as well be recognised at once that the scoring of essays is a complex process, with many variables in multiple combination influencing the reader differentially (Chase 1986). Only one of these is the content of the essay, and it could be that this is of only modest importance in determining score for an essay (Rafoth and Rubin 1984).' (Wood 1991: 53)

On one occasion I collected the marks of one photocopied essay that the assistant examiners had read in advance of the standardisation meeting. The maximum mark allowed was twenty. The senior examiners and myself had decided that the essay was worth eighteen, but I was not surprised to learn that some had given it as few as twelve. I was shocked, however, to discover a mark of twenty two. 'This must be a mistake' I declared. 'No', responded the individual concerned, 'I thought it was so good it deserved more than one hundred per cent'.

In technical terms this is known as 'between-rater variation'. Quoting Wood again: 'In brief, the problems are that different raters tend to assign different grades to the same paper, that a single rater tends to assign different grades to the same paper on different occasions, and that these differences tend to increase as the essay question permits greater freedom of response' (*ibid.*).

The team leader

Assuming the size of the examination justifies it, after a minimum of two years, assistant examiners who have proved themselves to be accurate markers, good administrators and who also indicate that they have the potential to lead others, are offered the chance to become team leaders. As part of their role they work through the photocopied scripts at the standardisation meeting and note how closely the assistant examiners in their team are to the agreed mark. It is often at this stage that it becomes clear that whilst the majority are more or less in line, some markers are 'lenient' and others 'severe'. This can often be accommodated at the standardisation meeting, but it may be that after the marking has finished that the profile of the scripts marked continues to show a consistent tendency one way or the other. Though this is by no means ideal, it is possible to adjust the marks accordingly. The difficulty comes when an examiner is inconsistent. When this happens it often means that the person will not be allowed to continue marking and will be asked to return their scripts to the examination board.

During the three-week marking period, every assistant examiner will send samples of their work to their team leader, who will themselves have their scripts sampled by the chief or principal. Certainly at the first sample stage examiners can have their marking modified. This is usually no more than saying that they are being a bit 'mean' on a particular question, or perhaps remind them of a decision taken at the moderation meeting, but if the marking is consistent the team leaders will allow them to continue, all the while keeping a close check for any further deviation. If discrepancies arise the team leader will continue to sample more and more of the marked work until a clear decision can be made; this may include having to re-mark all of the scripts.

The assistant examiner

This is the person whose main function is to mark the scripts. He or she will normally be a practising teacher, usually teaching the specification that is being examined and with a minimum of two or three years in the classroom. The job is a challenging one since it demands high levels of concentration over a quite lengthy period of time, usually around three weeks. It also requires an ability to accept criticism and modify work, as well as being an efficient administrator. In recent years the job has become increasingly difficult. For instance, at one time some mark schemes for a piece of extended writing or an essay consisted of a few sentences that indicated a general sense of the direction an answer might take. The assistant examiner then read the entire answer and awarded a mark, mainly based on experience and 'intuition'. Today things are quite different. As far as possible, factual information is supplied in the mark schemes, and for discursive answers 'levels of response' schemes are supplied (see Figure 4.1). The effect of this is to 'tighten' the process and to ensure, as far as possible, that when an answer is marked by two people, the result will be the same i.e. maximise reliability (though as Wood 1991: 62 indicates quoting an International Study (IEA 1988) there is no evidence that analytic is *necessarily* more reliable than impressionistic marking). This complexity in the mark schemes means that assistant examiners have to absorb much more information before they can start marking. Because they are paid on a piece rate, i.e. a rate per script, the time taken to learn the mark scheme necessarily affects the amount of money received per hour.

Other changes have also made the assistant examiner's job more challenging. Increasingly chief examiners are insisting that scripts are annotated, so that anyone checking them can see where marks were given, or not, and the reasons why. All this takes time, as well as increasing the pressure to get things right. Should recent proposals be put into effect whereby candidates' scripts are returned then there will be even more pressure as examiners' work comes under scrutiny by a wider audience. As the box below shows, all these changes that are adding to the work-load are beginning to have a cumulative and worrying effect.

'WHY EXAMS ARE FAILING'

In an article given the headline 'Why exams are failing', Vivien Anthony, the secretary of the influential Headmasters and Headmistresses Conference, which represents the leading independent schools, wrote about what he saw as the growing list of 'failures' within the examination system. 'Part of the problem' he wrote 'lies with the quantity and quality of examiners. While the boards say they can just about find enough examiners, they are stretched in subjects such as English and admit that the quality is not what it was. Not long ago chief examiners were from universities and there were several dons among the assistant examiners. Most teachers on the examining panels were either heads of department or very experienced. Nowadays it is rare to find examiners from universities and in some subjects the boards are appointing examiners with little teaching experience. . . .

A drive to recruit and retain more examiners is essential if the quality is not to diminish further. There must be better training and the work made more attractive. It is no wonder there are serious marking errors when examiners have to fit in their marking on top of all the other work going on at the busy end of term.'

(Anthony 1999: 45)

The job of assistant examiner has its rewards, however, which extend beyond the obvious financial ones. First there is admission into what at one time was an almost secret society. Learning how your own pupils' work will ultimately be marked provides insights that can be of enormous help within the classroom. For instance, an examination question can be set and the mark scheme issued to the students. They can then apply the scheme to their own work, or that of their peers if felt appropriate. Most are quite harsh critics of their own material in such circumstances, and they begin to understand what is really meant by words and phrases such as 'relevance', 'making all working clear and unambiguous' and so on. It not only prepares them fully for the examination, it also has a clear formative function because they begin to see that factual regurgitation is not *per se* a passport to instant examination success. For the developing professional, becoming an assistant examiner offers the chance to make contacts with others around the country. Finally there is the opportunity to influence the direction of the subject by becoming a part of the exam 'management team', either as team leader, reviser, principal or chief examiner.

The principal moderator

Where an examination has a coursework component, a principal moderator, leading a team of assistant moderators, will carry out similar functions to the principal examiner, although of course that person will be dealing with work marked by teachers. This adds a different dimension to the role because she or he will be required to liaise with schools directly in order to prepare staff for the examination, follow up their marking (especially if the work has been graded differently) and offer remedial help where necessary.

The assistant moderator

These are the examining boards' representatives responsible for teacher marked coursework. As their job title suggests, they compare marks awarded for different pieces of work, then compare them with other pieces from other centres and then adjust them as necessary. It is, after all, not surprising that marks from one centre differ from those in another, because teachers will only see the work of their own pupils, and that may simply be an unrepresentative sample. There may also be favouritism, though it is just as likely that teachers will be harder on their own pupils than the reverse (see Gipps and Murphy 1994, for a discussion on possible and actual stereotyping). Whichever the case, such deviations have to be ironed out, and it is the moderator's job to do so. It can be an unenviable task and one requiring a great deal of tact and diplomacy – there are few teachers who readily accept that their marking is at 'fault', but it is a learning process, and over time most come to accept that the moderator's experience and breadth of information gives him or her a unique perspective, which results in a fairer deal for all candidates. Not only that, but it professionalises teachers in other ways as well. For instance, they learn to operate levels of response marking schemes; to look beyond the superficial – such as presentation – and seek 'higher skills'; and they learn how to give constructive and formative feedback to pupils.

The awarding body officer

The awarding body officer, often still called a 'subject officer', is a crucial part of the examination organisation. He or she is a full-time employee of the Board with responsibility for ensuring that all the papers are set, moderated, printed and distributed within the required time-scale. The job requires liaising with government quangos, such as QCA, when required to and acting as the focal point for enquiries about an examination, or a series of examinations. As a result of often being the voice at the end of the telephone, teachers will get to know the subject officer, even if they are not themselves a part of the examining team. Traditionally subject officers are ex-teachers, usually in the subjects for which they are responsible. This offers considerable advantages. First, the subject officer can 'speak the language' that teachers understand at a general level, as well as being able to field subject-specific enquiries rather than having to put the teacher off and refer each one to the chief examiner. Second, the subject officer can understand and empathise with the pressures that teachers are under, especially during the marking period. Third, by being knowledgeable in the subject, the officer in effect becomes 'another pair of eyes' during the scrutiny period, so that ambiguities or inconsistencies can be ironed out at an early stage. Having to appoint an ex-teacher of the subject reduces flexibility however and with increasing competition there is pressure on the awarding body to keep costs as low as possible, so subject officers now have responsibility for a much wider range of subjects than they did in the past. This necessarily restricts the input they can have to any one alone.

The subject committee

Each subject will have a committee whose responsibility it is to scrutinise the proposed papers set by the chief and principal examiners and agree changes or modifications. Some, if not all of the committee will also be involved in the grade awarding procedures at the end of the examining process (see p. 53). Generally members of the subject committees are practising teachers though it is not uncommon for the Chair to be a member of a senior management team from a school or college – though with a background in the subject – or perhaps someone from Higher Education.

Mark schemes

As was indicated above (see p. 48) mark schemes have come a long way from the days when they were little more than a few sentences indicating a general 'feel' for what the examiners were looking for. Now, with a greater emphasis on positive achievement and specifying criteria, as far as possible they detail where marks should be given. For instance, if a graph is to be drawn, marks may be available for giving it a correct title, correctly labelling the axes, perhaps getting the scales right, and for drawing the curve or curves. Where the question is of the 'list' variety, the setter will almost certainly supply more answers than anyone might expect a candidate to offer. Thus if the question says 'Give four ways . . .' the mark scheme will probably show six or even more. Candidates are *not* expected to know everything. After all, they are working under stressful conditions and that has to be recognised. However, if they do list more than the required number they will not be penalised; indeed it is a good idea for candidates always to do so from a 'mark grubbing' angle, just in case one that they come up with is wrong!

POSITIVE AND NEGATIVE MARKING

Examiners now credit positive achievement. This was not always the case as Lloyd (1999) explains:

> A particularly striking example used to arise in the case of dictation in Modern Languages. . . . A mark was deducted for each mistake, so that if a passage was 100 words long and 20 marks were available a

candidate who got 80 words right would score no marks, since the 20 words wrong would have cost all the marks. . . .

Similarly in . . . Latin, it used to be the case . . . that candidates who omitted a word in translation could be penalized up to three marks, being deemed to have failed not only in their knowledge of the meaning of the word but also in its grammatical features, of which there were probably at least two. But a candidate who guessed a wrong meaning and correctly showed the grammatical elements would lose only one mark. Since examining Boards at that time did not publish their mark schemes . . . candidates did not know of this severity (unless their teacher also happened to be an examiner).

(p. 61)

In the case of discursive questions, mark schemes often follow what are called 'levels of response', which are said to follow a 'hierarchy', such as Bloom's taxonomy of educational objectives. The idea is to 'unpack' achievement so that a broader set of skills, understanding and more generic capacities can be rewarded, rather than straight factual content. Thus, in a twenty mark question, the first five might be available for content or knowledge recall, the second five for developing the argument so that a maximum of ten marks can be achieved, the third five, up to fifteen for analysis and the final five up to the maximum, for evaluation. This means that a candidate who simply lists twenty factual points can still only earn five marks. The idea behind this ceiling is to encourage a thoughtful approach rather than just rote learning – though as the box on p. 53 details, no one should underestimate the difficulty of memorising factual information. Nevertheless, rote learning can occur without any genuine understanding of the subject matter, and so the rewards are spread between different elements: content, analysis and evaluation. In theory one might be able to earn high marks for evaluation without passing through all the preceding levels, but in practice evaluation requires supporting evidence if it is to be seen as genuine, and not simply a conditioned response.

Readers should note that there is a recognition in the generic mark scheme that quality may vary in an answer. It is not expected that candidates will maintain the highest standard throughout. This can be a problem for examiners who may be tempted to 'mark down' a response when a part of the answer falls below expectation, and training is undertaken to ensure, as much as possible, that this does not happen. Note, too, that credit is given for the quality of SPAG, which stands for Spelling, Punctuation and Grammar. Sometimes SPAG marks are awarded separately, and sometimes, as here, incorporated in the overall scheme.

WHAT IS EVALUATION?

Encouraging students to reach what are termed 'higher level skills', such as analysis and evaluation, is a laudable ambition, but one that must be approached with caution. First there is the difficulty of definition. What precisely *is* 'evaluation'? It may be seen as the ability to come to some kind of conclusion having weighed up all the evidence, but it is possible for a candidate in an examination to *appear* to be evaluative, when they may in fact be doing little more than expressing a second-hand opinion or even a prejudiced position. It would be quite wrong, therefore, for an examiner to award between sixteen and twenty marks in an essay, unless apparently evaluative statements can be supported, which is where subject knowledge comes into its own. The statement 'Hitler was an evil man' is not in itself evaluative, unless evidence of a factual kind, such as mass genocide in the concentration camps of Auschwitz, Buchenwald and so on are brought in to support the argument. In a sense this turns the skills hierarchy on its head – it is relatively easy to remember Hitler as being evil; remembering the names of certain concentration camps to support this judgement can be a great deal harder.

Grading/awarding

Once the scripts have been marked, statistics begin to play a part in the process. Cumulative frequency graphs show the proportion of candidates at certain scores in each of the papers (or components as they are technically called). When the marks for all the components are summed, it becomes possible for the information to be graphed to give a picture of the examination overall. The rest of the procedure is a mixture of 'science' and 'art', and has been subject to some criticism.

The chief examiner will report, either orally or in writing (or both) on the way the examination was conducted. This may involve drawing attention to a question that caused special difficulties to candidates or to markers, and asking the committee members to take this into account when they look at scripts. It may happen that a question has to be removed from the process altogether – perhaps complaints have been received that a question was not a fair interpretation of the specification and the candidates' performances indicate that few had been taught the particular topic.

The report will also comment on the comparative performance of the candidates from one year to the next, bearing in mind that if the subject entry is sufficiently large, there should not be any great deviation. This is an important point to remember, because the assumption that each cohort will exhibit similar characteristics with more or less the same proportion getting As, Bs, Cs and so on is a form of norm referencing that remains in place, despite a

In marking history essays at Advanced and AS levels, examiners of history have two sets of mark schemes to work with, one generic and the other specific.

THE GENERIC MARK SCHEME:

Level 1

Either The answer demonstrates some relevant knowledge but provides little or no analytical focus. It follows an almost exclusively descriptive route, and the descriptions will have significant gaps and/or inaccuracies.

Or The answer implies an analytical response but is excessively generalised, being largely devoid of specific historical knowledge. The answer relies on assertion and not argument.

Writing skills are limited. Communication will normally be ragged and fragmentary. Frequent syntactical and spelling errors are likely to be found.

(0–6 marks)

Level 2

Either The answer depends disproportionately on the selection of material which, although it contains some detail and is substantially relevant, is not focused on the analytical demands of the question. There may be some gaps and/or inaccuracies in the historical knowledge.

Or The answer is predominantly analytical in intent and shows understanding of some issues relevant to the question. It will include some relevant detail but knowledge of the topic overall will be patchy and may include some inaccuracies.

The writing will show some coherence but will either be disjointed and/or poorly organised. Frequent syntactical and spelling errors are likely to be found.

(7–13 marks)

Level 3

The answer is predominantly analytical and offers a judgement showing some understanding of the issues relevant to the question. It will include a developed evaluation of some of these issues, although an analytical focus may not be maintained through the answer. The topic will be known in some detail and the analysis will be supported by mostly accurate and precise knowledge, but deployment of that knowledge may not be sufficiently selective.

Figure 4.1 History mark scheme

The writing will show some degree of both control and direction but these attributes may not be maintained throughout the answer. Meaning will be conveyed serviceably, although some syntactical and/or spelling errors may be found.

(14–20 marks)

THE SPECIFIC MARK SCHEME:

In answering the question below, examiners had a further five levels to work from:

Examine the view that US failure in Vietnam resulted more from losing the hearts and minds of the US people than from military defeats.

Level 1
Candidates will produce rather generalised material on the Vietnam war, possibly even including discussion on why the USA entered the war. There will be gaps and may be inaccuracies.

Level 2
Material about the war will mostly be accurate and there will be some detail, for example on the reasons why the USA was so often frustrated in the war. There is likely to be discussion of reasons for defeats and there may also be detail on domestic 'hearts and minds'.

Level 3
Focus will be predominantly analytical and candidates will have some detailed knowledge about defeats or setbacks in Vietnam and the growing opposition to deployment of US troops in Vietnam. Candidates may use knowledge about anti-draft campaigns. The essay should reach a reasoned conclusion although there may be a lack of balance.

Level 4
The analytical focus will be sharp and clear, and reasoned preferences about reasons for US defeat/withdrawal. Candidates at this level are likely to be confident in discussing the ideological or moral dimension as it surfaced during the 1960s.

Level 5
The insights will be sustained, the reasoned argument cogently sustained and it will be clear that the effective criteria for selection from a range of detailed material have been deployed.

Figure 4.1 continued

greater emphasis on criteria. However, it is a 'safe' position statistically (within certain 'confidence limits') and the one taken by the awarding bodies in the majority of cases.

The starting point for any review of scripts designed to determine this year's grade boundaries, therefore, are those achieved the previous year. So if 67 was the A/B boundary last year, it is assumed that there will not be a large deviation this time (this may not be a percentage figure – many papers are not marked out of one hundred, and the 'raw' figure is used). The committee members' first task, however, is to read 'archive scripts' from the previous year, to remind themselves, in the case of an A-level, of what an A, C and pass papers were like. Following this, the current year's scripts are read at or around last year's mark boundaries and decisions are taken about possible changes; this year the committee might believe 68 and not 67 is an A grade, for instance. If this is the case the statistics will then show how 68 translates into numbers and proportions of candidates getting A grades.

The result of such an exercise may be controversial, with the committee insisting on a mark that apparently changes the proportions of candidates getting particular grades quite significantly. The members may feel quite strongly about this, but the awarding bodies are more sanguine; they tend to believe that the statistics are more reliable, and so a committee which suggests radical change will have to argue its case very powerfully if it is to succeed.

It has to be said that awarding bodies are rarely persuaded, which makes sense from a logical standpoint: the entire system is geared to make one year's exam as close in terms of its difficulty as the last, and judging the value of one year's script against another, when the questions are quite different cannot be an objective exercise. After all, these committees are no different from any other: members may be swayed by the views of one influential person or even by a comment made about just one section of an entire paper such as, 'anyone who writes that cannot possibly get an A-grade in my book!'. There is another, perhaps more controversial point: from a marketing standpoint, an awarding body will not want an examination to display wide variations in performance year on year. What they ideally want, and of course what has been happening in recent years, is a slow but steady improvement in performance over time (see Chapter 2 for a discussion on norm and criterion referencing in this context).

Borderlining

Borderlining is the term used to describe the re-marking of scripts on the border of critical grades. This is carried out to ensure that candidates are awarded the correct one. Borderlining takes place after the mark boundaries have been set, when the statistics reveal those candidates whose work is at the border of certain grades. At A-level, these are A/B, C/D and E/N. Remember, of course, that the aggregate mark of all the components determines the grade (contrary to popular myth, a candidate does not have to 'pass' on all the papers in order to pass the examination overall). In order to ensure that a candidate who is one mark below the E/N boundary, say, has had his work fairly and accurately marked, all his papers are re-marked by the senior marking team, who will be unaware of the actual grade boundary and so will not be influenced in any way when they are presented with the scripts to mark.

The process of borderlining may also be used to check the work of paired examiners. If the examination has more than one written paper, the marks for each component within each centre will be compared. Assuming the examiners for the two papers were given the same centres to mark, the profile should more or less match. So examiner A's scripts will show 3 per cent A grades, 8 per cent B grades and so on. If examiner B's marking of the same scripts, but a different paper of course, shows no A grades, 2 per cent B and a higher proportion at the other grades then it *may* indicate that examiner A is too lenient, or B too hard, or perhaps there is another reason, such as the two papers examining different things in different ways (which is why it would not be appropriate to compare coursework with a final written paper). It is not true that any such deviation necessarily means poor marking, but it is an indicator that something may be amiss, and the subject officer will probably extract some scripts for the chief and principal examiners to sample in order to find out.

Appeals

Once the grades have been awarded to candidates it is possible for candidates, and indeed entire centres who feel aggrieved, to have their work re-marked. This is a service that anyone can use, though because it is quite expensive it is suggested that it is not equally available to everyone. Ten years ago very few availed themselves of this service – it was not known and not widely publicised. By the end of the 1990s it had become something of a problem, with senior examiners finding themselves marking scripts well into November and even later following a June examination, with the result that no one is satisfied. By then the result is too late to make any difference to university entrance that year, and the chief and principal examiners find themselves marking scripts from June to December almost without a break, at the very time they have not only to start writing the next series of examinations, but also to prepare for marking the January series. Modular examination can only add to the pressure in the system, a topic that we shall take up in Chapter 5.

APPEALS: REMOVING THE ONE-WAY OPTION

At the moment the rules operated by the awarding bodies mean that any re-mark can at worse result in the same grade and at best improve it. This means that anyone who can afford it loses nothing by appealing. One of the suggested solutions to the excessive number of appeals is to remove this 'one way option'. As the *London Evening Standard* reported in November 1999:

> Mr Blunkett has asked officials to investigate changing the rules to GCSE and A-level appeals, which at present only allow marks to be increased. Under the proposals, students unhappy with grades will be able to see the marked papers to help them decide whether to appeal.
>
> However, they will risk having their grade lowered if the appeal examiner feels the original marks were too generous.
>
> (30.11.99: 19)

The possibility of returning scripts to centres is controversial since it will clearly involve more expense and will place a further burden on examiners. Nevertheless, the benefits could be considerable. For instance, it may help teachers to ask important questions about content selection and organisation and help in their long-term planning. At an individual level, students sometimes believe they have done well because they have written a lot, whereas in reality most of it was irrelevant or inaccurate. This would show them why they received the grade they did.

In short, if one of the strengths of formative assessment is effective feedback, then why should that not apply equally in the more summative context of external examinations? (See Chapters 7–9, this volume.)

MARKING MYTHS

As the previous section indicates, the awarding bodies spend a great deal of time and trouble ensuring that candidates get as fair a deal as possible from examinations. One of the mantras often stated by chief examiners is 'always give the benefit of the doubt to the candidates', meaning that if an examiner is unsure whether to award a mark or not, then he or she should give it. The only time when that does not apply is when the examiner has to say, 'I *think* she means X or Y' because of course no one can predict what someone *meant* to say or write. That is why candidates should be encouraged to make all their thoughts as clear as possible in the examination. However, the development of this technique takes careful formative preparation and practice in the classroom and is a life skill whose benefit extends well beyond the examination hall.

The other false rumour is that markers are interested in 'catching out' candidates. Virtually all examiners are practising teachers and so they are aware of the stress that young people are under when they come into the examination room. These are 'high-stakes' tests and everyone is aware of that. Examiners are trained not to have 'perfect answers' lurking somewhere in their heads; every effort is made to remove such an idea, since it implies a negative methodology – all they have is a mark scheme that represents what a range of 16–18 year olds can achieve given the time constrained and stressful circumstances under which they are working.

Of course marking, other than that done by machine, can never be completely consistent, accurate and reliable. It is possible that a script read at the end of the day or the end of the examination period might receive a different mark than if it was seen at the start, but there are so many checks and balances that the possibility of a huge variation occurring and not being spotted is quite remote, though the increase in appeals in recent years may suggest that the general public does not necessarily accept that to be the case.

SUMMARY

- There is a hierarchy of part-time jobs in external examining that runs from the chief examiner to assistant examiners.
- The setting of papers involves a subject committee that also plays an important role in awarding grades.
- Marking is 'standardised' at a meeting where the CE aims to encourage everyone to think in a similar manner when faced with marking challenges.
- Mark schemes are written to award positive achievement and a range of skills.
- For a teacher new to the profession, becoming an assistant examiner is a challenging but rewarding experience and one that can help improve teaching.
- Increasing numbers of appeals aginst awarded grades suggest that candidates, parents and teachers are aware of the limitations inherent in the external examining system.

FOR FURTHER THINKING

1. Consider the pros and cons of making the examining system more transparent and accountable. You can do this from a number of different perspectives: students, teachers, parents and/or examiners.
2. We suggested that the increasing number of appeals indicates a growing awareness of the limitations of the system. There may be other reasons, however, ranging from the simple fact that more people are aware of the existence of appeals than before, to the more complex, where the 'no lose' option makes the gamble of an upgrade worthwhile. What is your view? Would allowing for downgrades as well as upgrades make any difference?

THE SYLLABUS/SPECIFICATION

One of the more significant changes that has occurred since the introduction of GCSEs in 1986, is the substantially improved specification of content (which partly explains why syllabuses are now called 'specifications'), alongside changes to mark schemes and other elements in the examining process. All the changes are designed to make the process more open and transparent, so that students can improve their examination performance and teachers are better equipped to help them do so. Thus, the specifications for A- and AS- levels typically contain the following:

- 'special features', such as coursework components;
- 'background information', which includes availability of assessment units and entry details;
- 'scheme of assessment', including aims and assessment objectives set out in a 'specification grid';
- 'subject content', which is set out in terms of essential knowledge and understanding and a commentary alongside to indicate the breadth and/or depth of treatment expected;
- the 'key skills' of Communication, Application of Number and Information Technology as they link with the subject, as well as 'Working with Others' and the spiritual, moral, ethical, social and cultural dimensions;
- notes on coursework if appropriate;
- 'awarding and reporting' including grading, 'shelf-life' of the qualifications and re-sits;
- 'appendices' which might include grade descriptors and overlaps with other qualifications.

SPECIFICATION CONTENT AND SCHEMES OF WORK

Specification content is not designed to supply teachers with a scheme of work. Indeed the awarding bodies are quite explicit in their statements regarding subject content. For instance:

> There is no implied hierarchy in the order in which the essential knowledge and understanding is [sic] presented, nor should the length of the various sections be taken to imply any view of their relative importance. The amount of guidance given is dependent on the nature of the topic and holds no implication for the depth or breadth, or for the amount of teaching time required.
>
> (AQA 1999: 15)

But specification content can be used as a framework, rather like the revised subject frameworks for the National Curriculum. The reason why this is so is fairly obvious: it guarantees that all the content areas are covered and that pupils will not be 'surprised' by something about which they know nothing when they enter the examination hall. On the other hand, simply 'lifting' the specification content and using it *as if* it were a scheme of work carries certain disadvantages. First, it makes no allowances for the strengths and weaknesses of the particular cohort of students. Numerical topics, for example, may be dealt with better at a later stage, or integrated with other topics to make them less threatening.

Second, the specification content does not necessarily reflect the emphasis each topic possesses in the mind of the chief examiner. Reference to past papers will help in this respect, showing how often a topic has been examined and to what depth. In addition, past papers will also provide practice questions, with accompanying mark schemes. These can be noted on a fully developed and thought through scheme of work, but an over-reliance on past questions and 'question spotting' is a mistake, if only because it may have a damaging backwash effect on more beneficial, diagnostic formative assessment (Harlen and James, 1997; Black, 1998).

Third, although specification designers generally construct the content with a logical sequence in their heads, this sequence may not be appropriate in all circumstances, and in any event, if the teacher is to feel ownership of the material she or he should reflect on sequencing and indeed ring the changes every once in a while, in order to remain fresh and challenged.

Fourth, and perhaps most significantly, 'specification content' is bereft of pedagogy. A scheme of work derives some of its effect by expressing the content in relation to teaching and learning situations. Simply adopting a specification driven approach will tend to emphasise content and may discourage the use of creative teaching approaches that would encourage deeper learning and understanding (which incidentally, is likely to have a greater examination grade pay-off) (Harlen and James, *op. cit.*).

AIMS, ASSESSMENT OBJECTIVES AND GRADE DESCRIPTORS

Teachers rightly pay close attention to the content pages of specifications. However, the rest of the document also contains a great deal of useful information that can be of considerable assistance in the planning of teaching.

First of all the aims provide an overview of what students should be encouraged to understand and be able to do by the end of the course. These aims are important because they offer an overview of the subject in a wider context. Referring back to them as the course proceeds will provide a focus that will help students when they come to the examination itself, since they are often evaluative in nature. Thus in English the aims might be to offer a critical response to literature, be able to construct and sustain an argument in written form, and be capable of writing creatively and personally. The close reading of a novel or poetry provides the vehicle for the development of such skills, which would be rewarded in the examination itself through the mark scheme.

The aims are supported by 'assessment objectives' and together they will lead to 'grade description' that will give a general indication of the required learning outcome at certain specified grades. These descriptions are of practical use to teachers when marking coursework, but they should also be considered when marking certain classwork exercises, so that the award of a high mark does indeed reflect the skills the examiners are seeking and the student comes to understand this also; it is another aspect of examination 'transparency'.

The grid below relates the assessment objectives of the examination to the overall scheme of assessment. In this case there are four assessment objectives, examined in three modules (called assessment units), to make an AS examination under the year 2000 regulations.

Assessment objectives (AOs)	Unit weightings %			Overall weighting of AOs (%)
	1	2	3	
Knowledge and understanding	10	10	10	30
Application	10	10	10	30
Analysis	7	7	10	24
Evaluation	3	3	10	16
Overall weighting	30	30	40	100

Note the relatively low weight placed on what are commonly called 'higher order' skills such as evaluation. This is one way the awarding bodies are distinguishing AS- from A-level. In the latter, the AOs of analysis and evaluation would carry as much weight as the first two.

Figure 4.2 A typical assessment objectives grid

Preparing students for an external examination is one of the most challenging contexts a teacher will face. These days specifications are large documents that need to be absorbed and then translated in a way that students can appreciate. The learning process should be enjoyable and not a dull trudge through content, which is where an appreciation of aims and objectives can help, informing other aspects of pedagogy and formative work that we shall be examining in Chapters 7–9 of this book. Nevertheless, there will come a time when the students enter the examination room and are 'on their own'. At this point the responsible teacher may pace nervously between the serried ranks of the candidates reading the paper and judging whether it is 'hard' or 'easy': two words often used in this context but perhaps rarely fully understood. In the next section we will examine them in more detail.

WHAT MAKES AN EXAMINATION 'HARD' OR 'EASY'?

Particularly in the context of A-level examinations, there is often a great deal of discussion surrounding the word 'rigour', which is rarely defined but appears, like virtue, to be self-evidently right and therefore impossible to challenge. In practice, what people sometimes mean by rigour is 'hard' or 'difficult', so it is worth spending some time investigating what makes an examination that way, or not.

Often prominent in people's minds is a question of depth 'versus' breadth. There is often an assumption that a more 'rigorous' examination is one that has more depth. In fact, learning *more*, even at what might appear to be a basic level, could be just as 'hard' as learning less but at greater depth. This is one reason why it is argued that modularity at A-level has made the examinations 'easier' (see Chapter 5; Stobart and Gipps 1997; Black 1998; Lloyd 1999). In fact there is a false polarisation here, as it is the *combination* of depth and breadth that offers real intellectual challenge.

The specification content is only one part of making an examination 'hard' or 'easy'. The design of the paper itself will provide a further challenge; for reasons of reliability one paper should be the same as every other from one year to the next, if they are to qualify people at the same level. In practice, one of the considerable challenges that setters of examinations have to face is trying to predict those topics that students will find easy and those they will find hard. Examiners are helped in this by their own experiences and from past papers, but they are often surprised to find a question answered well when they expected more difficulty, and vice versa. In fact, setting questions is a complicated and highly skilled activity, because there are so many considerations that together result in an overall examination being 'difficult' or 'easy', quite apart from the skill levels of the candidates themselves. What follows is an overview of the issues involved.

First of all, there are the components (papers) of the examination themselves. Open ended, or essay questions are better at testing 'high level skills' than multiple choice – more properly called Objective Item tests (Frith and Macintosh 1984) – but that does not necessarily make the latter 'easier', because if the objective test has a right answer and a very close alternative (known as a 'distractor'), the candidate may well lose the entire mark, whereas in a more discursive context she or he may well have picked up a good proportion of the marks on offer (see Gusky 1994). Nevertheless, the structure of the entire examination, the length of the papers, whether they are written or oral, sat at the end of the course or during it may well affect the performance of candidates. The belief that this is so resulted in limits being placed on coursework, which as Stobart and Gipps (1997) point out was originally at 'the personal wish of John Major' when he was Prime Minister (p. 85). Coursework is often perceived as 'easier' because it is less time constrained and does not take place in a conventional examination setting, but the reverse may be true. By adding a further dimension to the overall assessment it emphasises skills that might not otherwise be tested, possibly making it more difficult than conventional papers (Lloyd 1999).

Within each examination paper further complications can arise. Take, for example a situation where the skill of multiplication is being tested. To most people it is easier multiplying six by ten than six by nine, which in turn is far simpler than multiplying sixty nine by twenty four. What then would be a fair test of the skill – if someone can multiply one by two does that indicate sufficient mastery? In order to help answer this question, examinations depend heavily on the experience of the CE, as well as defined aims and assessment objectives.

There are other factors that make some questions more *accessible* than others. For instance, cultural factors will make a difference. Before decimalisation of the currency in 1971 most of the population of the UK, if asked, could add what now seem like impossible sums in their heads, involving four farthings to the penny, twelve pence to the shilling, twenty shillings to the pound and one pound and one shilling to the guinea! After decimalisation such mental skills have been marginalised, a situation further encouraged by the advent and universal acceptance of calculators, though this is sometimes seen as evidence of a 'lowering of standards' in mathematics (see Lloyd 1999: 50–52 for a discussion of the relationship between mathematical and arithmetical skills).

Even the way a question is asked can make a difference. As Pollitt *et al.* (1985) put it, 'it has become clear how the content and form of an examination question can *control* the extent and nature of the outcome space made available to the pupil' (p. 11, our emphasis). By 'outcome space' they mean the interpretation the candidate puts on the required answer to a given question. They showed, for example, that the same candidate displayed apparently low level skills of comprehension of an English passage in her answer to one question, but then demonstrated that she in fact had a high level of understanding by answering another on the same paper in a quite complex and detailed manner. The way the two questions were asked i.e. how the outcome space was defined, had prompted her to interpret the requirements so that she gave a low level response in the first and a high level one in the other (*ibid.* p. 89).

Other researchers (Hughes and Fisher-Hoch 1997) have identified 'valid' and 'invalid' sources of difficulty. Invalid ones are unintentional, that is to say, the setter does not intend to make the question more difficult, but by putting in irrelevant material or by using certain words or phrases it has the same result. In mathematics, putting a question in a context can have a considerable impact on the level of difficulty. Thus, asking a question on percentage increases became considerably easier with the context of train times removed. Even changing the particular context makes a difference. Thus a question that asked about the life span of a grasshopper was easier than one asking 'the mean time to bursting of fuel tanks on a space ship' (*ibid.*: 25).

Above all, perhaps, language can be a source of difficulty (either intentionally or accidentally). For instance, compare, 'After experimenting with various spanner lengths, it was found that a long spanner was required to remove a stubborn nut. Explain the principle involved that enabled the long spanner to be successful', with, 'Explain why a long spanner is better than a short spanner for removing a tight nut'. Both are requiring the same subject knowledge, but the first is asking for more than that. A second language learner, for instance, might be confused by the adjective 'stubborn' because of its colloquial nature and this may well affect his or her performance in Physics, the subject being tested (SCAA undated).

Other areas where language intrudes are in sentence construction, the use of the active rather than the passive form and so on. Even the words themselves can be harder or simpler. For instance, the use of Latin polysyllables: 'utilise', 'locate', 'adequate' rather than the simpler Anglo Saxon, 'use', 'find' and 'enough' are sources of difficulty, just as phrases such as 'prior to' rather than 'before' or 'in conjunction with' instead of simply 'with' (*ibid.*). It is important to recognise, of course, that the lessons learnt in external examinations apply just as much to the classroom; good practice is, after all, good practice, regardless of context.

In the final analysis, however, perfection in an examination is a goal to be aimed at rather than achieved. Nevertheless, the legitimacy of the entire system rests on what Eckstein and Noah (1993) say is 'a general sense that the examinations are honest, fair, and relevant, that is, administered in secure fashion, discriminating impartially amongst the candidates, and testing knowledge that is regarded as important' (p. 217). Given certain caveats, we would argue that the English examination system passes these tests.

GNVQ TESTING

So far this chapter has emphasised testing in what might be termed the 'traditional' examinations of GCSE and A/AS-levels. It is necessary to turn briefly to GNVQ, because its history and roots are somewhat different, with the result that the form of its assessment is also different.

Because GNVQs had their roots in the vocational arena (Dearing 1996), they incorporated much of the vocational qualification's philosophy, which emphasised competence. They also used the language of NVQs, so instead of *syllabuses*, GNVQs had *specifications* which were further broken down into *units*, *elements*, *evidence indicators* (what work the student had to produce) *performance criteria* (the extent of things a student had to do) and *range statements* (the subject content) (White Paper 1991; NCVQ 1993a; Hodkinson and Mattinson 1994; FEDA 1997). The assessment regime reflected this philosophy, so that candidates were required to complete a portfolio that demonstrated their competence. This was wholly teacher-assessed with moderation internally within the school or college, and externally through the awarding body (BTEC, RSA and City and Guilds). This, of course, sat in stark contrast to GCSE and A-levels, where, as we have seen, coursework was restricted to 20 per cent of the total mark.

There was one further anomaly. Because of their emphasis on 'competence', and because aspects of competence were generic (that is, not subject-specific) – Planning, Information Seeking and Handling and Evaluation – subject knowledge *per se* was not 'tested'. Instead, objective tests were set which were designed only to 'confirm knowledge' and so were considered by those brought up through the traditional routes as being unacceptably 'easy' (Capey 1995). Over time the tests have become much more equivalent, the terminologies of GNVQs, GCSEs and A/AS-levels have been altered to bring them into line and unit accreditation has been introduced to encourage transfer between the 'academic' and 'vocational' pathways (though no credit transfer is currently allowed). The amalgamations of the examination boards and the awarding bodies, the formation of QCA out of SCAA and the NCVQ and the DfEE from the DFE and the Department of Employment mean that as time passes it is hoped that such differences as remain will fade, largely, of course, because the stated aim is to establish the equivalence of qualifications. However, as we saw earlier, there remain strong cultural barriers in England that might prevent this happening for some considerable time (Green *et al.* 1999).

FURTHER THINKING

Look at some past papers in your subject, and evaluate the questions in terms of what *you* consider their level of difficulty. What is it that makes one more difficult than another? If you are in a position to do so, ask a class of students the same question of the same paper and see if their opinion coincides with yours. If they differ, find out why – their answers could be interesting and might well inform the way you teach them, and other groups in the future.

5 Exams, Exams, Exams

In Chapters 5 and 6 the debate over three controversial areas will be joined. Chapter 5 will look at developments in external, largely summative assessment at 16+ and 18+, whilst Chapter 6 will concentrate on the shortcomings of the examination process, as well as the notion of 'value added'. The UK is unusual internationally in having 'high-stakes' terminal assessment at 16+ (West et al. 1999), and with ever-increasing staying-on rates and changes to A-levels, there are those who call into question the need for GCSEs, arguing instead for a coherent 14–19 curriculum that recognises the growing maturity and changing aspirations of young people today. This has added weight given the mis-match that GCSEs have always had with the National Curriculum (Graham, 1993). At 18+, a substantial recent change to A-levels has been to separate AS and A2 courses and examinations. They will be largely modular – though that is itself controversial – and designed to widen the scope of study at that age, a laudable and perhaps long overdue reform in England and Wales. The chapter will argue that this may be a pious hope rather than expectation, and that these changes could well have a deleterious impact upon schools and colleges, as even more time and money is spent on preparing for and taking external examinations. This notion of the costs of external assessment: financial, managerial and opportunity will be further developed in Chapter 6.

THE NATIONAL CURRICULUM

In September 1999 the National Curriculum for England and Wales celebrated its tenth anniversary, for whilst it was set up under the 1988 Education Act, it did not begin to come into force in schools until the following year. Although it was essentially the brainchild of the then Conservative Education Secretary, Kenneth Baker, its roots lay in a speech made by a Labour Prime Minister, James Callaghan, some ten years earlier, in 1976.

A brief history

Callaghan argued for what he called a 'Great Debate' on education. With hindsight this signified the end of a period of what Lawton describes as 'pluralism', which had developed after the 1944 Education Act and the expansion of state education for all. By this he means 'different kinds of school and curricula for different types of children' (1996: 2). In some sense the Callaghan speech also articulated, in a public way, the trend towards central-isation in education that had been gaining ground throughout the 1960s and 1970s and which continues to this day (Davis 1999; Green *et al.* 1999). Not only was there a continuing move towards comprehensive schools by LEAs of both political persuasions (the period that Lawton (1996) calls 'comprehensive planning'), but national bodies were also created during the period to look at wider curriculum issues, starting with a small Curriculum Study Group in 1962, followed by the Schools Council for Curriculum and Examinations in 1964. In addition, Her Majesty's Inspectors of Schools (HMI) were increasingly using their experiences nationally to produce reflec-tive papers, which complemented material coming from university departments of education.

Nevertheless, because of the devolved nature of education budgets, power and influence still rested with LEAs. To the incoming Conservative govern-ment in 1979, headed by Lady, then Mrs Thatcher, this was frustrating. The Rate Support Grant from central government almost exactly matched LEA's expenditure on education (some £9 billion in 1986–7 money), and yet many LEAs were Labour controlled, including the Inner London Education Authority which, as Lady Thatcher described it, 'spent more per pupil than any other educational authority and achieved some of the worst examination results' (Thatcher 1993). This tension raised an issue of accountability (Lawson, 1992), but also one of power. As Aldrich says, 'curriculum is not just a matter of content, but also of control' (Aldrich 1996: 24). Lady Thatcher saw the need for centralisation as a first step in the defence against a fundamental threat to her beliefs – the next step would be to devolve power directly to the people (Young 1989; Thatcher 1993; Lawton 1994). As much as she disliked LEAs, she distrusted the teachers' trade unions more as members of what she called the 'vested interests' of the educational establishment, namely HMI and perhaps somewhat surprisingly, officials at the Department of Education and Science (Thatcher 1993).

Nevertheless, it was Kenneth Baker who forced through the ten subject National Curriculum in 1988, against the wishes of Lady Thatcher, who consis-tently argued for a simple version containing just three subjects: English, maths and a science (Graham 1993). What both agreed on, however, was the need to make schools and teachers accountable, especially to parents, who would be encouraged to make choices about where to send their children. This element of choice, allied to the financial rewards to the individual schools that would accompany success, could only be satisfactorily achieved if it was an informed decision. Given that all schools would now be following the same curriculum, it was possible to make comparisons, but of course that meant that performance had to be tested. Furthermore, since each school would have a vested interest in the results, their staff could not be trusted to mark the tests, and so a new system of external assessment had to be devised for that purpose. The logic of this argument is important because it continues to drive policy to this day, despite the change of government; but of course its conclusion rests on a significant value judgement about teachers; one that in our view is deeply flawed.

Translating the theory of a National Curriculum into practice proved immediately difficult, perhaps because there was no consideration of the overall aims and objectives (White 1988, 1998), and thus no holistic notion of what the final learning outcomes should be. Instead, Kenneth Baker established Subject Working Groups, consisting of specialist lay people but few teachers – to define the content that all pupils should follow. These groups, working within very tight time constraints, understandably found it easier to add material than to remove it. Inevitably, therefore, each one tended to over-load its proposed curriculum, with the result that when added together the prescribed material, alongside its associated tests, occupied far in excess of the 80 to 85 per cent of teaching time which it was supposed to.

At the same time as the working groups were attempting to establish subject content, the issue of how the National Curriculum was to be assessed was being addressed by The Task Group on Assessment and Testing (TGAT), which reported in January 1988. It was required to cover a number of objectives (DES 1988: Appendix B), some of which were conflicting (Murphy 1990; Chitty 1996). On the one hand it was politically imperative that test data were available in order to ensure accountability as well as offering parents 'informed' choices. On the other, the tests were supposed to monitor and improve pupil progress and achievement. There was then, a confusion between the aims and objectives of the tests, most particularly whether they were summative or formative. In one respect, however, there was agreement between educationalists and the political right, and that was in the use of criterion referencing. The theoretical arguments for criterion referencing were persuasive, but their practical application was beset with difficulties, as overseas experience and work on GCSEs had already shown (Wolf 1995b; Daugherty 1995) and which was quickly revealed by the working groups. For instance, the first set of proposals from the Science Working Group contained no fewer than 354 statements of attainment, grouped into ten levels in each of twenty two separate attainment targets!

CRITERION REFERENCING RE-VISITED

As was outlined in Chapter 1, the principle behind criterion referencing is that the criteria for success are defined in advance of the test so that each candidate has an equal chance regardless of the performance of others – the example often cited is the driving test where, in order to prove 'competence', certain skills have to be displayed. Although there is a tendency in some books to use criterion testing and competence testing as the same thing, they are not. Competence testing, which tends to predominate in vocational fields – the driving test, NVQs and so on – is a specialised version of criterion testing (Wolf 1995b).

The advantages of criterion testing are:

- The test will be 'transparent' to everyone involved: the examiners, the candidates and the public. There can be no hint of favouritism and the test will gain in status as a result. This is because the criteria are built around what are called 'domain descriptors' that are 'so clear and unambiguous that reliable, parallel assessments can be derived from . . . [them] . . . directly' (*ibid.*).
- Especially in a vocational context 'competence' against the criteria is demonstrated unequivocally. Thus in GNVQs, the existence of a port-folio of work will be matched against assessment criteria to determine success. This will therefore avoid any hint of 'norm referencing', that is to say it will in no way be affected or influenced by the perfor-mance of other members of the class, or school, or year-group.
- The existence of criteria means that part-qualification is possible and candidates can continue to work on areas where they have not met the criteria until they achieve success.

Against:

- In practice, defining the domains is extremely difficult. There is a tendency to break them down into smaller and smaller units in the search for greater clarity, but whilst the number of specifications increases, transparency does not.
- Although the existence of criteria should ensure consistency between each testing occasion, the assessor is affected by the context of the test and by his or her bias (Gipps and Wood 1981; Wolf and Silver 1986; Pollard *et al.* 1994).
- Criterion referencing often implies multiple choice tests, because they are the only type that can come close to defining the domains. But even in an objective test there are difficulties in ensuring precision, not least because of some of the challenges of establishing what is

hard and what easy between two different questions (Popham 1984 and Chapter 4 this volume).

- Once the scores from different domains are aggregated in order to give an overall grade, technically known as 'compensation', it becomes impossible to determine the underlying performance unambiguously. So, if there are two domains, and four candidates in turn score 2 and 3; 3 and 2; 1 and 4 and 4 and 1, are they all the same? It might be considered reasonable for all of them to be awarded a 'C' grade since they have accumulated the same total, but clearly they have all revealed different skills from each other. Nevertheless, users of the information such as employers and further or higher education accept the limitations of a grade, recognising that the alternative would be a lengthy and bureaucratic process describing the performance on each of the domains.

- Setting criteria are supposed to release tests from the 'tyranny' of norm referencing (see Chapter 1), but in fact setting standards actually involves recognising some kind of norm in the whole population. The UK driving test has recently been modified because it was believed that the old one no longer matched what most people believed was an adequate test of competence for driving in this country. Similarly, once the tests are used for purposes of selection, which is often the case in non-vocational contexts, judgements have to be made about relative rather than absolute performance.

The 'ten level scale'

Part of the challenge in creating a national curriculum assessment system was the adoption of a radical idea, namely that the attainment of young people, regardless of their age, could be measured by a single set of subject criteria encouraged to achieve the highest level possible. Ten 'levels of attainment' were described by identifying statements of attainment[1] for each subject. In theory, therefore, a child aged seven could be at level ten and one aged sixteen at level one. As Daugherty says:

> Most pre-existing assessment systems, in the UK as elsewhere in the world, were age-related. The TGAT view of progression . . . not only presented the system-designers with the challenge of defining attainment criteria. Those who were given the job of drafting the criteria would also have to write them in such a way that they could be used in describing the performance of a pupil of any age between 5 and 16.
>
> (Daugherty 1995)

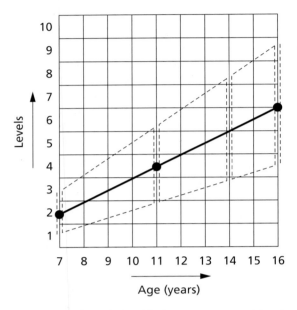

Figure 5.1 The relationship between age and levels of attainment
Source: TGAT Report, DES (1988)

Yet it was self-evident, and presumably an aim of education generally, that children would improve through their years of schooling, and this reality had to be accommodated. In order to clarify what was intended, the graph shown in Figure 5.1 was drawn. On it the ten levels are matched against the age of the pupils, but added to it is a curve – conveniently a straight line – which represents a 'median' child's progress. On either side of this line are bands that represent the likely spread of 80 per cent of the students at each Key Stage, bearing in mind that testing would only take place at ages 7, 11, 14 and 16.

Thus at each stage students had to meet 'attainment targets' in their 'programmes of study', the latter being mainly content-based. Within what were described as 'expected' results, there was, necessarily, an allowance for different levels of performance because of course, the criteria were not age related. So it would be possible for children to be in the same class because of their chronological age (comprehensive schools in England have tradition-ally not 'held back' under-achievers, or 'pushed on' high ones, however 'achievement' is defined) but working towards entirely different levels. Understandably, the issue of classroom differentiation in such circumstances would be daunting to say the least. But then it always was; this system, though, was designed to bring diverse student attainment into the open.

Crucially, though, because the system was criterion referenced *and* (supposed-ly) *unrelated* to the child's age, it did not lend itself easily to reliable reporting at the end of each Key Stage. This problem remains today, despite a slimmed down National Curriculum that now only has tests in English, maths and science. On the other hand, the radical impact of this system can barely be overstated. The reason why the Secretary of State is able to set himself targets (with a promise to resign if they are not met) is the existence of a legible 'national grid' (Figure 5.1). But the government should worry about promoting some kind of objective level four standard for 11 year olds. Take the case of Barrie Day, a head of English, reporting his SATs (Standard Assessment Tasks) results for 1999 at Key Stage 3. Despite a mark scheme that was 'commendable in its detail', he argues that the external marking was poor, and as a result his pupils' peaked at level four. But he then goes on to make an important general point:

> My wife who teaches in a primary school, has been celebrating 81 per cent level 4 and above at Key Stage 2. Great for them. But curtains for us. Bright-eyed Year 7s arrive with level 4s. And three years later? They've achieved . . . 4! Seemingly we've taught them nothing. Parents understandably raise serious questions.
>
> (Day, B. 'Testing Times' in *The Teacher*
> September/October 1999, p. 16)

It might be that the Key Stage 2 marking was generous and that at Key Stage 3 mean, but for whatever reason, unambiguous comparisons between schools cannot be made; in short the test is not reliable, even accepting its validity, which many commentators have also questioned (*inter alia*, Black 1993; Gipps 1993; Chitty 1996; Daugherty 1995; Lawton, 1996).

Lawton argues that fundamentally the National Curriculum confused one curriculum model based on subject content, with another based on assessment. Indeed, assessment remains a bone of contention, as we have already seen, for not only are there problems with the ten level model, the fact that the tests are another form of 'high-stakes' assessment is putting pressure on pupils and teachers in areas of schooling that in the past were relatively free from them. Thus we see the proliferation of 'Revision Guides' at the Key Stages, of pupils suffering examination stress and teachers using inappropriate summative testing techniques in place of formative ones (Black 1998: 120; Assessment Reform Group 1999).

'The nightmare of Key Stage Four' (Graham 1993)

GCSEs were a serious stumbling block for the ten level scale at Key Stage 4. Indeed the retention of GCSE courses (each of which takes a minimum of 10 per cent of curriculum time), plus a proposal to allow 14–16 pre-vocational and vocational courses, suggests that the National Curriculum now effectively ends at Key Stage 3. For some this is quite logical and opens up the possibility of a 14–19 curriculum, which they argue is more appropriate to the needs of both the students and the country. In the meantime, however, we turn in the next section to what is still the main 'currency' in secondary schools, the GCSE examination. This examination exerts enormous influence on teachers, pupils and parents and is likely to remain in place for the foreseeable future – though in the long term its future is questionable.

In summary, the National Curriculum of 1988:

- represented a centralising move in the curriculum which had begun at least ten years earlier;
- was politically inspired and largely represented the views of one Secretary of State;
- lacked a clear curriculum rationale and confused content with assessment;
- was excessive in its demands on teaching time and administration;
- introduced a radical assessment methodology that was criterion referenced and not age related; and
- never satisfactorily resolved the Key Stage 4/GCSE interface.

GENERAL CERTIFICATE OF SECONDARY EDUCATION (GCSE)

Why was it that the overlap of the National Curriculum at Key Stage 4 and GCSEs became such an issue? First, there was the politically somewhat uncomfortable fact that GCSEs had been announced by Sir Keith Joseph, then a highly influential Education Secretary, only four years earlier. Indeed the first candidates sat GCSEs in 1988, the same year as the Education Reform Act, which introduced the National Curriculum. To abandon the exams just as they were coming on stream would have been politically unacceptable, as well as a massive waste of resources.

Second, there was a strong tradition of testing at 16+, and the public and user groups were familiar with the outcomes. An ambitious, yet unproved new national assessment system would have caused considerable confusion.

Third, GCSEs were a genuine advance, which had taken many years – almost twenty in fact – to come to fruition. Compared to the National Curriculum at least, they had been carefully researched and thought through, were popular and are to this day considered a success (Stobart and Gipps 1997). They enjoyed support from a wide range of influential bodies, including the examining boards, LEAs and teachers in general (Tattersall 1994). They promoted the idea of 'cascade' in-service training, which was well funded and organised and which in some ways became a model for INSET and professional development (Torrance 1986).

Finally, the independent sector was not bound by the National Curriculum. Although it might have been forced to adopt the grade descriptors had GCSEs been abandoned, such indirect coercion would simply not have been acceptable, especially to a Conservative government.

The background to GCSEs

It is important to remember that the school leaving age was raised to 16 as late as 1974, and up to that time there was a proportion of the population that was denied the opportunity to acquire qualifications at 16+. However, even when the leaving age was raised, only a relatively small proportion of each year group carried on to sit GCE O-levels, which were designed to cater only for the top 20 per cent of the cohort. For the remainder, Certificate of Secondary Education (CSE) examinations were available to cater for the next 40 per cent of the 'ability range' below the top 20 per cent, and while they certainly had a 'second-class' feel to them (Lloyd 1999), they were quite innovative in a number of ways that we shall explore below. From this it is easy to see that the system functioned on the assumption that 40 per cent of each age cohort of students was denied the chance of acquiring formal qualifications, which was as educationally, economically and socially unacceptable as it was demotivating for the students.

Certificate of Secondary Education (CSE)

Before moving on to the GCSE reform, however, it is worth noting the ways in which CSEs were innovative. First, they pioneered coursework assessment; indeed some were 100 per cent coursework. This also involved new methods of moderating marks between schools and teachers, which in turn encouraged greater liaison between teachers and became a form of continuing professional development.

Second, groups of schools, perhaps organised by an LEA adviser, got together to create so-called 'Mode 3' examinations in which the syllabus and examination were devised, set and marked locally (a conventional examination set and marked by a board is a 'Mode 1' and a 'Mode 2' is one created by individual schools or groups of schools but which is set and marked by a board). These consisted of syllabuses designed for the specific needs of the area and the pupils in those schools. They were often highly creative and some went on to be adopted nationally.

Third, CSEs were organised by examining 'Groups' that were defined geographically. Although they had ties with examination boards, they also involved and engaged teachers at a local level, as well as the LEAs. Finally, there was an attempt to identify national standards, in that the highest at CSE was regarded as 'equivalent' to an O-level pass.

GCSEs: a successful innovation

The history of the transition from O-levels and CSEs to GCSEs is an interesting one, especially since it took almost twenty years to happen. It was bound up with the move to comprehensive schools.

Perhaps because GCSEs took so long to come about, they introduced a number of innovations that are taken as read today. One such is the specification of both 'General Criteria' and 'Subject-Specific Criteria'. Another was the debate over the form of their assessment which became increasingly sophisticated. One of the results of this discussion was the intention to move away from a *norm* referenced examination system to one that was built around *criteria*. In practice this attempt turned out to be only partially successful, as we shall discuss in more detail below, but it at least forced specialists to examine the fundamentals of their disciplines. Certain areas were given their own criteria, but in minority subjects this was not considered an economic exercise, so General Criteria were written instead. This exercise, in determining what was the essential underpinning of knowledge in each subject, also changed the positions of the examination boards relative to the government agencies in charge of assessment, because from this point any syllabus had to seek approval before it could be offered, and each one had to conform to the criteria. Thus every syllabus now states that it conforms to the subject-specific, General and Key Stage 4 Criteria. The introduction of the criteria also served another purpose, that of encouraging equality of standards across examination boards; because the main areas to be examined were common, the results should as far as possible 'mean' the same thing.

Another change brought about by GCSEs was a clear emphasis on positive achievement. One of the early 'catch phrases' of GCSE was that the examination should try to determine what students 'know, understand and can do'. Thus papers were not to be written in a way that might catch the unwary, or prevent some from achieving; instead they should encourage students to get things right. This was connected to the notion of setting assessment criteria. Thus, if the criteria for a baseline level of achievement were clear, once the candidate had met those criteria a mark could be awarded. Any additional information would be matched against further criteria and so more marks could be given, and so on. This was designed to encourage the use of all the marks, especially at the top end where examiners, especially in discursive topics, are sometimes disinclined to give the maximum possible on the grounds that there is always, theoretically, room for improvement. What the criteria said was that 'perfection' is an impossible dream that cannot be satisfactorily defined; all that a candidate has to do is to match what is reasonably achievable in the circumstances of an external 'high-stakes' form of assessment in order to be rewarded. This decisive move to reward positive achievement goes a long way to explain the consistent, steady improvement in grades awarded nationally (critics argue that it represents the examination becoming 'easier').

Along with the notions of achievement and specified criteria in GCSEs came the principle that testing should not be confined to terminal examination papers alone. CSEs had pioneered coursework and had proved that it could work (as well as indicating the safeguards required to ensure fairness and consistency). This principle was carried over to GCSEs. As a result coursework was introduced to students who would otherwise not have had the opportunity, because O-levels rarely offered such an option. Coursework extended the opportunity to test attributes that would otherwise be hard to examine, such as the ability to research, make decisions and so on. Some subjects even introduced the testing of group work, sometimes with novel approaches such as oral assessment, so the development of life-skills such as working with others could be encouraged and rewarded.

As Eckstein and Noah (1993: 235) point out, 'teachers must have training and the opportunity to accumulate experience and *enjoy a sufficient degree of public and professional trust* to lend legitimacy to their decisions' (our emphasis). The then Prime Minister John Major betrayed the limits to trust when he restricted the amount of coursework allowed in public examinations, which is not seen by some to be as fair and honest as externally marked work. Indeed, as Daugherty (1995) and Black (1996) have demonstrated, there appears to have been a conscious policy throughout the 1990s to remove teachers from assessment in both the GCSE and the National Curriculum. If one accepts the principle of increasing control through greater centralisation then such a policy makes perfect sense, though it should be pointed out that unions are often keen to reduce the burden placed on teachers by this marking, which is usually unpaid.

GCSEs also introduced the notion of clearly defined 'Aims' and 'Assessment Objectives'. Syllabus booklets began to take on a new form which attempted to offer a holistic view of what a successful candidate might know, understand and be able to do by the end of the course.

Today the aims and assessment objectives are both subject-specific and generic, so that the ability to select, apply and evaluate material is put in context. These then have to be translated into examination papers. In practice this is a difficult task for the team that sets them. Precisely defining what percentage of a ten mark question is for 'selection' and what is allowed for 'evaluation' is impossible, and the chief examiner who writes the specification grid of assessment objectives by component does so knowing that they are only spuriously accurate; but that their very frailty lends them a certain robustness (see Chapter 4). That said, aims and objectives are useful for all involved as a broad-brushed means of ensuring a fair test of skills, in the same way that the syllabus content should also be tested fairly. The intention is to provide comparability and fairness for candidates taking the same subject with different awarding bodies. The need for fairness and comparability has of course increased markedly as we enter the age of performance-related pay dependent at least in part on examination results.

One of the problems with examinations predating GCSEs was that they were norm referenced, meaning that success or failure was judged against the performance of the whole population taking that particular test. The box on pp. 70–1, described some of the advantages and disadvantages of criterion referencing, but it was in GCSEs that the theory was first applied, in order to support the principles of fairness and positive achievement. As Eckstein and Noah (1993) write:

There is nothing natural about the idea of arranging for a sizeable fraction of the country's teenage youth to complete their secondary schooling by producing externally graded written answers to a series of externally set questions. The esteem enjoyed by such an examination system derives primarily from the public's estimate of its legitimacy. This in turn depends on the general sense that the examinations are honest, fair and relevant.

(p. 217)

Fairness, of course, relates to the overall aim of the examination, which, as we have argued in Chapter 3, has always been to offer opportunities to people, regardless of their place in society. Norm referencing intuitively suggests unfairness; being judged against a group of other people depends on the make-up and qualities of that group – like the six feet four inch rugby player deemed 'too small' to play at international level. Criterion referencing, on the other hand, suggests equality of opportunity – as long as you can swim 25 metres in a certain time you receive a certificate, whether or not you come home in the first three places. The argument is persuasive, and was equally so when GCSEs were proposed.

Alongside subject and general criteria discussed above, GCSEs also specified grade descriptions, which offered in a holistic and composite way, meaning to each of the grades. Thus if a candidate achieved a C grade he or she would know, understand and be able to do 'X'; alternatively an A grade would mean he or she knows, understands and is able to do 'X + Y', and so on. This was not only potentially helpful to candidates and others, it was also extremely useful to examiners, because it offered a yardstick against which they could judge the aggregated marks of several components, to see if they translated into a fair and true view of a complete performance by the candidate. Such was the success of this innovation that it remains in place today, although grade descriptors may be called by a different name. One such is a 'Level of Performance' table. This device is especially useful in assessing coursework, where each piece can be unique and thus not easily moderated. By applying grade descriptions in addition to the marking scheme, an examiner can match criteria to the assignments to help judge each one's worth.

Although grade descriptions were a success, the original GCSE proposals went a great deal further. It was suggested that in addition to the generalised statements about a C-grade or an A-grade candidate, specific criteria should be established for each subject in certain 'domains': knowledge, understanding and skills. Then each domain had to be referenced against each of the grades of what was to be achieved in subject terms. Like the National Curriculum that followed GCSEs, this exercise became unworkable because of the complexity involved and, as we saw in Chapter 3, because of the inherent technical difficulties with criterion referencing, which result in tasks being broken down into smaller and smaller elements in order to be unambiguous.

GCSEs: 'a single system for examining at 16+'

Alongside the problems and difficulties of defining achievement at certain grades, was the challenge faced by setting an examination that would fairly test the entire population of a particular age group. From a purely practical point of view, a setter would be faced with the dilemma of either asking questions that could be answered by the 'least able', but which would not challenge the 'most able', or setting ones for the 'most able' which would perhaps exclude the majority.

So right from the outset GCSEs were termed 'a single *system* for examining at 16+', rather than a single examination. This distinction allowed for the existence of what are called 'tiered papers'. Originally set in maths, modern languages and the sciences, pupils (and their teachers) had to decide in advance which paper was to be sat, the higher tier offering A to C grades (the A★ grade was a later addition) or the lower tier C to G. Both could also be termed 'unclassified'. Although tiered papers overcame the practical difficulties of setting papers across the whole ability range, and as a result have become the norm, they carry certain disadvantages.

As Lloyd puts it, tiered papers mean that 'In effect the old GCE/CSE divide has been reintroduced by the back door' (Lloyd 1999). This was perhaps more apparent when there were only two tiers, but now there can be three: Basic, Standard and Higher. The Basic stretches from grades G to D, Standard F to B and Higher C to A, with 'additional awardable grades', C for Basic, G and A for Intermediate and D and A★ for Higher. The reason for these 'extra' grades is that early research showed that grade limits on some tiered papers did not properly reward the performance of certain candidates, so that, for example, work that merited the award of a B grade could only earn a C because that was the limit of the tier. This has now been addressed by allowing for 'exceptions' beyond the normal grade limits, which is also important in terms of motivation. A student who knows that he or she cannot achieve what is commonly accepted as a 'pass' (i.e. a C grade) will often 'turn off'. To a certain extent the availability of exceptional grades has countered this, but it remains a problem and one often requiring careful 'negotiation' with students and parents.

Nevertheless, the fact that students have to be entered for one of the tiers means mistakes can happen. Thus in the first GCSE examination no fewer than 38,000 maths candidates who had been entered for the *higher* tier were 'unclassified', perhaps because parents resisted the notion of their child being unable to gain a 'pass', i.e. a C grade, through the lower tier (Stobart and Gipps 1997: 83). Similarly, in the early days of the GCSE there was some evidence that girls in particular were being wrongly entered, on the grounds that they could not take the 'exam pressure', though as other research showed, there was no sign of this in their examination performance (Stobart *et al.* 1992).

Where it is possible to gain the same grade from different tiers, it has been shown to be easier to do so from the lower than from the higher (Good and

Cresswell 1988). This may be because markers expect more from higher grade candidates, or because judged normatively against, say, an A★ script, a C grade script looks poor, whereas against a G grade script a C looks good. For whatever reason, this may result in candidates being entered for the lowest tier that offers the possibility of the much sought after C grade, because in league table terms, that represents an important signpost.

A few GCSE subjects do not have tiered papers, mainly those where, in technical terms, 'differentiation by outcome' is realistic. Thus in art it is possible to set a common task that all candidates can address without it seeming demeaning or, at the other extreme, condescending, and then judging the result. Similarly, coursework tasks can be taken by all. In the case of history it was successfully argued that setters could provide questions across the ability range, using 'levels of response' mark schemes to differentiate between candidates (see Chapter 4). There are other modifications as well, such as in modern languages, where a Basic paper is sat by all and candidates have the choice of proceeding to the next tier, and then on to the Higher. All these cases have to be approved by QCA and there does appear to be some flexibility in the system; what Lloyd calls 'fine tuning' (1999: 118). In contrast Stobart and Gipps (1997) argue:

> We believe the earlier, less constrained, GCSE met many of the requirements of a 'good' examination in that there was a mix of coursework and examination (determined by 'fitness for purpose'): it encouraged teachers to be innovative and respected professional judgements; it motivated students through coursework, and through more imaginative syllabuses than those of the GCE it replaced. The politically imposed limits on coursework (the personal wish of John Major) have weakened the model, as may the reduction of syllabuses and teacher freedom.
>
> (pp. 84, 85)

In addition to these points, the existence of 'league tables' based around A★ to C grades continues to influence the way the examination operates. This is, to rehearse an argument we shall return to repeatedly in this book, an example of confused purpose. Despite GCSE's main one being the certification of individuals, GCSEs are now seen as a way, by aggregation, of certifying the whole school. There must be a very real danger of the well-being of individuals being subordinated to the perceived needs of the institution. And there is evidence that this is happening, for just as the numbers of A★- to C-grade candidates has shown a steady increase over the years, there has been a matching decline in performance at the bottom end of the ability range, with all that that implies for social inclusion and participation.

LEAGUE TABLES, POLARISATION AND RATIONING

Research undertaken by David Gilborn and Deborah Youndell was reported in the *TES* on 26 November 1999 under the headline, 'Weakest not at the table'. Gilborn and Youndell found that schools were 'rationing their attention so as to concentrate on children at the "borderline" between grades D and C'. They found that whilst schools were keen to recruit 'high achievers', 'once through the school gates, they are no longer the centre of attention'. 'At the other end of the spectrum, however, are those children thought unable to contribute to the five A-to-C benchmark. They are relegated to bottom sets; taught by less experienced teachers; and fall further and further behind.' (p. 13)

To a certain extent, however, the debate has moved on. Although compulsory schooling ends at 16, de facto for the majority it is now 18. As we saw above, the National Curriculum at Key Stage 4 has never really melded with GCSEs, and there is an acceptance that at age 14 young people should be given a wider choice of subjects, not least the possibility of introducing vocational elements into their curriculum. It may therefore be time to examine the possibility of the prescribed National Curriculum ending at Key Stage 3 (perhaps not being as tightly age determined as it has in the past) and then allowing for a coherent curriculum for Key Stages 4 and 5, which for the majority would mean the ages of 14 to 19. Within such a curriculum GCSEs would be unnecessary – such high-stakes testing at this age is very unusual internationally – and would allow for a number of routes to be followed, perhaps 'academic', perhaps 'vocational', perhaps a mixture of the two, allowing credits to be accumulated through a modular system. These credits could then be taken forward for application in lifelong learning.

Unfortunately, to suggest the abandonment of a 16+ examination is like proposing that we drive on the right-hand side of the road – distinctly foreign and likely to lead to nasty accidents! The preoccupation that the English system has for externally assessed summative, high-stakes assessment remains paramount. There is no better evidence of this fact than the story of Advanced levels, and it is to that we now turn.

'THE GOLD STANDARD'

In 1988 the Higginson report on the future of Advanced levels recommended fundamental changes (DES 1988). It was by no means the first serious inquiry into the post-compulsory examination in England and Wales, but in an act vividly demonstrating the increased centralisation of the English educational system, the government dismissed the proposals on the same day as they were published. The justification for this peremptory move hinged around a phrase that has since become part of educational history: the A-level 'Gold Standard'. Translated, this meant that no change would be contemplated that threatened the fundamentals of this particular examination, which was seen to embody 'quality' for the system at large.

Advanced levels are, to a large proportion of the population recognisably rigorous in both language and expectation, 'untainted' by coursework assessment, being externally marked, and 'protected' by apolitical gatekeepers, the universities. Perhaps as a result of these factors the examinations are held in high esteem; a perception that is especially strong amongst those who have passed them and who go on to form the backbone of the influential middle class (Stobart and Gipps 1997). The universities in particular have an important role, and one that has been pervasive since the examination's introduction in 1951. A-levels are de facto university entrance examinations, a function that is refined still further through the specificity of the grades. These carry a clear message that is often followed through to the final degree, from the A and B offers of the ancient and 'red-brick' universities to the Ds and Es of the 'new' universities.

Furthermore, because A-levels require young people to become specialists at a relatively early stage in their education, those who go on to university generally do well in their chosen subject, and despite what is by international comparison a relatively short (and cost effective) undergraduate course, the system turns out people who can compete with the very best in the world. Thus any proposed change to the system, and there have been many over the almost half century of their existence, has always run up against the universities' power and influence, supported in turn by the independent sector, both using the apparently irrefutable argument that the examinations are 'rigorous'; after all, in education, rigour is 'like virtue – (something) nobody would oppose' (*ibid.*: 98)! Overall, then, there is a great deal of inertia preventing change in what Stobart and Gipps describe as the 'most high stakes qualifications in the land' (*ibid.*: 89). What has happened over time, however, and especially in the last ten years or so, is a change in the A-level market. The examinations are increasingly serving a purpose that no one intended them to have when they were first introduced.

A changing population

Forty years ago the school leaving age for the majority was 15, whilst access to many professions was made at 16. As a result, only a relatively small proportion in any year-group even sat A-levels. University places were few and hard to come by – they existed for an elite. As time passed this situation changed. In the 1960s the number of places in higher education expanded rapidly through the building of universities such as Sussex, Essex and Warwick; the Polytechnics offered an alternative route for those showing a more vocational aptitude. At the same time the school leaving age was raised to 16, and the professions increasingly looked for candidates with A-levels. Inevitably, therefore, the examinations became more and more inappropriate for many of the students who took them and for others provided too high a hurdle, resulting in either 'failure' or a reluctance to stay on in education. For policy makers this presented a conundrum: how could post-16 participation rates be improved so as to match international levels, whilst at the same time maintaining the A-level 'Gold Standard'?

It became increasingly apparent throughout the 1980s and into the 1990s that the question could not be ducked. The UK's post-16 participation rates were amongst the lowest in comparison with the country's closest economic rivals, and this low participation was also reflected in poor levels of achievement (Finegold *et al.* 1990; Raffe 1992). At the same time the UK had the highest numbers of 'economically active' 16–19 year olds in the OECD but also the highest levels of youth unemployment. In addition, work-based training was 'low level' and as many as 30 per cent were 'involved in emergency training schemes, such as the Youth Training Scheme which . . . developed a reputation for low quality and low qualifications outcomes' (Hodgson and Spours 1997: 5). It was therefore important to encourage students to stay on in full-time education beyond the age of 16, *despite* the existence of A-levels, and this is indeed what happened, as Figure 5.2 shows.

This expansion was achieved through a mixture of incentives and penalties, the details of which lie outside the scope of this book, but the result was a massive growth, especially in Further Education colleges, so that whereas in 1991–2 full-time education in schools and colleges accounted for 42.5 per cent of the cohort, by 1996–7 this had risen to 49.7 per cent, and most of these students were following A-level courses. Inevitably this wider participation meant that traditional A-levels were inappropriate for the majority and would become more so as the economy increasingly demanded a flexible, re-trainable workforce (Dearing 1996). The corollary of this wider participation was either that A-level standards would become diluted, or more students would 'fail'. In

Academic Year	FT education			PT education	Training	Total Participation
	Schools	FE	HE			
1991–2	19.1	23.4	4.8	12.3	10.0	69.5
1992–3	20.2	25.8	5.7	10.2	10.5	72.5
1993–4	20.9	28.0	6.1	9.2	10.4	74.0
1994–5	21.0	28.3	6.5	8.7	10.2	74.9
1995–6	21.6	29.1	6.4	8.3	10.3	75.6
1996–7	21.7	28.0	6.4	8.0	11.3	75.4

Figure 5.2 Participation of 16–18 year olds in education and training (%)
Source: DfEE News 159/97

order to solve this seemingly intractable problem, the government appointed Sir Ron Dearing, who had successfully saved the National Curriculum from collapse in 1995, to attempt the same with the 16–19 curriculum.

The Dearing review of 16–19 qualifications

In 1996 Lord Dearing reported on the future of qualifications for 16–19 year olds. As we have outlined above, he faced a huge challenge. On the one hand he was instructed to retain the rigour of A-levels, whilst at the same time accepting the reality of a changed sixth form environment containing students, who only ten or so years earlier would not have considered staying on at school or college. Many commentators believed he was given an impossible brief, but he managed it by the simple but clever expedient of offering no fewer than 198 recommendations, which

> may explain why it was so well received by all parties – it had something for everybody: more rigour; more breadth; more status for vocational qualifications; more key skills. The *Daily Telegraph* wryly commentated: 'any initiative that receives a unanimous welcome in so contentious a field as education should set alarm bells ringing' (26 March 1996).
>
> (Stobart and Gipps 1997: 86)

In the years since 1996, the Dearing recommendations have been modified. Perhaps most importantly his idea of a National Diploma and the insertion of key skills into all A-levels have been dropped, but what has been accepted is the idea of a 'half way house' AS examination designed to broaden the curriculum, at least in the first year of a sixth form course.

AS-levels

Again, like so many reforming ideas concerning A-levels, the notion of offering some 'mid-point' has been around for many years; with slightly odd-sounding titles such as 'Q' and 'F', and 'N' and 'F' instead of 'AS' and 'A'. Of these, only AS examinations have been introduced, although somewhat confusingly in two forms, one spanning 1989 to 2000 and the second as half of an 'Advanced' course from September 2000 onwards.

The first AS examinations were not a success. This is because they suffered from a fundamental misunderstanding of examinations, which we shall detail below, but also because of the A-level 'Gold Standard'. Because they could not threaten this standard, they were required to have as much depth as a normal A-level but half the content, so the term 'advanced level' applied as much to an AS syllabus as it did an A-level: there was no such thing as AS-*level*. Not only were schools unwilling or unable to spare the resources required to timetable separate AS courses, students were quick to recognise that universities were, on the whole, continuing to demand the usual A-level points, which meant that the extra effort required to add an AS to three A-levels simply wasn't worth it, whilst dropping to two A-levels and one AS did not carry enough weight.

There was, in any case, a misunderstanding of what makes an examination 'difficult' – the notion we examined in the previous chapter (pp. 63–65). 'A-level-ness' is a combination of both depth and breadth of knowledge, and so one cannot guarantee the same depth simply by cutting the content in half. As Lloyd (1999) points out, the idea that a linguist can reach the same level of fluency in half the teaching time is a nonsense; more exposure to any language will necessarily improve standards. In any case, what exactly does it mean, in the context of learning a language, to reduce the content by half – halve the vocabulary, study half the number of books? It was the same for most syllabus designers; trying to separate content from depth was very difficult, especially since existing A-level syllabuses were designed with a coherence in mind. Trying to create a similarly coherent AS (at the same depth) but with half the content was almost impossible.

Fortunately at least some of the lessons from the original AS were learnt. The 'new' Advanced Subsidiary examinations are coherent because they are designed to be taught in the first year of a two year course. They have separate syllabuses (like all public examinations, now called 'specifications') and separate examinations. Of course, this will mean separate teams of examiners and all the other paraphernalia of an external exam. Inevitably costs will rise as a result, but these AS-levels may well offer the first genuine opportunity for a broadening of the sixth form curriculum for many years, though the issue of how schools, especially those with small sixth forms will fund them, remains to be seen. However, there is another important aspect of their introduction and that is that they fit into an increasing trend that has been developing in the past decade, namely the move towards modularity.

Modular A-levels

It may be that the conundrum that we outlined above: expanding numbers but retaining the 'Gold Standard' has been 'solved' in a subtle, evolutionary way rather than by a Higginson style revolution that would have provoked both controversy and confrontation. This 'solution' is the growth of modular A-levels.

Modular A-levels have proved to be popular for a number of reasons. First, of course, they offer an alternative to the 'high-stakes' terminal examination that requires the synthesis of two years of study in a highly stressed environment, where little or no allowance is made for nerves, illness or any other variable that might affect performance 'on the day'. They are also arguably more valid than conventional terminal examinations. This is because a situation where everything is so dependent on a 'once and for all' performance may test the ability to deliver under such circumstances more than it tests the subject itself.

To many teachers who have noticed a 'slackening' of effort after GCSEs and a slow start to post–16 study, modular exams encourage constant and consistent effort throughout a course rather than 'last-minute' effort and revision. In addition, modular examinations reward part-completion. This is especially important if the notion of lifelong learning is taken seriously. It is argued that people can and should be encouraged to accumulate qualifications as and when they feel able to or when their circumstances allow, rather than having to commit themselves to a lengthy period of study that might in the end only result in apparent 'failure'.

Connected to this final point is the opportunity for re-submission of modules and possible grade improvement. If one of the aims of A-levels is to improve educational standards, and if higher grades indicate such an improvement (both of these assumptions are, of course, contentious) then allowing candidates to re-enter modules is perfectly acceptable, in the same way as anyone can re-enter for conventional A-levels.

From a purely practical and pragmatic perspective, modular A-levels are easier to align with vocational or general vocational qualifications, which have traditionally used modular structures to credit achievement. Given the aims of (1) 'parity of esteem' between 'academic' and 'vocational' courses, (2) broadening the 16–19 curriculum and (3) encouraging credit accumulation over a lifetime, the 'bite-sized' nature of modules fits better than the large chunks of conventional A-levels.

Finally, and probably crucially, modular A-level examinations are probably more accessible to a greater range of students than conventional A-levels, either because less information has to be learnt and recalled, or because they do not require such deep learning (Stobart and Gipps 1997). For whichever reason – and we know that depth and breadth are inextricably linked when it comes to the relative difficulty of an examination – modular exams face opposition, because they are seen as a devaluation of the 'Gold Standard' (Hodgson and Spours 1997; Black 1998).

Opposition to modularity takes many forms. For instance, it is argued that modular A-levels distort comparability. If they are 'easier' than conventional (linear) examinations it is impossible to compare candidates (and perhaps even schools and colleges), which is crucial given their role in qualifying for higher education. Furthermore, whilst it is true that a conventional A-level *can* be re-sat, in practice such a move is rarely successful, because the re-sit will occur several months after the summer series, too late to affect university offers. In contrast, modules (in theory) can be re-done while a student is still at school or college, with relatively little disturbance to other study and none to university entrance. On the other hand, sitting a 'high-stakes' modular examination frequently, inevitably adds to the pressure on the students, even though they may have the opportunity to re-sit papers. There is also the impact upon the curriculum and formative assessment, which may be curtailed or abandoned to be replaced by an unrelenting diet of 'past papers'.

It is also suggested that, in the same way as the original AS examinations lost coherence by 'dividing up' conventional A-level syllabuses, modules also lack coherence, with artificial groupings of subject areas or topics. Furthermore, by offering options it may be possible for candidates to avoid 'difficult' areas. Both of these problems were illustrated in one of the most popular A-levels, business studies. This is a subject which can be divided up, in the same way as a business may divide up its functions: accounts, marketing, human resources and so on. Nevertheless, to have an advanced knowledge of the way a business functions, an individual needs to study all these elements and then make holistic or synoptic judgements, gathering data from each one. This is what linear syllabuses in business studies set out to do. The introduction of modules encouraged students to think only about one or two elements at a time and furthermore, until the practice was identified and stopped, for a time business studies students could actually avoid the study of 'difficult' but fundamentally important areas such as finance and accounting.

As the arguments show, there are concerns about modularity and government agencies, in particular SCAA and its successor QCA, have been concerned for some time about ensuring equity between candidates. As a result such syllabuses are subject to certain rules, the most important of which govern the number of re-sits a candidate can take, and the mandatory requirement to sit a final, synoptic paper that tests across the entire syllabus.

A-levels in the future

The latest changes to AS- and A-levels represent another attempt to modify the existing system, which once again increases the number and frequency of external examinations. We believe that the costs to individuals, schools, the awarding bodies and society are too high and will not be sustained for any length of time. It is hard to escape the conclusion that A-levels are in need of – yet another – radical review, which we would argue should be made within the context of a thoroughly thought through curriculum for 14–19 year olds. Tampering with A-levels in their existing form, either through the introduction by the front door of new AS-levels, or the back door via modularity, cannot achieve that objective. The school population is different from the one when A-levels were introduced, and our ideas of a broad and balanced curriculum suggest that the conventional three A-level diet, even if supported by four or perhaps five AS-levels, is no longer appropriate for the needs of the twenty-first century, characterised as it is by rapidly changing work and social patterns. The needs of universities are still important, of course, though that sector has itself changed through expansion and the growth of modular courses, but it is equally uncertain about the efficacy of a system of 'conditional offers' that so often turn out not to be accurate. Add to this a movement towards a four-term year in schools, the importance of lifelong learning and the inefficient use of scarce social capital when schools are closed, and it is clear that there is room for radical thinking, similar to that required when Britain came off the *real* gold standard in 1931!

FOR FURTHER READING

Anyone wishing to put the National Curriculum into context would be advised to read Denis Lawton's work. One of the best ways to understand the curriculum thinking of the Conservative Party through the 1980s and 1990s can be found in his 1994 publication *The Tory Mind on Education 1979–94*. Alternatively his book *Beyond the National Curriculum: Teacher Professionalism and Empowerment* (1996) contextualises the National Curriculum in a way relevant to all teachers, both new and experienced.

An 'alternative' discussion of the National Curriculum in the 1990s is supplied by Aldrich and White. They have written a pamphlet on the way the National Curriculum might be revised, using the aims of education in a way that was not explored by the original. This brief work called *The National Curriculum beyond 2000: the QCA and the Aims of Education* (1998) is well worth reading because it suggests that we need first to explore where we want to get to in our curriculum, before we decide the way we might get there, as has been the tendency in the recent past.

For those seeking more information on the development of GCSEs, Gipps's (1986) 'GCSE: some background' in *The GCSE: An Uncommon Examination* and Nuttall's (1984) 'Doomsday or a new dawn? The prospects of a common system of examination at 16+' in P. M. Broadfoot (ed.) *Selection, Certification and Control* will supply interesting and illuminating material.

NOTE

1 Statements of attainment proliferated in a vain attempt by specialist working groups to specify attainment unambiguously. Unwieldy and unworkable statements of attainment have now been replaced – in all National Curriculum subjects – by composite level descriptions (rather like GCSE grade related descriptions in form).

6 Can We Trust Examinations?

This chapter will argue that in England and Wales we have developed something of an obsession with summative assessment. This is partly the result of historical trends and partly because of recent political moves designed to increase 'accountability'. We argue that the concentration on high-stakes external assessment is expensive, adds to the pressures on young people and importantly, distorts the learning process because teachers are forced to measure achievement rather than finding out more about their students as individuals. In other words the emphasis on summative assessment tends to drive out 'genuine' formative assessment, an issue taken up more directly in Chapters 7–9.

INTRODUCTION

The previous three chapters have offered considerable detail on the practices and processes involved in external, largely summative assessment. We have argued that the system that has developed in England and Wales has resulted in a level of 'high-stakes' assessment almost without equal in western countries (West *et al.* 1999). Such a system carries high costs, some of which are tangible and some more hidden. The tangible ones are largely financial, but opportunity costs are also significant. Whilst students are sitting examinations they are not able to do anything else, they cannot be taught and they cannot expand their knowledge; whilst schools and colleges are paying for examination entry fees the money cannot be used for other things that might be seen as more beneficial. Above all, the creative processes involved in formative assessment may be lost or subsumed, and an emphasis on 'teaching for the test' may result in sterile, unimaginative classroom exercises that are justified on the sometimes spurious grounds that such work will help in the final exam.

INTERNATIONAL RESEARCH ON THE IMPACT OF EXAMINATIONS

In a study for the United Nations Educational, Scientific and Cultural Organization (UNESCO), Christine de Luca looked at the impact of examination systems on curriculum development in the following countries: Columbia, Egypt, Japan, Scotland, the USA and Zimbabwe. She identified positive and negative factors of examinations on the curriculum, and came to the following conclusion:

> Examination systems can have a powerful impact on curriculum development, and while the potential for positive effects can be impressive, the overall impact as experienced by pupils is, more often than not, tilted towards negative effects. This is especially the case if the examination is high stakes for pupils and schools.
>
> (1994: 123)

At the same time, of course, no one would deny the value of summative assessment that is undertaken through external examinations; in one form or another all European countries use it (*ibid.*). Such assessment allows certification to take place, providing a baseline for those who wish to proceed to the next stage in their education or towards a career. It can also have a positive impact upon the curriculum, as GCSE showed. These exams de-emphasised the factual rote learning and regurgitation so prevalent in O-levels and replaced it with a more creative assessment regime that included a measure of continuous assessment (see Chapter 5). Finally, and this is perhaps its strongest point and indeed the reason for its existence in the first place, external summative assessment is seen to be *fair* to all candidates. If final examinations are based on a syllabus that everyone knows and has access to, if scripts are sent to independent professionals who have no contact with the students whose work they are marking, and if the entire process is controlled by organisations that have a reputation for ethical working and who are in any case controlled, or at least monitored by a government agency, then, as the saying goes, the playing field is seen to be 'level', and the 'most able', whatever their circumstances, will rise to the top.

Unfortunately, and perhaps unsurprisingly given their complexity and the involvement of so many people in the process, examinations are not the perfect instruments their advocates might suggest. There can be few people who go through the system in England and Wales who have not considered themselves, or one or more of their contemporaries, either 'lucky' or 'unlucky' in an examination, in that their result did not reflect their ability, their commitment or both. The simple fact is that in spite of all the best efforts of the examinations industry, mistakes are made, some subjects appear to be easier to pass, or to get high grades in than others and, rightly or wrongly, the awarding bodies are themselves perceived to have variable levels of difficulty. As Stobart and Gipps (1997) put it:

> Much of the discussion concerning rigour revolves around whether subjects, syllabuses and assessment schemes are equally demanding. This is essentially an issue of reliability. The perception is that, with six examining boards offering over six hundred syllabuses, comparative standards may be difficult to guarantee. The same is true at GCSE. A particular concern is that some subjects appear easier (i.e. give more higher grades or give higher grades to students with weaker GCSE results than in other subjects), a problem when university entry may be decided on total grade points.
>
> (p. 91)

What then is the issue of reliability to which Stobart and Gipps refer?

RELIABILITY

The personal experience we described above, of having been 'lucky' or 'unlucky' in an examination, illustrates a lack of reliability. Let us follow this through with an example. Assume that we and our teachers 'know', by means of evidence accumulated throughout the two years of an A-level course, that we should have got, say, a D grade in history, but in the examination proper we are actually awarded an A (perhaps an unlikely, but not an impossible scenario). As Stobart and Gipps suggest above, this 'false' result then leads to all sorts of generalisations, not only about our ability in history, but also about our level of intelligence overall. That A grade may enable us to train to become a doctor, enter one of the top universities, or be offered a post in one of the prestigious law or accounting firms, when our more lowly D would not. In each case certain pivotal individuals will look at our A-level result and conclude that we must be articulate, able to prepare an argument, synthesise information and so on; all conclusions that might reasonably be drawn from someone who genuinely deserves an A grade in A-level history. Put in this way, the stakes of such an examination are high indeed; mistakes can have a massive and perhaps a disproportionate impact on our lives, especially perhaps if the example is reversed, so that instead of an A grade we end up with an D, with the result that university and career ambitions are denied.

All of which explains why, the higher the stakes, the greater the emphasis on reliability and comparability. But more reliability, as we saw in Chapter 2, carries a cost, not only in terms of assessment instruments that may be more *valid* but also, and this is central to our argument, of 'imaginative teaching and effective learning' (Stobart and Gipps 1997), utilising formative techniques.

In the example of the history grade, an error has occurred. We are incorrectly making a generalised comment about the individual's 'ability' on the basis of a particular event (Wood 1991; Black 1998). The source of such error can be either through the examining process or through the candidate's performance on the day. We shall look at each of these potential sources in turn.

AN ERROR IN THE EXAMINING PROCESS

Arithmetic mistakes

The examination process, as we have seen, is complex, and one that involves the intervention of large numbers of people. It is therefore unsurprising that mistakes happen. At the most basic level there are many points in an examination where apparently simple, arithmetic errors can occur. For instance, the examiner may incorrectly add up the marks of an individual question, or of all the questions on a paper. Then he or she may incorrectly transfer the marks from the script on to the mark sheets. These sheets are read by a computer, so the number may not be correctly transposed into a machine-readable form, and so on. Of course the awarding bodies go to great lengths to avoid such errors by double and even triple checking additions and by not re-appointing examiners who consistently make such mistakes, but, as re-marked scripts often demonstrate after results have been issued, errors do still creep through.

Mark scheme errors

Other mistakes are caused by examiners not interpreting the mark scheme correctly. They may forget about changes made at the standardisation meeting, or they may have a 'blank' about a part of a question, confusing it with another part, fondly believing it was to be marked out of six, say, when in fact it was out of eight. As we saw in Chapter 4, this may be picked up when the marks across two papers are compared, and the examiner may be 'scaled' as a result, or it may be spotted when scripts are sampled, resulting in a complete re-mark of that particular question but, in the nature of statistics, this cannot always happen.

Machine errors

Although this is extremely rare, it has happened that new computer processes have led to mistakes. Some years ago such an incident took place in an examination consisting of two papers, the first marked out of one hundred and the second out of one hundred and fifty. Unfortunately the computer had mistakenly been programmed to recognise both papers as being out of one hundred, and so it simply added together the raw marks on both papers and halved them. This had two effects. The first was to give the relatively poor candidates i.e. those who had scored raw marks between zero and ninety nine on the second paper, a disproportionately high percentage mark (99 should have been worth 66 per cent, not 99 per cent). The second was to penalise the relatively few, high scoring candidates (i.e. those who achieved 100 or more out of 150), because the only way the computer could deal with raw marks above what it had been told was the maximum, was to give those candidates a mark of zero! Fortunately this error was spotted by the chief examiner before the results were issued, but it does demonstrate how, even in areas that might appear to be foolproof, mistakes can still occur.

Marking 'errors'

The marking process is, of course, itself subject to inconsistency, despite the best efforts to train, monitor and check individual examiners. The more discursive the style of examination, such as an essay paper, the less likely it is that two identical answers will be awarded the same mark (Wood 1991). This is unsurprising, of course, and is sometimes advanced as an argument for not including such components in an examination. The predilection in the USA for machine marked objective tests was largely founded on the principle that reliability was over-arching, even though validity might be lost. In England and Wales it has generally been accepted that the loss of some reliability is a price worth paying in order to test a range of skills. A way around this is to set an examination that consists of a variety of components such as multiple choice, coursework and extended writing (essays), so that in theory at least, it is possible to have both valid and reliable papers overall. Nevertheless, it is clear that the simple intervention of human beings in the marking process will introduce inconsistencies. It is unlikely, for instance, that the twentieth script of the day will receive the same attention as the first; an examiner who is under domestic or professional pressure is unlikely to mark as well or as consistently as one who is not; it is even possible for markers to be become complacent after a few years: one chief examiner was always more alert to check his 'best' markers after three or four years, for this reason alone. There is also the borderline decision, when an answer might reasonably be awarded one more, or one less mark. In such circumstances no one can offer a clear argument either way and so both are in a sense the 'right' mark. It may seem that such a decision is relatively trivial or unimportant, after all what is one mark out of one hundred, but over an entire paper it can make a difference, especially when grade boundaries are close.

Grade boundaries

Translating raw marks into all-important grades is another potential source of error. Although examiners are always encouraged to award across a range of available marks, in practice they rarely do, especially where the question is discursive. There is a reluctance to award, say twenty out of twenty for an essay, just as there is a similar resistance to giving another one zero. The result is bunching, so that in effect the marks are not ranged between zero and twenty, but instead they become, say, between five and sixteen. If this situation is repeated across a number of questions, the good candidate is penalised whilst the poor one actually does better. To take an extreme example, say the good candidate should have received twenty, eighteen and eighteen for three essays, but instead gets sixteen, fifteen and fifteen. The total mark is therefore forty-six as opposed to fifty-six. In contrast the poor candidate who should have got two, zero and zero for the same questions gets seven, five and five. This results in a total of seventeen instead of two. The poor candidate has a score that is approximately 37 per cent of the good one's instead of 3.5 per cent – a ten-fold difference. This is bad enough in itself, but when grade boundaries are set the problem gets worse. The fail grade has now to be seventeen, whereas the A/B boundary will not be forty-six (because we are discussing an *outstanding* candidate), let us say it is forty-two. So if we want grades A to E and then fail we have a range of only twenty-five marks to play with. Assuming each of the grades are equal in size, this results in:

Grade	Mark
A	42+
B	36–41
C	30–35
D	24–29
E	18–23
F	0–17

In other words each grade is only five marks wide on a paper worth sixty marks. It is easy to see how two examiners, faced with the possibility of giving one or two extra marks on each question may, quite legitimately, decide either to do so or not, with the result that two 'identical' candidates become separated by an entire grade, which may make the difference between university acceptance or rejection.

Although it might be argued that such a scenario exaggerates the situation, as more components are added to an examination the danger of bunching may become more acute. Of course the awarding bodies are aware of and sensitive to this threat and constantly emphasise the need for examiners to use the entire range of marks available. In addition, they carry out 'borderline' marking exercises, where the scripts of candidates at certain 'key' boundaries are re-marked by senior examiners to see if errors have been made.

New syllabuses

The examining process is, for teachers as well as students, something of a lottery, although as we saw in Chapter 4, considerable strides have been made in recent years to make the process more open and accessible. Nevertheless, imponderables remain, such as the way the chief and principal examiners interpret a syllabus. This is even more the case when a new syllabus is introduced, and it is quite possible for a teacher simply to misinterpret the way it will be examined – not perhaps in substance, but in detail – with the result that an error occurs in the grades awarded to candidates. Such a possibility may result in teachers, students and parents avoiding new syllabuses wherever possible, and that is often the case, but innovations are always attractive to some, and clearly it is in everyone's interest to make the process as pain free as possible. Thus the awarding bodies do their best to avoid misinterpretation by issuing specimen papers and mark schemes, offering free INSET run by the chief and principal examiners, providing 'help desks' and so on.

AN ERROR IN THE CANDIDATE'S PERFORMANCE

Health and environmental issues

It is inevitable that outside factors will cause candidates not to perform as well on some days as on others. Quite apart from the mental stress of knowing, or believing in the potential impact upon their futures that success or failure will bring, physical health is also likely to influence an individual's answers. Equally, it is easy to speculate that the environment in which so many examinations take place will also have an effect. The converted gymnasium, hot and stuffy in summer, cold and inhospitable in winter, allied to the dread step of the invigilator pacing, far from noiselessly up and down the serried ranks of poorly constructed and inadequately sized temporary 'desks', is an image branded into the minds of countless generations; one hardly designed to encourage candidates to perform at their best!

The examination regime

The length of the paper itself can be daunting to some candidates. In recent times this has been reduced, but it is still not uncommon for candidates, at least at A-level, to find themselves incarcerated for up to two hours, writing more or less constantly without a break. This is not a 'natural' environment either in a school or work context, and it is unlikely to encourage the best from all candidates. There are still some people who see examinations as a kind of endurance test, designed to weed out the 'weak' from the strong, and it appears that this is taken to mean weakness and strength in a far wider context than simply an educational one.

The examination paper as a barrier

The paper itself may prove to be a barrier. Different results will be obtained from an identical topic because it is examined in a different way, or because the question uses more complex, more obscure or even 'sexist' language or contexts (Gipps and Murphy (1994) argue that sexism can be 'explicit' e.g. stereotypical images in the exam paper, or 'non-explicit' such as in the choice of texts tested, and so on). More recently it was suggested that the 1999 Key Stage 2 tests showed a considerable improvement in the performance of boys' reading and comprehension scores because the chosen topic was 'spiders': apparently a subject that appealed to them more than the ones used on different testing occasions (Wragg 1999).

Samples from the syllabus

Questions on papers necessarily sample from the whole syllabus. It may be that the one chosen for a particular year does not enable candidates to display their skills, and there are quite complex statistical measures that can be applied to determine whether a paper is 'internally consistent' (for a more detailed discussion on this topic see Black 1998: 39–42). As we saw in the last chapter, as far as possible the awarding bodies try to prevent changes year-to-year, but it is inevitable that even if a topic is examined regularly, the particular aspect will suit some more than others, and that may lead to a false result.

Choice of questions

Where a paper contains a choice of questions, the ones a candidate chooses to answer can have an impact. This is because, for the question setter, attempting to divine which questions candidates will find relatively 'easy' and which 'hard', is almost impossible. There are structures that help achieve this, as we saw in Chapter 4, and of course experience both in and of classrooms is invaluable, but in the end it is something of a leap of faith. Consider two essay questions and the ways in which they can be perceived by candidates as 'easy' or 'hard':

- It could be the topic itself. Within any syllabus there are areas that are popular and others that are not. In business studies, for example, questions on accounting are often avoided, those on marketing almost always answered.
- It will make a difference whether the question is multi-part or not. Generally a multi-part question will lead the candidate through the answer; in effect supplying a structure that will help to accumulate marks.

- As we saw in the previous chapter, the words used in the question will affect candidate performance. These words can be either technical, i.e. the language of the discipline, or not, but either way, if they are not understood they will form a barrier.
- There are the requirements of the question. In the past it was often felt enough to write a stem, such as a quotation, and then follow it with the simple (but actually highly demanding) word, 'discuss'. Today it is recognised that such a word offers little or no guidance as to what candidates are required to write. Instead a sentence or two will be given to indicate the required depth. These changes are all bound up with the principles of openness and fairness that we have detailed in earlier chapters.

Conclusion

It may seem that the above discussion indicates that we believe the system to be seriously flawed. That is not our intention. For every candidate who feels aggrieved, there are many hundreds who believe their result is about right. Nevertheless, what we are suggesting is that externally set and marked summative tests are not some kind of universal panacea that will guarantee a precise and accurate reflection of students' abilities, free from any bias that might creep into teacher assessment. Simply adding more high-stakes external exams into the lives of young people will not automatically raise standards; indeed, we suggest that the financial, human and opportunity costs involved in doing so are becoming excessive, and that, if we really are concerned about achievement, a fresh look needs to be taken at the balance between formative and summative techniques.

FURTHER THINKING

1. What is your view of external, summative tests? Have you always felt them to be fair and to give an honest result, bearing in mind that if you have a degree you are likely to be someone for whom this system has worked well?
2. What are the opinions of your teacher-colleagues, and importantly have their views or perceptions changed in recent times?

ASSESSING SCHOOLS: VALUE ADDED DATA

Introduction

In the last decade or so a new approach to judging achievement has been introduced, one which in some senses forms a bridge between summative and formative assessment. This approach uses 'value added' measures, which claim to show the learning *gain* as a result of a course of study, rather than simply a raw score. The focus, then, is on the individual student, as an indicator of progress. However, by aggregating the data, value added becomes a way of measuring the 'output' of a school. This is an important distinction (and confusion), and one that returns us to the emphasis on 'fitness for purpose' made throughout this book: by asking a single assessment device to do 'too much' there is a danger that its original purpose becomes 'diluted'.

Raw examination data and the measurement of school performance

By the start of the 1980s, attention was increasingly focused on the performance of schools (and staff) as much as individual students. The 'simple' way of measuring this performance was through 'raw' external examination results (i.e. with no allowance for social factors). They were, after all, apparently 'objective', they were trusted by user groups and they offered evidence that could be used to compare performance across schools. If any stakeholder, and especially government, wanted to know how well a school was performing, external examination results gave apparently bias-free measures of output. And the results had to be 'raw'; in 1993–4 'the Secretary of State . . . was adamant that results which were anything other than "raw" must be "cooked"' (Saunders 1998: 2).

   The government is of course, a crucial stakeholder in education, not just as a provider of financial resources, but also as the elected guardian of the nation's future. It is unsurprising therefore, that successive governments, regardless of party, have increasingly sought ways of holding schools to account. To achieve this they have created and supported an interrelated and interdependent package of 'league tables' which are based around 'raw' examination results, and backed up by regular visits by OFSTED inspectors. The initial justification for such a system was that it would result in more 'informed' parental choice and a distribution of assets towards the most 'successful' schools (Davies 1999) in a straightforward, some might say simplistic notion of the 'market mechanism'. As de Luca found in her international study,

> In Columbia, Japan, France, Scotland and the USA, publication of results of high stakes examinations by school, and generally also by region or district, has become a fairly recent fact of life. In all cases

these results are raw results, and in most cases, the publication is associated with a move to a more 'market-orientated' model of education. While such information *can encourage schools to look carefully at the curriculum and examination preparation techniques, it can also encourage simplistic interpretation of what is essentially a very complex situation. . . .*

(de Luca 1994: 123, emphasis in original)

The cornerstone of the system in England and Wales was external examination results, but to some researchers this was factually misleading and encouraged invidious comparisons to be made. In their research on *Effective Schools and Effective Departments*, Sammons and her colleagues conclude that the publication of raw examination results is undesirable:

Our study makes it quite clear that the current publication of raw 'league tables' of schools' public examination results is not justified as a mechanism for accountability. As we have shown, schools vary markedly in the nature of their student intakes and valid comparisons cannot be made without reference to this.

(Sammons *et al.* 1997: 184–185)

This was a call to avoid simple judgements based on simple data. And yet the related agenda of raising achievement and obtaining 'value for money' from 'effective' schools has grown in prominence. As Stoll and Mortimore put it:

The last decade has seen a burgeoning of interest in the twin fields of school effectiveness and school improvement by policy makers and practitioners. For some, the drive has been to raise standards and increase accountability through inspection and assessment measures, believing that the incentive of accountability and market competition will lead to improvement. Alternatively, reform and reconstructing have led many people in schools to create their own agenda and ask, 'How do we know that what we are doing makes a positive difference to our pupils?' and 'What can we do to provide pupils with the best possible education?

(Stoll and Mortimore 1995: 1)

Thus there has been great interest in techniques that can use examination data in a way that can help teachers answer *their* questions and at the same time provide clear and fair accountability data for school managers, inspectors and government. The difficulty though, is that operating at the level of the individual student is not the same as working in aggregate, and it is necessary at all times to consider the question of fitness for purpose. As Goldstein put it:

> If an assessment system is to prosper and if it is to retain intellectual integrity, it must avoid claiming that it can serve conflicting aims simultaneously.
>
> (Goldstein 1993: 33)

School effectiveness and value added analysis

For school effectiveness researchers, and for others (e.g. Goldstein, *ibid.*), raw examination data was simply not good enough on its own, because it took no account of the baseline performance of pupils. If a school intake consisted of a high proportion of children who were second-language learners and/or possibly traumatised refugees, it was unrealistic to expect the same proportion to achieve A★ GCSEs as in a school where children came from backgrounds built on stable personal relationships and homes filled with televisions, computers and books. It was therefore necessary to find other ways of measuring performance. Thus:

> Ultimately, school effectiveness research searches for appropriate and reliable ways to measure school quality. . . . In this paper we define an effective school as one in which pupils progress further than might be expected from consideration of its intake. . . . Value added is a technique designed to make fair comparisons between schools.
>
> (Stoll and Mortimore 1995: 1)

Intuitively, the idea of value added in an educational context is a simple one: student achievement is measured at the start of a course and then at the end, recognising that starting points will vary between individuals. Thus, if two students start an A-level course, one with eight GCSE A★ grades and another with eight C grades and both finish with three Grade A A-levels, it is apparent that more value has been added to the second one than the first.

Perhaps unsurprisingly, however, behind such simplicity lies considerable complexity. If an institution such as a school or college claims to add greater than expected value to students, it may be very difficult to say how exactly this is achieved: greater spending on textbooks, or ICT or a carefully judged combination of both? Or is it the quality of pastoral relationships, or tutorial support? Are the subject teachers better, and if so, how? And remaining stubbornly in the background is the notion that any improved performance is the result of individuals working harder, or better, rather than anything the institution itself does. It could be, for instance, that between GCSEs and A-level the student has simply 'grown up' and realised he has to work harder in order to do well, admittedly something that may be better encouraged in some institutions in comparison with others where sixth formers are not encouraged to take responsibility for themselves and others; or home circumstances may have changed and created a more attractive learning environment; or simply the fact of being able to concentrate on a limited number of subjects of greater interest encourages deeper learning, and so on.

To the student it is the raw data (three A-grades) that is important (Stobart and Gipps 1997; Thomas *et al.* 1997), and there is certainly a danger that adding a great deal of value on to very little may still leave an individual student ill-equipped for life. Value added is used as an aggregate measure – a way of judging schools or parts of schools – as well as a means of judging individuals, and in compiling the data it is of course the ultimate intention to improve the performance of each person. Thus it is increasingly familiar for school managers to ask department teams to identify aggregate 'targets' for the number of GCSE A–C grades they expect in their subject. Once such a decision is made the aggregate targets are 'translated' to individual student contexts: individuals are given targets appropriate to the level of achievement to which they can reasonably aspire.

Saunders, in her overview of value added argues that,

> The term has become a handy way of describing a whole range of connected but distinct activities, including:
>
> * making *'like with like'* comparisons of schools' (or departments' or classes') performance;
> * representing pupils' *progress* as well as their achievement;
> * identifying which schools/departments/classes are *currently performing above or below predictions*;
> * identifying which individual pupils *are likely to perform above or below predictions*.
>
> (Saunders 1998: 1, emphasis in original)

Saunders goes on to argue that each of the above is not equally 'susceptible to statistical analysis' and that such analysis 'is more appropriate to ... aggregate past performance than to the prediction of individual current or future performance' (*ibid.*: 2). Nevertheless,

> Value added analysis attempts to strip away factors which are associated with performance – either positively or negatively – but are not related to institutional quality. These include pupils' prior attainment, sex, ethnic group, date of birth, level of special educational need and social disadvantage. *Typically, pupils' prior attainment plus the overall level of social disadvantage in the school (as measured by free school meals) can account for as much as 80 per cent of the apparent difference between schools.*
>
> (*ibid.*: 2, emphasis in original)

If true, this makes value added a powerful tool, because it holds out the mouth-watering possibility of a completely 'level playing field', with schools and colleges being *fairly* compared in an open and transparent way. We should note Saunders' opening sentence, however, and her use of the word 'attempt': it sounds a note of caution. Later on in this chapter we shall detail some of the ways in which value added analysis has to be treated with a degree of circumspection, but first we shall look at a possible practical application of the data.

Using value added

One of the most immediately usable and effective ways of applying value added data is to plot school performance on a matrix (Figure 6.1), with unadjusted scores on one axis and adjusted ones – allowing for 'student' and 'school' factors on the other. More technically the scores are termed *residuals*, meaning an estimate of the difference between an actually observed score and a score predicted from previous attainment (Thomas *et al.* 1997). There are four segments on such a matrix into which it is possible to plot school performance and say something meaningful about them.

Schools falling into Box A would have below average raw results, and would therefore not have a high position in the league tables. However, they would be adding considerable value to their students. Using raw data alone, the staff may feel demoralised because of the 'league' position, whereas in fact their teachers are doing well by the students. The benefit in using

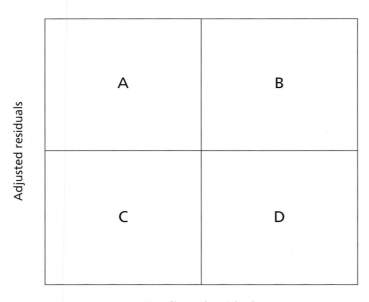

Figure 6.1 A value added matrix

Source: based on Saunders and Rudd (1999)

value added data is therefore apparent because the school can be shown to be 'effective'.

In contrast, schools in box C have both below average raw and below average added value scores. They would therefore be vulnerable to the accusation of 'failing', especially if they move further towards the origin. Again the strength of this information can be seen, as presumably such schools are in need of some kind of intervention (of exactly what kind, however, is likely to be contested!).

Box D schools might be categorised as 'complacent'. They have above average raw scores, and are therefore high in the league tables, but they are not greatly adding value. The need for such schools to use value added data is arguably considerable; for management in the medium- to long-term such information is vital — any slip towards segment C could be critical.

Box B schools are the 'beacons'; not only are their results above average, but they are also adding considerable value. They might use the information to discover where particular success stories are, perhaps within individual departments, so that good practice can be disseminated more widely.

It can be seen from this analysis that the potential benefits of using value added data are high, though, as we indicated above, extrapolating the information can be potentially misleading and should be treated with caution. And although the data may be interesting descriptively, they do not and cannot offer explanations in different school and department contexts. For those readers interested in how schools use this information and the detail from which Figure 6.1 was derived, see Saunders and Rudd (1999).

Value added: a summary

The entire notion of school effectiveness depends on being able to measure improvement (or deterioration). Value added uses sophisticated statistical techniques to offer insights into the way schools are performing, but it does not and cannot tell the whole story. Schools and colleges are complex micropolitical institutions, each one unique in terms of its space, its people and its dynamic and so the use of an aggregate, macro-tool carries clear dangers. So what are its limitations?

- As Saunders and Rudd state, 'What value added data cannot do is *prove* anything' (*ibid.* 1999: 1); it is simply an indicator.
- Training needs to be given on the use of the data once it arrives in schools. There is some evidence (West and Moore 1998; Saunders 1998; Saunders and Rudd 1999) that it is being used as a managerial device for change without the full cooperation of all staff. On the other hand it has caused managers and classroom teachers to question a simplistic 'gut reaction' along the lines of 'I know what's right for my students, whatever the numbers say' and to show them ways forward.

- Of course the very fact that value added *data* are *data* raises important questions. The danger with any statistics is that they can offer spurious accuracy, especially to those unfamiliar with their limitations. Thus it is important to be aware of confidence limits, which can show the likelihood of an event occurring simply by chance, rather than having any causal connection (Thomas *et al.* 1997). Goldstein's research showed that 'for the GCSE examination, value added analyses yield "uncertainty intervals" which are so large that only schools with extremely small or extremely large value added scores can be separated from the remainder. In other words, it is not technically possible with any reasonable certainty to give an unequivocal ranking of schools in a league table' (Goldstein 1993: 34).
- Connected to the last point is the sample size; the smaller the sample the larger the margin of statistical error or uncertainty. Goldstein criticises the Newcastle A-level Information Service (ALIS) on this basis, because it 'reports comparisons on a subject–department basis where numbers may be very small indeed' (*ibid.*: 34).
- Then there is the way a student intake can change for no apparent reason. As Davis (1998: 17) points out, 'cohorts of pupils simply do vary year to year', and the smaller the sample the more likely this is to be the case.
- Davis (*ibid.*) also questions whether it is possible to test students on entry in respect of certain knowledge and skills and then later on test the '*same* knowledge and skills'. 'Adding value' he says 'seems to imply that on entry pupils can be discovered to be in possession of a given level of something, and later can be discovered to be in possession of *more* of that something' (p. 18, emphasis in original).
- Then there is the inevitable reaction to testing that we have explored in a number of places in this book. Once schools know they are going to be measured against their intake score, they will do everything they can to depress that score so that the output measure shows as large an increase as possible.

In the end, value added is simply another, albeit new and sophisticated, device that can help managers, teachers, governors, parents and governments improve student performance. Yet it tends to be used as an aggregate measure, in the same way as external examinations results have come to be applied. Indeed, there has been an inevitable emphasis on macro-issues in this discourse; to what extent do we over-examine compared to other countries; how do we ensure fairness for all candidates; have standards overall gone up and so on? All of these are matters of concern to individuals, of course, but part of our argument is that discussion of assessment at an aggregate level has come to dominate, to such an extent that the all-important micro-issues of what happens in classrooms in a day-to-day sense is in danger of becoming lost. It is therefore that topic, and the role that formative assessment plays, to which we now turn in Chapters 7–9.

FURTHER READING

Paul Black's *Testing: Friend or Foe* (1998) offers a more detailed look at areas of reliability and validity in Chapter 4. In particular he describes variability between pupils from question to question (pp. 39–41) in more detail than is appropriate here.

As its name suggests *'Value Added' Measurement of School Effectiveness: An Overview* by Leslie Saunders (1998) provides a summary of what value added is, how it came into being, its key lessons, its use in schools, and its likely future. There is even a practical section entitled 'Hints for senior managers on using value added'! Anyone interested in the subject, and that should include virtually everyone in the teaching profession, ought to read this quite brief but accessible paper, and perhaps follow it up with the *'Critical Review'* published the following year.

7 Classroom Assessment: Making a Case for Formative Assessment

Chapters 7–9 explore the mounting interest among educationists and teachers in developing formative assessment theory and practice. This is a relatively underdeveloped field but one with dramatic potential impact on practically all aspects of teaching and learning, from the fundamental theories we may hold, implicitly or explicitly, about the nature of intelligence or how people learn, to the way we manage classrooms, mark work and interact generally with pupils on a day to day basis. Chapter 7 is about making a case for adopting formative, classroom assessment practices in which we shall see that the terminology, let alone coherent and fully developed understanding, is far from settled. Chapter 8 then focuses on the theoretical underpinning of classroom assessment and the key mechanisms linking theory to the effective practice of formative assessment – namely the use of feedback and the involvement of pupils in self-assessment. Chapter 9 discusses the implications of adopting such practices and will offer some critical perspectives, particularly on issues of fairness. This chapter also critically examines a particular aspect of day-to-day classroom assessment known as marking, within the context of the broad issues raised in the previous chapters.

This chapter provides arguments for adopting formative assessment practices in school. The arguments are strong and offer powerful and convincing reasons to change certain common, often habitual, assessment procedures and assumptions about what assessment is for and how it 'works'. These arguments are challenging to many teachers, particularly perhaps, to beginning teachers for whom establishing good classroom relationships is complicated enough already. However, we wish to suggest that once comprehended and translated into practical action, formative assessment provides the theoretical framework to deepen and improve the quality of teaching and learning in the classroom. Although quite different in form and purpose from external, summative assessment practices – indeed some writers argue that the rising interest in formative assessment amounts to a 'paradigm shift' (Shinn and Hubbard 1992) in the field of educational assessment – we would emphasise from the start that we do not advocate an all or nothing approach here (as the use of *the word paradigm might imply). That is, we are not suggesting the wholesale dumping of external assessment, even though from our analysis we do conclude that a state of over dependence on external assessment mechanisms (and the system in England and Wales may be perilously close to this), can distort healthy classroom processes. As with most issues and problems in teaching and learning, we are urging that distinctions are made and an effective balance be struck between competing principles and purposes. Individual teachers need to be vigilant in this respect and have a role to play in striking such a balance.*

WHAT IS FORMATIVE ASSESSMENT (FA)?
A DISCUSSION

It appears that classroom assessment, particularly the form of practice that some writers have dubbed 'assessment for learning' (e.g. Sutton 1995), occupies an ambiguous and uncertain position in the world of education. It is not well understood, and partly as a result, practice is found, by inspectors and researchers alike, to be patchy. For example, OFSTED concluded that

> day-to-day assessment . . . is weak and the use of assessment to help planning of future work is unsatisfactory in one in five schools. What is particularly lacking is marking which clearly informs pupils about the standards they have achieved in a piece of work, and what they need to do to improve; whilst marking needs to be supportive of efforts made, it also needs to be constructively critical, and diagnostic of both strengths and weaknesses.

> (DfEE 1997)

This is a very interesting quotation. It purports to be based upon the dispassionate observation of hundreds of lessons over a four year period and is stamped with the authority of the government's education standards agency. But of course observations can never be entirely 'independent'. What is observed, and what sense is made of the observations, is informed or mediated by theory – either explicitly or implicitly. The OFSTED comment above, though this remains unacknowledged, is directly informed by judgements emanating from the educational research community. It makes statements about classroom assessment which are framed in the language of 'formative assessment' (FA). We, in turn, use the quote to help frame this chapter and though perplexed slightly by the apparent precision and authority of OFSTED's judgement (unsatisfactory work in 20 per cent of schools!) take as our starting point the notion that the kind of good practice inspectors say they want to see is not exactly easy to find.

That good FA practice is hard to find is also somewhat perplexing, for we imagine that many, if not most, teachers would say that they do it. Perhaps inspectors do not see it; and it is the case that, unlike formal summative assessments in the form of tests, for example, FA may well be relatively invisible, in the teacher's head rather than in some form of documentation. Or perhaps 'good practice' is so difficult to pull off that it is in fact rarely seen operating in a fully developed manner. If we take a close look at the OFSTED quotation we can see that what they have in mind is indeed demanding: they are looking for assessment that:

- helps teachers plan future work;
- informs pupils of the standards they have reached;
- shows pupils what they need to do to improve;
- is diagnostic of strengths and weaknesses; and
- is constructively critical.

But how does one demonstrate using assessment to inform planning? Against whose standards do we measure pupils' achievements? And in a class of thirty Year 8 pupils, which a teacher may meet twice a week for forty minutes, how does one undertake diagnostic work on which to base individually tailored advice?

Such questions require responses which draw from both theoretical and practical perspectives, ones which we shall progessively uncover throughout this section. But first, let us try to clarify our definitions of formative assessment by pulling in additional positions and statements found in the literature and by offering a brief historical account which will, so to speak, show where the ideas that underpin FA have come from.

Torrance and Pryor (1998) maintain that although debates about the formative *potential* of classroom assessment have a long history, it is only really since the 1980s that they have come to the fore in the UK. This resulted from attempts to raise the level of validity of the external assessment system, particularly through the introduction of the GCSE and its incorporation of coursework which could be monitored by teachers and improved by pupils responding to teacher feedback. In the same decade, 'profiles' and Records of Achievement (RoA) were widely introduced as an assessment instrument which placed value on the *process* of assessment as much as the product: that is, teacher–pupil *dialogue* was necessary in order to discuss strengths and weaknesses and negotiate targets and learning outcomes (see for example Broadfoot 1987; Hitchcock 1986).

As we have noted in Chapters 3–6, the introduction of the GCSE, which was itself a significant and long awaited reform, was in a sense overshadowed by the root and branch changes heralded by the 1988 Education Reform Act. Clearly, the proposal to introduce a national curriculum of ten subjects for all children between the ages of 5 and 16, in order to 'lever up' standards (to use the rhetoric of the day), required a national assessment system. The Task Group on Assessment and Testing (TGAT) was therefore established in 1987 with the urgent mission to invent just that: a system of assessment which would calibrate and help raise national standards of educational achievement. Here is not

---

The four purposes of the national assessment system advocated in the TGAT report

Assessment should be:

- formative   supporting learning: planning next steps
- diagnostic   identifying learning difficulties
- summative   systematic recording of attainment at ages 7, 11, 14 and 16
- evaluative   judging effectiveness of local education authorities, schools and teachers by using assessment data as performance indicators

---

Figure 7.1 The diverse roles of the National Curriculum assessment system
Source: DES/WO (1988)

the place to recount the whole detail of the task group's proposals (DES/WO 1988), nor the subsequent story, but see, for example Daugherty 1995, and Chapter 5 in this book. Suffice it to say here that the Group concluded that a national assessment system, properly designed, could and should pursue *both* formative and summative ends. That is to say, it would produce data on a national scale so that nationwide standards could be monitored and evaluated *and* provide diagnostic data at the individual pupil level so that future learning could be planned and supported in the classroom (see Figure 7.1)

Arguments have continued to the present day as to whether a single assessment system can possibly serve such diverse and conflicting aims (as we discuss later in this chapter). Nevertheless, the report articulated the formative function of the proposed assessment system in a most helpful manner:

> Promoting children's learning is a principal aim of schools. Assessment lies at the heart of this process. It can provide a framework in which educational objectives may be set, and pupils' progress charted and expressed. It can yield a basis for planning the next educational steps in response to children's needs . . . it should be an integral part of the educational process, continually providing both 'feedback' and 'feedforward'. It therefore needs to be incorporated systematically into teaching strategies and practices at all levels.
>
> (DES/WO 1988: paras 3/4)

The TGAT report was accepted by the government of the day and following the Education Reform Act in 1988 the education system of England and Wales had, at least in principle, an assessment framework which encouraged the kinds of ambitious formative assessment practices that, subsequently,

OFSTED inspectors reported they were looking for. Again, close examination of the TGAT quotation is useful. It recommended assessment practice which,

- informs planning;
- articulates standards ('feedback');
- shows pupils what to do next in order to improve ('feedforward'); and
- becomes an organic part of teaching and learning.

This list is remarkably similar to our previous one based on the OFSTED quotation. Arguably, it goes a little further in that it equates assessment with teaching, in effect saying that the two cannot be separated, although it may be that teaching is what OFSTED had in mind with the phrase 'constructively critical'. This is, however, a very significant point to contemplate and helps counter the claim that busy teachers have 'no time' to engage seriously with formative assessment practices: this, the argument runs, would be tantamount to saying they have no time to teach effectively! The shift in thinking represented by the TGAT quote takes us away from an assumption that assessment is something done after the teaching is finished and towards the notion that it is integral to teaching; you cannot claim to be teaching without undertaking forms of assessment and by implication, this assessment activity helps ensure the quality of what is taught and learned (and how).

Torrance and Pryor (1998) appear to agree: 'Our own position is that formative assessment is an "inevitable thing", *i.e. all assessment practices will have an impact on pupil learning*' (p. 10, original emphasis). In saying this they make a further distinction, albeit one which they argue is difficult to maintain in practice, between 'routine classroom assessment' and true formative assessment. The latter, they argue, is '*intended* to have a specific and positive impact on learning' (*ibid.*, our emphasis) whereas the former may have purposes with little or no direct relationship to learning. Such a view echoes a comment made in Black and Wiliam's (1998a) review of the research evidence on assessment and classroom learning (referred to frequently in this and the following two chapters), that much 'feedback' to pupils in secondary schools has limited impact, being 'social and managerial' rather than focused on learning. This distinction requires further discussion.

There are occasions when routine classroom assessments (say, returning a project or a homework task) may legitimately turn into a session with a focus on discipline, motivation or behaviour. But this ought not to happen too frequently because there comes a time when pupils stop listening, especially if such feedback is to the whole class and is therefore conducted at a level of generality that allows individual pupils to switch off. It is salutary to learn from a survey commissioned by the National Commission on Education in the early 1990s that nearly half of Year 7 children claimed that their teachers never spoke to them individually *about their work*.

The poor quality of some lessons may be attributed to teachers not being qualified in the appropriate subject area, but there is also evidence of more general problems with teachers' support of learning. We commissioned a survey of the views of pupils in the early years of secondary school. It found that 44% of year 7 pupils and 45% of year 9 pupils indicated that they never talked individually to their class teachers about their work, and 42% of year 7 pupils and 41% of year 9 pupils indicated that they never talked individually to other teachers about their work. Only 55% of year 7 pupils and 50% of year 9 pupils indicated that all or most of their teachers praised them when they did their work well.

(NCE 1993: 205)

That may not be how the teachers see things, but what the pupils seemed to be telling teachers here, and what this may mean for classroom practice, requires some consideration. We find it difficult to agree with Torrance and Pryor that FA is an 'inevitable thing', therefore, because we do not accept that all that is done in the name of classroom assessment necessarily has any impact *on learning*. For a start, if it is taking place, a large number of pupils do not seem to recognise it! – at least not in terms of individual dialogue with teachers about their work. To be fair, the authors seem to accept this, acknowledging the complexity of the processes involved: in the end they argue,

> formative assessment is not a 'thing'; rather it is a construct, a name given to what should more accurately be characterised as a social interaction between teacher and pupil which is intended to have a positive impact on pupil learning, but may not.
>
> (Torrance and Pryor 1998: 10)

This is similar to the way routine classroom assessment has been described by one of us elsewhere as essentially a 'getting to know you' activity, whereby the teacher's intention is to *find out* about the individual pupils as learners (Lambert 1996; see also Rowntree 1987). The acid test would be the question 'Do I know enough about each of my pupils' understanding (their motivations, their mental blocks, their special talents) to help each one of them?' Ideally, this is a useful question to have in mind when preparing for parents' evenings too.

Thus, classroom assessment has the potential to be formative, but is not necessarily so. Getting to know pupils as learners – an essential but difficult, and sometimes a painfully slow process – *is by itself not enough*. The intention to help the learner improve, through effective feedback and feedforward, is also a crucial aspect of FA. These are also evidently difficult processes to get right and integrate into teaching (but see the following chapter in this book). The simple possession of the pious intention to help pupils learn is therefore not sufficient in itself to bring this about (although it is probably a necessary precondition). As Sadler observed over a decade ago:

> the common but puzzling observation [is] that even when teachers provide students with valid and reliable judgements about the quality of their work, improvement does not necessarily follow.
>
> (Sadler 1989: 119)

Whilst we note that this quotation fails to acknowledge the role of *feed-forward* identifying the next steps, Sadler's wider discussion in fact makes the point that 'showing' the next steps is probably still not enough. Pupils need to be taught strategies for improvement based upon a shared understanding with the teacher of what the standards and expectations are. What we conclude from this is the great significance of ambitious moves over recent years (and again, embodied by GCSE to some extent and then in a big way by TGAT) to base educational assessments on pre-specified *criteria*. Sadler's point was that to be truly effective, classroom assessment needs fully to reach its formative potential (see summary p. 113), which ultimately requires pupils to be self-monitoring:

> for students to be able to improve, they must develop the capacity to monitor the quality of their own work during actual production. This in turn requires that students possess an appreciation of what high quality work is [and] that they have the evaluative skill necessary for them to compare with some objectivity the quality of what they are producing in relation to the . . . standard.
>
> (Sadler 1989: 119)

In Chapter 8 we therefore consider together approaches to *feedback* and *feedforward* and ways to involve pupils in meaningful *self-assessment* – as a means of encouraging them to internalise the standards and expectations through using directly the assessment criteria.

But before this, in the next part of the present chapter, we shall consider the *impact* of FA. *What difference does it make?* After all, despite official 'endorse-ment' in the national assessment structure following the TGAT report, it seems to have acquired little more than the status of a good idea. Millions of pounds have been invested in external assessments for the national curricu-lum core subjects, and GCSE and A-levels continue to consume a large slice of the annual budget of secondary schools and colleges. By comparison, the development of FA strategies and techniques has received minuscule financial support. No wonder OFSTED finds it difficult to track down good practice!

SUMMARY – WHAT IS FORMATIVE ASSESSMENT?

According to Sadler:

> Formative assessment is concerned with how judgements about the quality of student responses ... can be used to shape and improve the student's competence by short-circuiting the randomness and inefficiency of trial and error learning.
>
> (Sadler 1989: 121)

It does this by

- yielding information that is useful in helping to improve *teaching*, helping teachers to get to know pupils and to plan work with appropriate pace, access and challenge;
- yielding information that is useful in helping to improve *learning*, helping pupils to understand how they learn best, and how well they have learned;
- providing the basis for effective *feedback and feedforward* for pupils to help them *realise their unfulfilled potential*; and
- providing experiences and activities that enable pupils to *involve themselves* in assessment and monitoring their own achievements.

THE IMPACT OF FORMATIVE ASSESSMENT: DOES IT MAKE A DIFFERENCE?

Impact studies are difficult to undertake in education. Despite the obvious attraction of measuring the 'effect' of undertaking a particular action or teaching strategy, for example, attempting to do so is fraught with difficulty. Teaching and learning encounters are complicated because of the number of individuals involved and the myriad influences on the conditions in which they take place (many of which cannot be scientifically 'controlled'). Researchers of 'impact' are therefore always left with a problem: How can we be sure that any measurements or observations of 'cause and effect' are not just coincidental, and that the really significant influences on learning do not remain hidden or unrealised? The classic analogy used to illustrate this point asks us to consider the regular weighing of small babies as part of standard post–natal health care provision. Objective observational records will show that weighing babies is closely correlated with their steady increase in weight: do we conclude from this that to encourage rapid weight gain in small babies we should weigh them more often? So, assessing pupils regularly may well show that they 'improve': but we should be careful not to attribute too much to the act of assessment itself.

Specifically in the field of assessment, there are further problems. As we have seen in Chapters 3–6, any test or examination is an abstraction or sample of what the pupil knows, understands and can do. Thus, if summative assessment scores are used in order to measure the outcome of a series of lessons, how can we be sure that the test fairly represents the pupils' learning? For example, a highly *reliable* (see Chapter 5 of this book) multiple choice test of scientific knowledge may grossly under-represent gains in confidence in the way pupils handle that knowledge. Such a test may lack *validity*, therefore, but there may be aspects of achievement that tests in general simply do not measure well (see also Moore 1999, Chapter 7).

While holding reservations such as these very firmly in mind, it is nevertheless still natural to pose the question: what impact does FA have on pupil achievement? Or more precisely: is there evidence that the use of formative assessment raises standards?

In response to such questions we can turn to a review of the research literature undertaken by Black and Wiliam in 1998a. They introduce the study by emphasising that,

> One of the outstanding features of studies of assessment in recent years has been the shift in the focus of attention, towards greater interest in the interactions between assessment and classroom learning and away from concentration on the properties of restricted forms of test which are only weakly linked to the learning experiences of students. This shift has been coupled with many expressions of hope that improvement in classroom assessment will make a strong contribution to the improvement of learning. So one main purpose of this review is to survey the evidence which might show whether or not such hope is justified.
>
> (Black and Wiliam 1998a: 7)

On the basis of a process which identified 681 recent (i.e. since 1988) and relevant publications from around the world, narrowed down to 250 which were of sufficient quality to examine in detail, the authors were able to conclude that: 'innovations designed to strengthen the frequent feedback that students receive about their learning yield substantial learning gains' (*ibid.*: 7).

This statement is in a form of shorthand for as we have already seen, there is more to effective formative assessment than providing frequent feedback. Black and Wiliam show this conclusively, and state from the outset that the other main purpose of their work was to shine a light on the key practical and theoretical aspects of FA identified in the diverse research that had been undertaken during the review period. Much of the following chapter is reliant on the platform which their review provides, but before turning to this, we need to examine more closely their primary claim that effective FA yields substantial learning gain. First, what do the authors mean by 'learning gain'?

Learning gain is a term used by educationists, derived from attempts to measure improved performance resulting from an innovation of some kind.

It is described in terms of a statistic which shows the 'effect size' of the performance registered in the experimental or research group compared with that of 'control' groups (i.e. groups of pupils who have not experienced the innovation). The effect size, therefore, is the ratio of A divided by B, where

A is the average improvement in pupils' scores on the selected test and
B is the range of scores found for typical groups of pupils on the same tests.

Formative assessment studies in the research read and evaluated by Black and Wiliam produced typical effect sizes of between 0.4 and 0.7. Bald statistics like these are of course difficult to interpret. But they appear to be highly significant. For example, an effect size of 0.4 can be crudely 'translated' as bringing improved GCSE grading by between one and two grades. An effect size of 0.7, if felt across all schools, would, according to the research review, have the potential to raise England into the top five (from a middle ranking position) of the forty plus countries in recent international mathematics attainment studies (a startling claim, if one believes international league tables have any credence). In one study (Kulik and Kulik 1989) the strategy under scrutiny resulted in an effect size of 0.82, 'which is the equivalent to raising the achievement of an "average" student to that of the top 20%' (Black and Wiliam 1998a: 41).

Such findings are dramatic enough. But the use of FA techniques would appear to be of particular significance to teachers grappling with underachievement in school. The evidence indicates that formative assessment processes help the (so-called) low attainers more than the rest. Thus, the impact of FA is said not only to raise attainment overall *but at the same time to reduce the spread of attainment.* As the reviewers go on to observe in their summary (Black and Wiliam 1998b), this suggests that any 'tail' of low achievement is a portent of unfulfilled and wasted talent. Thus, the research review suggests, if the messages emanating from the research can be successfully applied then the traditional and persistent problem of the English education system (underachievement, except among the high fliers) ought to be possible to tackle. Educational experiences planned for pupils which do not tackle the question of how to support learning as an integral part of the teaching stand a good chance of producing young people who come to believe that they are unable to learn.

The evidence briefly described above is presented persuasively. It is worth noting however that it was the authors' clear intention to distinguish FA from external summative assessment (SA) in a way that maximised the potential benefits of the former in contrast to the largely taken-as-read limitations of the latter. They find and present the evidence for improving FA practice in the absence of any consideration of SA. This could result in unwary readers assembling a misleading picture or model of assessment, for it is our view, following Biggs' (1998) critique of Black and Wiliam's review, that it is not helpful to think of FA and SA as being 'mutually exclusive' (Biggs 1998a: 106).

To be sure, SA impacts on teaching and learning, as we have seen in Chapters 3–6. The assumption often made is that such impact, referred to as the 'backwash' effect of examinations to distinguish it from more positive sounding 'feedback' associated with FA, emphasises a surface approach to learning in contrast to deeper approaches encouraged by FA – and is therefore largely negative. It would be a shame if in trying to redress the balance between the FA and SA, the potential for good to be found in channelling the backwash from external examinations and tests in order to improve learning was inadvertently obscured or forgotten; after all it is possible to identify 'where teaching to the test is exactly what you want because it is teaching the intended curriculum' (Biggs 1998: 108). In other words external summative assessment structures can be used formatively – if the criteria for assessment and the test design are valid.

SO WHY IS GOOD FORMATIVE ASSESSMENT HARD TO FIND?

It was noted at the beginning of this chapter that OFSTED regards FA as relatively difficult to find in operation. If this is the case, what prevents teachers from adopting classroom assessment practices that fully exploit their formative potential? It may be that the persuasive evidence of its potential impact noted in the previous section is not widely known. Perhaps the mechanisms of FA are perceived in practice to be too daunting even for the most committed classroom practitioner: indeed, the Standards for the Award of QTS lay down some ambitious qualities to be expected during day-to-day teaching practice (see Figure 7.2). But it may simply be that the kind of practice that effective FA implies requires too much of a leap of faith on the part of teachers, and (as we shall see subsequently), by pupils too. In other words, the hegemony of the external examination system, which as we have seen in Chapters 3–6 can bring about constructive and positive curriculum change, is such that it also has the potential to distort teaching and learning relationships (de Luca 1994). The rest of this section discusses these possible resistances to the widespread adoption of FA in more detail.

Figure 7.2 quotes from the DfEE 'standards', but only those statements which describe classroom assessment practices with formative potential. It is interesting to compare these with the statements of OFSTED and TGAT identified earlier in this chapter, on pp. 108 and 110: there is a consistent 'official' line promoting the adoption by teachers of techniques which enable them to analyse pupils' work, resulting in feedback to individuals and feed-forward to ensure raised levels of attainment. But the implementation of such practices is demanding, and OFSTED inspections of initial teacher training have shown that these standards are amongst the most challenging faced by training mentors in schools whose job it is to support the development of practical teaching skills among trainee teachers.

An extract from the Standards for the Award of Qualified Teacher Status

'those to be awarded QTS must, when assessed, demonstrate that they:

a   assess how well learning objectives have been achieved and use this assessment to improve specific aspects of teaching;

b   mark and monitor pupils' assigned classwork and homework, providing constructive oral and written feedback, and setting targets for pupils' progress;

c   assess and record each pupil's progress systematically, including through focused observation, questioning, testing and marking, and use these records to:

    (i)   check that pupils have understood and completed the work set;

    (ii)   monitor strengths and weaknesses and use the information gained as a basis for purposeful intervention in pupils' learning;

    (iii) inform planning;

    (iv)   check that pupils continue to make demonstrable progress in their acquisition of the knowledge, skills and understanding of the subject;

i   use different kinds of assessment appropriately for different purposes'

Figure 7.2 Classroom assessment standards

Source: extracted from DfEE (1998)

Similarly, Dwyer (1994) has found that for beginning teachers the skills demanded by the alignment of teaching goals, learning activities and assessment are the most difficult to acquire. Novice teachers, for example, are often found not to be able to distinguish classroom activities from learning goals, conflating the two as if the 'means' and the 'ends' of teaching were the same thing. Some find it difficult, therefore, to conceive their teaching in terms of an integrated cycle of establishing desired learning goals and taking steps to verify pupils' progress towards achieving them. As a result, assessments may be selected that do not provide teachers with the quality of information they require in relation to the specified goals. It is perhaps not unreasonable to assume that unless established early on in a teaching career, such vital technical skills are unlikely to be assimilated readily, particularly if teaching is conceptualised as essentially a matter 'of "covering" the curriculum – ensuring that students are exposed to a body of knowledge or the contents of particular texts' (Dwyer 1998: 134). But why are these aspects of teaching so challenging when, all other things being equal (and teaching is seen as something more interactive than merely delivering the list of contents), they seem so reasonable and sensible? *Of course* we want to use assessment to understand pupils' learning, improve pupils' performance and develop our teaching! So why does it often appear that we do not do this?

Perhaps the answer lies in further analysis of the perceptions of 'assessment' held by teachers – and new teachers – pupils and parents. As we have seen in Chapters 3–6 of this book, the shadow cast by the enormously influential *examinations industry* on what we perceive the primary purpose of educational assessment to be, is long and deep, and to some extent immovable. Even though much progress has been made in recent years in clarifying the roles and purposes of assessment, it is widely accepted that in practice it remains the Achilles heel for many teachers. Thus, Dwyer (1998) writes convincingly:

> Assessment is most often viewed by teachers as being imposed by external forces (and as such, the responsibility of others). Moreover, they are disinclined to label their own collecting of evidence about students' learning as 'assessment', despite their strong endorsement of the importance of such activities as monitoring students' understanding in order to adjust instruction.
>
> (p. 134)

The point about external assessment is that it usually has a 'high stake' attached to it: that is, the test scores really matter; a lot depends on them. Thus, when the *stakes are high* (as undoubtedly they are, for example, in the GCSE for pupils, teachers and schools), the tendency is for the system to reduce to the minimum any possibility of external factors affecting the scores. In other words *reliability* concerns dominate, significantly skewing the form of the assessment, and the way in which pupils are prepared for it.

Daugherty and Lambert (1994), for example, reported evidence in geography that some teachers perceived National Curriculum 'teacher assessment' also to have high stakes attached to it, even though it was supposed to be essentially internal and a matter for teacher judgement. However, moves to raise accountability of schools and individual teachers were gathering momentum at that time, through the publication of league tables. As a result, it seemed that many teachers concentrated their energies on devising and managing tests and examinations that aped the 'rigour' of external assessment, in preference to more ipsative approaches (see also Lambert and Daugherty 1993) which may have been used more formatively.

Evidence indicates that teachers may attach great value to high-stakes external assessment (for understandable reasons) and consequently attach much weight to the principles that underpin it, notably reliability, applying such principles willy-nilly to *all* aspects of their assessment practice. Research in the USA has evaluated low-stakes testing designed to support learning, and the impact of raising the stakes, which has usually involved test results being used in comparisons of schools, or testing becoming part of the high school graduation requirements. The evidence suggests that teachers move quickly to a situation in which concentration on raising scores conflicts with what are widely considered to be other aspects of sound educational practice, such as applying knowledge to new situations in order to deepen understanding, cooperative learning strategies and so on. School administrators in this research acknowledged that the emergence of specific, almost game-like ways to raise test scores, including chanting text and the widespread use of mnemonics was entirely for political reasons, not to improve standards of teaching and learning, but to look good.

Madaus (1988), drawing from his work on high-stakes testing in the USA (also reported in Stobart and Gipps 1997: 5–6), found that the great power of the external assessment industry to influence day-to-day practice is essentially perceptual: that is, it matters little whether a test *is* a high-stakes one or not, but whether the participants *believe* it to be so. Stobart and Gipps maintain that this explains the symbolic powers of tests in the school system at large: 'Policy makers realise the high symbolic value attached to testing, and by requiring testing to take place, they can be seen to be tackling the problem of standards.' (*ibid.*: 6). We are tempted to extend this argument somewhat and speculate that when teachers themselves are placed in a 'high-stakes/low-trust' context, which includes regular inspection, published league tables and payment by results, the natural tendency is to believe that all assessment has a high stake attached to it (including National Curriculum teacher assessment). Softer, low-stakes assessment (that which happens informally on a day-to-day basis, and remains mainly between the teacher and pupil, being classroom-based rather than external in nature) does not really count in such a perception. It is perhaps small wonder that good formative assessment is hard to find when the classroom context is analysed in this way: teachers (especially during an OFSTED inspection, perhaps) apparently believe they need to emphasise the principles of 'rigorous' external assessment, and play down informal methods.

As the late Desmond Nuttall concluded early in 1989, in the context of the national assessment system as proposed by TGAT (DES 1988):

> You cannot combine formative, summative and evaluative purposes in the same assessment system and expect them all to function unaffected by each other. By making the stakes so high we are making sure that the evaluative function predominates and that the pressure for comparability and rigid systems of moderation that will make the system as cheat-proof as possible will drive out good formative practice and the facilitating conditions that allow pupils to put forward their best performance.
>
> (Nuttall 1989: 7)

FOR FURTHER THINKING

1. The basic organisational structure of this book is to distinguish classroom assessment (Chapters 7–9) from external assessment (Chapters 3–6). In so doing, we have tended to associate the former with

formative assessment and the latter with summative assessment. In what ways do you find this approach to be justified, and in what ways are such distinctions less clear cut?

2.   Write down your own descriptions of the key assessment purposes referred to by Nuttall above: formative, summative and evaluative. Show how these purposes interact with each other (i.e., are not mutually exclusive).

3.   Read the Nuttall quotation above. If you find yourself in agreement with it, in what ways can raising the stakes of external assessment drive out 'the facilitating conditions that allow pupils to put forward their best performance'?

    If on the other hand you disagree with the statement, in what ways may Nuttall be mistaken?

4.   We have claimed in this chapter that good formative classroom assessment is sometimes difficult to find in practice. What do teacher colleagues in your school understand by the term FA?

Re-examine the relevant NQT Standards on classroom assessment. Make notes, based upon your own conversations and classroom observations, on what policies and practices support good FA and where opportunities exist in lessons to engage in good FA.

CONCLUSION

Perhaps the OFSTED quotation used at the beginning of this chapter serves merely to show the accuracy of Nuttall's prediction repeated at the end of the chapter. However, as a final word, we do not wish to be misconstrued. We are hypothesising in this section that effective formative assessment practice is not as widespread in schools as the evidence suggests it ought to be because:

- the high-stakes external examination system has a powerful backwash effect and influences how teachers (and others) perceive the role of assessment in their work;
- certain principles that underpin external assessment – notably the importance of reliability – are carried forward and influence unduly aspects of classroom assessment; and
- moves to increase the public accountability of teachers and schools has also tended to raise the stakes in assessment and increase the propensity in teachers to rely on formal tests.

As a result, we suggest, for teachers to move more fully to the adoption of FA requires a considerable shift in their beliefs and perceptions: a 'leap of faith'. Also implied in our discussion was that many teachers understand and indeed practise FA, although within a context which causes them to undervalue it in comparison with more formal assessment practices.

What we also wish to return to and emphasise, however, is the need to assimilate the evidence and discussion assembled earlier in this chapter to underpin radical reflection on practice. We do not wish to suggest that formative assessment is uncontested in meaning, nor that its practice is itself unproblematic if only the circumstances were more friendly. The climate may be resistant to forms of assessment practice driven solely by *educational* goals (i.e. better teaching and improved learning) because of the overriding influence of what Nuttall (above) called the 'evaluative function' of assessment, or what we have referred to as accountability, based on external tests and examinations. But even if the stakes attached to external summative assessment were held in better balance (were toned down somewhat), there is, in our view, no guarantee that effective formative assessment would flower in its place. This is because:

- Formative assessment needs to be understood fully; what it is for and what it can and cannot do. Not all classroom assessment is *necessarily* formative.
- The relationship between our conceptions of teaching, learning and the role of assessment may need radical review before we can *believe* formative assessment to be worth pursuing.
- Following this, the implications of implementing formative assessment fully into classroom practice also need to be understood fully.
- Practical strategies need to be identified and developed which enable teachers, under pressure to 'cover' the curriculum, syllabus or specification, to organise (or reorganise) their classroom teaching in a way that incorporates formative assessment.

In other words, FA requires the application of relentless mental and physical energy, excellent classroom management and organisational skills and what the DfEE (1997) refer to as 'secure' subject knowledge. What *we* understand by the latter is the ability of the teacher to analyse the pupil's work within the 'bigger picture' of the disciplinary context. That is, more than ticking the right answers and correcting errors, it implies a growing understanding of the pupil as a learner – what causes him or her to shine, get stuck, irritated, enjoy the struggle and so on. This chapter has attempted to make a case for why we believe such goals are worth striving for.

Figure 7.3 offers a summary which provides two kinds of information. First, some points which have emerged during this chapter are identified and second, further points are raised which in some ways are anticipated by the discussion in this chapter. Thus, we feedforward to the following chapter which centres on implementation, though not without attempting to be explicit concerning underlying theory.

Formative assessment in the classroom

What is it?

'Formative assessment is concerned with how judgements about the quality of student responses . . . can be used to shape and improve the student's competence by short-circuiting the randomness and inefficiency of trial-and-error learning.'

(Sadler 1989)

What does it do?
- Yield information that is useful in helping to improve teaching and learning
- Provide the basis for effective feedback to pupils to help them realise their untapped potential

Theory – how does it work?
- Increasing motivation
- Helping pupils understand how they learn (best)
- Assisting pupils (and teachers) deciding what to learn
- Showing students what and how well they have learned

Pros and cons
- Good formative assessment seems to require a leap of faith by many teachers
- Strong evidence that good formative assessment promotes substantial 'learning gain'
- Good formative assessment is embedded in the classroom 'black box'
- Good formative assessment is not easy to achieve
- Formative assessment seems to be undervalued at the system level

---

Figure 7.3 A summary of classroom-based formative assessment

FOR FURTHER THINKING

1. 'Teachers should know enough about the understanding of their pupils to be able to help each one of them.' Do you consider this to be both worthwhile and realistic?

    If you answer negatively, or even have your doubts, what are the implications for you as a teacher?

2. From your observations of classrooms in your department or school, in what ways do teachers organise lessons to facilitate teacher–pupil interaction of various kinds? In what ways are classrooms devoted to the growth of pupils' confidence and self-understanding?

FOR FURTHER READING

P. Black and D. Wiliam (1998) 'Assessment and classroom learning', in *Assessment in Education* 5(1), pp. 7–74.

P. Black and D. Wiliam (1998b) *Inside the Black Box*. This thorough research review (summarised in the pamphlet *Inside the Black Box*) examines the relationship between assessment and classroom learning and is essential reading for the student of formative assessment. This chapter has drawn heavily from it.

C. Gipps (1994) *Beyond Testing: Towards a Theory of Educational* Assessment. This is a readable discussion which, partly in response to National Curriculum assessment developments, put forward a coherent critique of a system over-dependent upon a rigid and narrow understanding of assessment in education and its potential to support learning. *Beyond Testing* is referred to in Chapters 10 and 11 of this book.

R. Sutton (1995) *Assessment for Learning*. This is a short and highly accessible book which usefully links a number of key educational concepts together, helping to facilitate 'joined up' thinking about formative assessment and its place in classrooms.

8 Implementing Effective Classroom Assessment: Theory and Practice

This chapter seeks to encourage the reader to move from a dispassionate discussion of the principles of formative assessment (FA) to the consideration of what it could (or should) look like in practice. It aims to take the reader from ideas to the messier world of classroom implementation.

It begins with a short reprise of the thinking that underpins FA: How is it supposed to work? How is a belief in the potential of FA linked to theories of learning? Referring to a fairly long list of strategies and tactics which singly or together enable classroom encounters to become formative assessment opportunities, the point is emphasised that FA is no 'add on' to teaching: it is a part of teaching and cannot be planned in a way that imagines it as existing outside day-to-day classroom life. At the same time, care is taken to point out some of the traps which exist for the unwary: common sense cannot be relied upon to avoid some of the difficulties involved – including, for example, the research finding that the use of praise by teachers is not always productive; it depends how, and in what circumstances, it is offered. Thus, adopting ready-made FA strategies is no 'quick fix' solution to better teaching.

The chapter then concentrates particularly on two broad FA strategies which together encompass a wide range of practical possibilities. First we consider in detail the meaning of feedback and the central role it plays in developing FA. Second, we examine 'pupil involvement', particularly pupil self-assessment, both in terms of its considerable theoretical potential for enhancing student achievement and the more practical business of making it happen.

HOW DOES FA WORK IN THE CLASSROOM? EXAMINING SOME ASSUMPTIONS

The assertion is that formative assessment, formative feedback, can and will aid learning. But can it? What theories of learning give us grounds for believing this? And if they seem plausible, what does it look like in practice: what does the interactive process involve and how might it work?

(Torrance and Pryor 1998: 14)

There is comparatively little empirical research which, as it were, unlocks the classroom door and lets us in to see good formative practice at work (though Torrance and Pryor (1998), is an accessible exception). In other words, much of what is written on the topic is heavily dependent on currently accepted theories of learning and sometimes not a little exhortation and rhetoric. This is at least in part due to the fairly self-evident difficulties in investigating such a complex and slippery construct as FA, which itself is not a stable term, being used seemingly interchangeably with others such as 'classroom assessment', 'classroom evaluation', 'curriculum based assessment', 'feedback', 'formative evaluation', 'assessment for learning' and so on (see Wiliam and Black 1996). For example, how can researchers be convincing about what to investigate if, as we have implied in the previous chapter, FA is organically part of teaching and learning, and classroom process: is skilled debriefing through questioning a teaching skill or an assessment skill – or both? If we were to set up an experiment to examine, say, self-assessment strategies with a class or teaching group (with other groups as 'controls'), how could we separate out all the interrelated parts of such a process so that we are in a position to say how *it* worked, or what the key mechanisms were?

On the other hand, there are those who assert that *conviction* based on direct experience is a perfectly adequate basis on which to develop practice. For example, on the subject of pupil involvement (an important theme taken up later in this chapter), Ruth Sutton (1995) writes

> I'd like to be able to say that my conviction about the usefulness of student involvement in assessment sprang from my knowledge of the research findings on the issue, but I confess that it didn't. First and foremost I believe in involving learners in the assessment process because I myself have found it useful and effective.
>
> (p. 131)

Even she admits, however, that she has since found 'research evidence from around the world' to support her position, (but one is left wondering what she would have done with evidence that did *not* support her position!). In the end her stance is not entirely satisfactory because in personally claiming pupil involvement to be 'useful and effective' as a reason to follow her lead may not be entirely convincing to others: someone else might personally find the reduction of pupil involvement just as useful and effective, for example, claiming back educational processes from harmful 'progressive' influences. It is helpful, therefore, that claims for the efficacy of FA can be identified and located. Even if empirical evidence is lacking, it is useful when a statement such as 'pupil involvement in assessment processes is important' can be positioned in terms of the assumptions that underpin it: on what grounds is this claim made?

In Sutton's case, she explains that her conviction is really based on her assumption that teachers should be encouraging learners to become autonomous, and that this 'will not be achieved merely by wishing it so' (*ibid*. p. 132).

- The learner believes he/she is capable of learning
- She knows enough about herself to set learning targets within her extended grasp
- He is willing to make the effort and commitment
- She is aware of different ways of tackling a learning task, and able to make good decisions depending on circumstances
- He has access to useful resources and knows how to use them
- She is not afraid of failure and knows how to learn from it

Figure 8.1 Preconditions for successful independent learning
Source: Sutton (1995: 132)

She then lists six further assumptions (see Figure 8.1) about what she considers to be the preconditions for successful independent learning.

Not one of these criteria can be considered to be entirely innate to the individual or capable of development unaided. They express how Sutton understood her job as a teacher in relation to a very broad educational goal. They describe, in other words, the way in which she believes pupils' potential can be released, by encouraging them to become autonomous, independent learners. Attempting to spell out the theory that underlies the practice she advocates in this way is useful: and it has the power to convince others, even though hard evidence may still be somewhat elusive.

For example, it helps us to establish the basis on which to judge, and perhaps act on, a number of key questions which logically follow the over-

These questions concern the balance of responsibility and involvement between teachers and pupils:

1   Who decides what is to be taught and learned, and on what basis are such decisions made?
2   Who determines the starting point of the teaching, and on what evidence?
3   Who decides how the learning is to be organised: what teaching and learning methods are to be employed?
4   Who provides, describes and exemplifies the criteria for success in this learning, when is this done and how?
5   Who is responsible for the assessment: when and how is it done?
6   Who records the outcomes: where, how, when and for what purpose?

Figure 8.2 Planning the teaching and learning cycle
Source: adapted from Sutton (1995: 133–134)

arching guiding principle she proposes. These questions (see Figure 8.2) are in effect a practical guide to the planning and implementation of the teaching and learning cycle (see Figure 8.3). Using the 'preconditions' (the assumptions listed in Figure 8.1) provides a theoretical basis, enabling us to *judge* the significance and relevance of the key questions in promoting the broad educational goal already identified.

The questions in Figure 8.2 are searching ones which force us to confront what we understand by that lofty and worthy educational purpose of encouraging 'independent learning'. Take the first question. At one end of a continuum, it may be accepted almost as a truism, that it is the teacher's job to decide what to teach; but if we seriously intend that pupils see their involvement in the educational process as more than passive recipients, we may feel that taking steps to 'negotiate' the contents of lessons would be beneficial. At the very least, teachers may feel they need to *justify* what they decide to teach (and if they cannot, be prepared to change).

The second question shown in Figure 8.2 is clearly redolent of that well known adage in teaching: 'start from where the pupils are at'. But how do we know where the pupils are? Because of the inherent difficulties here, we occasionally hear about teachers embarking on a new topic assuming nothing in terms of prior knowledge or experience in the pupils. This is often a recipe for boredom and perhaps alienation. But if we accept that building on pupils' existing ideas, information and understanding is good sense, there is an imperative to find out what this is: teachers probably need to ask certain kinds of

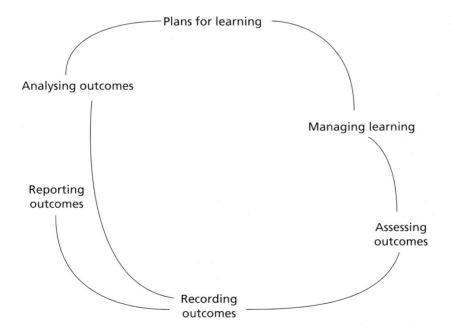

Figure 8.3 The planning, learning and assessment cycle
Source: Sutton (1995:2)

questions, listen to the varied responses across the class and plan teaching accordingly. In this sense teaching does not precede assessment. They go hand in hand, the outcomes of early informal assessments helping shape the teaching programme. Thus, the teaching programme cannot, according to such a model of teaching and learning, be predetermined totally.

We shall return to these questions later in the chapter when we discuss feedback and self-assessment, but it is clear that in all cases they *feature the nature of the teacher–pupil relationship*. Though we began the present discussion with the identification of certain assumptions that were thought to underpin what we presumed to be 'good practice', what by now is also becoming clear is the way assumptions such as these are themselves shaped by deeper theories of teaching and learning. Teacher–pupil relationships are to some large extent governed by underlying theories of teaching and learning (see the first book in this series: Moore 2000), and it is useful to be able to identify how – see Summary.

SUMMARY: SOME THEORETICAL LINKS

The discussion presented in this chapter on how formative assessment is said to 'work' rests quite heavily on a broadly *constructivist* model of teaching and learning. Learning is not a steady, incremental accumulation of knowledge, being more provisional and involving building and sometimes changing meanings and understandings in the light of new experience or challenge. Bruner's model of a 'spiralling' curriculum, in which pupils' learning is 'scaffolded' with appropriate support, is influential here, as is his idea of 'intersubjectivity' as the foundation of educational relationships (see Bruner 1960). These ideas insist that teachers need to know the minds of their pupils in order to arrange and promote learning most effectively. Also strongly implied is the need for pupils to know their teacher's mind – at least to the extent that the criteria for success in the learning are known and understood.

THEORY BEHIND FA – A SUMMARY

The question we posed at the beginning of this chapter was 'How does FA work?' We have responded to our question by exhorting the reader to look for theoretical rationale and justifications for FA practice. The ultimate value of this is to provoke self-reflection and understanding with regard to the underlying theories of teaching and learning which govern the assumptions shaping our practice. Though at a policy level teachers are bombarded with the need to base decisions on 'evidence', the point we are making in this section is that most classroom decision making is rarely so simple as to implement 'proven success'. It would be hard to prove *how* FA works, even though there is some evidence (see Chapter 7) that FA does have positive impact on learning. Not only are the processes involved super-complex, but they are highly dependent upon particular contexts: thus, what works for *you* in *your* classroom, may not work for *me* in quite the same way.

We are arguing that although empirical evidence on FA mechanisms may be lacking (it is), theories of learning are, in contrast, well developed and help us rationalise and indeed justify classroom practice. Note the main emphasis in this discussion is more on learning than on teaching (the following chapter offers a sharper focus on classroom organisation and teaching practice). For the sake of simplicity we will briefly examine in turn two fundamentally contrasting theories of learning, both of which have had positive impact on the ways teachers do their jobs, and also help make the case for making classroom assessment formative in practice:

- behaviourism and
- constructivism.

For many years, including to the present day, behaviourist models of learning have been very influential. Essentially, *behaviourist thinking* requires the clarification and definition of specific objectives which are then taught and learnt in carefully graded stages. It lies behind the objectives-led model of curriculum planning and, arguably, has been the main theoretical element (though largely unstated) in the creation of the National Curriculum in England and Wales. Behaviourist theory may be more appropriate in some subjects (e.g. mathematics?) than others (e.g. geography?) but its influence can be traced across the curriculum. In particular the National Curriculum 'levels', describing achievements from the more simple, concrete, specific, closed and descriptive to the more complex, abstract, general, open and explanatory, are the statutory embodiment of the behaviourist model. What it says to teachers is 'break down the learning into its constituent parts, get the hierarchies of learning right and organise the teaching (suitably differentiated!) accordingly'. What it says in relation to our discussion on FA is powerful:

- the learning objectives of lessons should be clearly articulated to the learners;
- the criteria by which the teacher/assessor will judge achievement in relation to those objectives should be explicit and understood by the learners; and
- the results of assessments (possibly graded tests) should be fed back to the learners so that they can build a picture of their progress in terms of strengths, weaknesses and 'next steps'.

However, it is not a behaviourist conception of learning that drives the kind of approach to classrooms exemplified by Ruth Sutton (see p. 126) who sees learning as essentially interactive: hence the importance ascribed to teacher–pupil relationships. Such *constructivist perspectives* of learning see educational encounters as interactive in the sense that both teacher and learners bring material (in the form of information, ideas, imagination, etc.) to them. The quality of teaching and learning depends on communication based on mutual understanding. Teachers are not satisfied (merely) with the identification of objectives and testing how well they were met (note the past tense), but with trying also to find what the pupils *could* achieve with help. Thus assessment is an integral part of teaching and learning, its main purpose being to look forward and help pupils realise their learning potential through self-knowledge. What a constructivist vision of learning contributes to our discussion on FA is also powerful therefore. It helps us understand that:

- the processes of assessment are at least as important as the products (marks or results);
- assessment processes, inasmuch as they can help pupils understand new concepts or refine old ones, are an integral part of teaching; and
- because assessment processes are orchestrated with a future orientation, the role of feedback needs expansion to include notions of feedforward, with pupils *shown* strategies to promote improvement.

We should emphasise at this point that the two dominant theoretical perspectives outlined here are not offered as polar opposites which teachers are meant somehow to choose between in an all or nothing kind of way. To follow constructivist thinking does not, or need not, require the total abandonment of other models of learning such as that suggested by behaviourists. Though fundamentally different, requiring different approaches to teaching as well as learning, they are not mutually exclusive within the context of the whole repertoire of teacher actions. Current educational thought in virtually all aspects, from theories of 'multiple intelligences' (see for example Gardner 1983) to the need to differentiate varied 'teaching styles' (see Leask 1999; Joyce and Weil 1986) and to theorise learning (see Moore 2000), recognises and accommodates diversity. It is perhaps one of the most challenging teaching skills that practitioners face day in and day out, to hold in mind, and deal with, the deeply conflicting needs and perspectives that constantly inform educational transactions in relation to constantly changing circumstances. Single dogmatic solutions are illusory. But the crucial point for the present discussion is that, albeit for significantly different reasons, *both theoretical perspectives on learning (behaviourist and constructivist) justify formative assessment practice, in terms of accounting for how it works.*

Teachers need a strong understanding of assessment, and such theoretical perspectives help build this. What we are suggesting here, and is a continuing theme of this book, is a sophisticated understanding of what has been called '*educational* assessment' (Dockrell 1995a; Gipps 1994). We return to this discussion in Chapters 10 and 11.

In the meantime it is worth recording, as we do in Figure 8.4, the range of classroom activities that may also be seen as assessment opportunities. The

Sources of assessment evidence

Oral	*Written*	*Graphic*	*Products*
Questioning	Questionnaires	Diagrams	Models
Listening	Diaries	Sketches	Artefacts
Discussing	Reports	Drawings	Games
Presentations	Essays	Graphs	Photos
Interviews	Notes	Maps	Web page
Debates	Stories	Overlays	
Audio recording	Scripts		
Video recording	Newspaper articles		
Role play	Bullet point lists		
Simulation	Poems		

Questions to consider when planning lessons

- Which of these are produced frequently in your classroom?
- Which are produced rarely?
- In what ways do these activities provide different assessment opportunities?
- Can you add others to these lists?

Figure 8.4 Learning activities presenting potential evidence on which to base assessment

list, which is by no means exhaustive, suggests that virtually any learning activity is an assessment opportunity – even a period of uninterrupted teacher exposition (although it is very difficult to assess accurately pupils' understanding, just by the expressions on their faces!). Some assessment opportunities therefore are of more value than others, but the list does clearly show once more, that assessment, teaching and learning are all parts of the same circular process. The precise use to which the assessment opportunities are put, and possibly their impact, depends on the teacher's priorities at the time and indeed what model of teaching and learning is in operation.

WARNING: FA IS NO 'BANDWAGON'

The purpose of this part of the chapter is to provide a link between the 'theoretical' and the 'practical'. The previous sections outlined convincing theoretical justifications for using FA to support teaching and learning, though we were at pains to point out the relative difficulty in producing clear cut empirical evidence to 'prove' its impact in practice. Part of the difficulty lies in the very nature of FA: what exactly counts as formative assessment practice? Is it possible (or even necessary) to distinguish assessment skills from teaching skills? This difficulty provides a clue to the practical context or setting which we explore briefly here, namely the reluctance of classrooms to lend themselves to quick, clean 'fix' by the introduction of some kind of FA technology.

FA is not some kind of passing bandwagon that we need to be seen to jump on to to be proved 'with it', or up-to-date. Even so, sometimes it seems that the educational world is prone to the promise of magical solutions: it is as if problems can appear to be so deep and intractible that the next radical insight which seems to suggest a solution can be enticing to both policy makers and teachers. This tendency has led to disappointment in the past, for the research insights and recommendations rarely contain blanket 'solutions'. Thus battles have raged over the grouping arrangements adopted – mixed ability or setting; over ('traditional') whole class teaching or ('progressive') group work classroom organisation; and even whether to mark pupils work for 'effort' or 'achievement'. But these are all false polarisations. Wherever possible 'or' could be changed to 'and', in which case the teacher's job becomes one to evaluate the pros and cons, or the costs and benefits, of available alternatives in relation to particular contexts, the pupils and the teaching and learning goals.

And so it is with FA. As Black and Wiliam (1998b) point out, the research on classroom assessment practice shows that there is no 'silver bullet', no magic solution that can simply be bolted on to existing practice.

FA is any activity undertaken by teachers, including their students assessing themselves, which provides feedback that has *consequential validity*. By this we mean that formative assessment is valid when it can be shown to have positive consequences in terms of learning outcomes: for example, it makes pupils better learners; it increases their confidence; it raises their level of self-awareness or encourages learning autonomy; it enables them to perform better in examinations. The research shows that FA has consequential validity when it involves new ways to enhance feedback, but that this usually requires significant changes in classroom practice. The active involvement of pupils seems to be necessary, especially in self-assessment activities of various kinds.

Before examining feedback and self-assessment in turn, it is worth identifying and discussing briefly the potential traps and dangers that Black and Wiliam's reading of the research suggests exist in much current assessment practice in schools. The following list (based on Black and Wiliam 1998b) could form a useful agenda on which to base a critical evaluation of observed classroom practice in your school, the kind of assessment that you witnessed yourself as a school student or your own first attempts at classroom assessment during your training.

● Too much generous unfocused praise is unhelpful to pupils

Praise can, of course, be a positive force and is considered by most teachers to be motivating. But praise can be misused. Indiscriminate praise can be debilitating because it soon becomes unclear to pupils what exactly is worthy of praise. In some classes, putting hands up yields massive blanket praise. In some classes, individuals who answer a question wrongly receive a 'good' or a 'well done'. And it has been known that a whole class, which has been ill-mannered and uncooperative for the best part of the lesson is praised for 'working so well': perhaps the teacher's relief at hearing the bell gets translated into well meaning sentiment, but it is one which does not carry a clear positive message. If the whole group gets praised for virtually any response, how can a teacher meaningfully congratulate real, gutsy, hard-won achievement?

● Teachers' tests encourage surface learning

As we have seen in Chapters 3–6 of this book, devising and designing examination questions which test real understanding is a highly skilled occupation, and not easily achieved. Even the best questions are constrained by the circumstance: they have to be readily assimilated by the candidate and answerable within the time frame, for example. For reasons such as these, and the manner in which pupils are often prepared with past papers, revision sheets and prompts, tests and examinations tend to focus attention on the kind of 'performance' that will 'gain credit', rather than on deep learning which may encompass uncertainty and doubt as much as correct answers. Test scores are also perceived by pupils to be final entities, measuring their position, or the quality of their performance, on a simple objective numerical scale. They are not seen as a means of learning more about themselves as learners.

In this sense, there is a vital question to ask of regular testing regimes which may be more 'serial summative' than formative in their impact. Torrance and Pryor maintain that there is a widely shared perception by teachers that 'rigorous' assessment needs to be governed by procedures and processes that derive from external assessment, which may badly reduce the formative potential of assessment. From their research they conclude that:

> Overwhelmingly, . . . assessment was perceived as a formal activity oriented to producing valid and reliable summative measures of performance, and teacher assessment was assumed to be part of this process.
>
> (Torrance and Pryor 1998: 23)

● Classrooms, even in the same department, are 'black boxes'

This is arguably less the case now than in the past, as peer observation of lessons has become widely adopted as a component of professional development. Yet still there is a tendency to imagine that the nature of classroom interaction between teachers and pupils is best left to sort out individually behind closed doors. We feel that this may be at least in part a result of the conflicts and subsequent uncertainties implied in the previous point leading to a kind of 'performance gap' which (many teachers imagine) is best kept private. Again, Torrance and Pryor's research alludes to such insecurities:

> while some [teachers] might act largely intuitively, they often felt insecure about this and felt the need for guidance from their headteacher and/or LEA advisory service; others had well worked out plans for conducting assessments in the context of particular topic work, but often felt uneasy about this and yearned for more flexibility and spontaneity in the way they could respond to individual children.
>
> (Torrance and Pryor 1998: 23)

It is probably a mistake for teachers who feel such conflicts and tensions not to open up and share professional practices with others in the same department or school.

● Quantity and presentation tend to be overemphasised

We shall look at marking in some detail in Chapter 9. Regular assessment needs to be properly constituted and reach beyond the level of superficial impression. It needs to be sure to incorporate judgement and possibly analysis of individuals' concept acquisition or development so as to ensure that subject-specific guidance and advice can be given, tailored to individual need. Often the marking load imposed by school policy on secondary teachers is such that a surface skim of the pupils' work is all that is thought possible in the time available (Brant et al. 2000). Often this results in little more than monitoring that the work has been done, marks and comments being unduly influenced by quantity and presentation.

● Marks and grades are grossly over emphasised, and the comparison of marks rather than personal improvement becomes the focus

This point links with the earlier one concerning the 'serial summative' nature of tests. Many teachers are acutely aware of the dangers being alluded to here, and in some schools work is marked without reference to grades as a result: a 'comment only' system is used instead. The dilemma here revolves around the question of how to get pupils to centre their attention on the process of learning rather than only the measured product of their performance.

Refusing to value their work with a grade, however, seems harsh and, arguably, an abrogation of the teacher's responsibility. Pupils surely can legitimately ask 'how good is this work?' and expect some kind of grading of its value in return. Therefore, we have a serious dilemma. It can, in our view, be resolved satisfactorily only by accepting (as argued earlier in this chapter) that assessment is an organic part of teaching: this has implications for classroom processes as we shall discuss in Chapter 9. The stumbling block for some teachers is the strongly felt need (for accountability purposes – to the head-teacher, to parents, to inpectors . . .) to collect assessment data in the form of a full mark book, but which can prevent them breaking through to focus on subject-specific and pupil-specific learning needs. To put this another way, the dilemma (to grade or not to grade) is greatly reduced if assessments are criteria referenced, in a way that the criteria can be shared effectively with the pupils.

● Teachers' feedback is mainly 'social and managerial' at the expense of learning functions

We touched on this observation in the previous chapter. This issue is also closely connected to the discussion on 'praise' above: granting the class indis-criminate praise at the end of a lesson (in an attempt, perhaps, to raise the 'feel-good factor') can have no positive learning outcome, and may well have negative consequences. But what is implied by this point is a more general proposition that *any* whole-class feedback is likely to miss the learning needs of individual pupils. Of course, providing individual feedback is more diffi-cult to organise and manage – but at least is more likely to have impact.

● Teachers can predict external results – they understand the tests but may have less understanding of learning needs

It is often impressive to see how well an experienced teacher can predict external examination grades for the pupils he or she teaches. But it can be a mistake to assume that this means they have acquired a good knowledge and understanding of the pupils' needs. What it can mean instead is that the teacher has a fine knowledge and understanding of the needs of the examination (not the pupils): because the teaching has been shaped by the needs of the exam-ination the teacher is able to assess likely performance outcomes of the pupils. Some theorists would argue that there is sometimes an element of 'self-fulfilling prophecy' about this, as we have seen in Chapters 3–6 of this book. In the context of our present discussion, this points up the tension once more between the needs of the external examinations and the learning needs of pupils. Teachers need to combine these influences. It is perhaps worth speculating that too heavy an emphasis on the former probably excludes the latter, whilst serious attention paid to the latter can reap dividends in relation to the former.

In summary, although formative assessment has a strong theoretical rationale, and its principles can be enunciated quite readily, there are serious obstacles to its adoption in practice. Effective FA is easier said than done. The following two parts of this chapter examine the fundamental practical preconditions for its success, delivering effective feedback, and involving pupils in self-assessment.

DELIVERING EFFECTIVE FEEDBACK

In the previous section of this chapter we showed how FA had both behaviourist and constructivist theoretical justification. It was strongly implied in the discussion that constructivist perspectives were more difficult to put into practice, but probably more effective, than the simpler less elaborate behaviourist models of teaching and learning. In considering how to use feedback with pupils, we have to confront this realisation directly. Feedback stands some chance of being 'consequentially valid' (see p. 132) when the initial assessment produces evidence on which teaching (and learning) decisions can be based. In other words, the communication of this evidence, in a way that 'makes sense' to the learner, lies at the heart of delivering effective feedback.

Paul Black put it this way:

> Surveys of the practice of formative assessment in several countries show that its potential to improve teaching and learning has not been exploited. . . .
>
> Overall, such visions point to a very demanding programme of development. Formative feedback implies more than correction of errors. It really needs understanding of their causes, which would tax the best learning experts.
>
> Furthermore, the student's main resource in self-adjustment is the model provided by the teacher. Students must get into the frame of reference of the teacher, to share the model of learning which gives meaning to the criteria that are reflected in assessment.
>
> (Black 1998: 122–123)

In Chapter 7 we discussed why FA was apparently so hard to find in schools. This quote firms up our conclusion that it is hard to find because it is hard to achieve. But more than that, it even suggests that developing effective classroom assessment may be impeded within a general framework of teaching and learning that does not realise its potential. As we suggested in Chapter 7, teachers may think they are doing it, but it may be in such a restricted manner that it fails really to register as *valid* formative assessment; i.e. it may lack *consequential* validity. Let us explore this contention further, specifically in relation to feedback.

If we show people where they make mistakes will they avoid them in future? We might imagine that such an assumption is not unreasonable, particularly if the people concerned have a clear vested interest and the motive to do better. Such an essentially behaviourist view works for some. But it is less likely to succeed if pupils fail to understand *why* they have made mistakes and *how* they can avoid them in the future. In this case new meanings have to be constructed, which is why we say communication is important, implying dialogue between teacher and pupils.

Such dialogue needs to focus on the particular qualities of the work, with advice for improvement. This takes a lot of practice, which could start with the written comments made on pupils' work (see Chapter 9), directed by the words 'you can improve this work by . . .'. What completes the sentence should be specific, subject centred advice which, if possible, shows the pupil (individually) how to proceed. But feeding back by written comment has limited impact (and is very laborious) – partly because it is essentially only one way communication. The importance of dialogue is its potential to enable the teacher to learn about the pupil, and therefore provide 'shared meaning' (to paraphrase the Black quotation above).

Figure 8.5 outlines two practical strategies identifying potentially effective feedback opportunities. Note that in both instances the actual moment of teacher–pupil communication is part of a bigger picture and cannot be fully understood in isolation. However, although they encourage us to see the potential in *existing* classroom practice for effective dialogue to take place, this may be a little over-optimistic as a general model. Black argues that fulfilling the potential of FA 'cannot be realized by change of assessment alone. The changes have to be part of a coherent programme in which curriculum and pedagogy are also restructured' (Black 1998: 123). At the very least, feedback needs to be planned for, not as a separate or even special component but as a regular and integral part of the lesson plan. Feedback in its various forms, becomes a regular component, or episode, of lessons, and therefore features explicitly in lesson plans.

So far we have described the delivery of effective feedback in a holistic kind of way, equating it mainly with forms of teacher–pupil dialogue. It is helpful, perhaps, to pause at this point and 'unpack' the idea so as to provide a summary of what we have been proposing. To maximise effectiveness, feedback should:

- be conducted at the level of individual learners, and avoid comparisons with other pupils;
- emphasise ipsative functions – individualised, challenging but achievable 'targets';
- should be criteria referenced, and steps taken to ensure that the criteria have shared understanding between teacher and pupils; and
- consist of precise recommendations for improvement in relation to particular subject skills, concepts or knowledge.

If such principles are taken fully on board, there are a number of other points that emerge which are important in demonstrating the scale of the broader changes in attitude (of both teachers and pupils) which are necessary in some school settings before real feedback can happen:

- Teachers and pupils converse (and 'get to know' each other – see Lambert 1996) within a 'culture of success'.
- Pupils learn to take risks, and accept that making mistakes is a positive attribute in the sense that it enables learning to take place.

Developing feedback strategies: practical examples

A

In its simplest form we could illustrate the importance of 'feedback' with reference to a fairly widespread policy in relation to spelling. Which is likely to be more effective in the long run, correcting all the pupils' spelling mistakes on every occasion, or selecting a small number of misspelt words (three or four, on a regular basis) to be learned individually? With some discernment over the selection of words, a teacher can help the pupil learn them. This approach can transform the self-image of a pupil from someone who 'can't spell' to someone who can learn to spell.

This approach can be translated into most subject settings. Think of how pupils can come to see themselves as 'no good at maths' when on the receiving end of lots of conscientiously corrected errors.

B

Read this excerpt from the observation notes made by a training mentor on a student teacher's lesson:

> The second phase of the lesson starts well: the students are all quickly engaged in pairs, working on the task. . . . But the teacher seems strangely lost: it is as if he does not really know what to do now – mark some books, plan a lesson, read the paper! What he decides to do is to 'circulate' rather like a cocktail waiter: are you ok? any problems? do you need anything? My challenge is this: tell me how this episode of the lesson (25 minutes) could be spent more purposefully by the teacher.

If feedback depends on dialogue between teachers and pupils, the stumbling block is often considered to be 'making time'. But there is often time to be *taken* (it does not have to be made). When the class is on task, individuals, pairs or small groups can benefit immensely from the occasional five- or ten-minute focused feedback session concerning specific learning points. Over a period of half a term everyone in the class can be 'seen' in this way – with the help of careful record keeping (see Chapter 9 on marking).

Figure 8.5 Using existing opportunities to develop effective feedback

- Teachers and pupils may need to renegotiate the 'contract of contentment' which can so easily take hold in classrooms when they become filled with 'busy work' such as finishing the graph or copying notes. Crudely, this is when teachers and pupils seem to have made the tacit agreement: 'you don't challenge us and we won't challenge you'. See the box, below, which indicates the level of professional skill required of teachers to overcome this problem.

> In his book on the theory and practice of assessment and testing, Paul Black writes:
>
> > A review of evidence about teaching and learning styles needed for effective group work illustrated further these general lessons. It showed that the ways in which teachers control and react to pupils' performances is a delicate and critical factor. Apart from the most able and confident, many pupils are self-protective and will negotiate a level of task which does not expose them to public failure or criticism. Thus, a careful response to their work, in an atmosphere where empathy is established, is essential if challenging and worthwhile tasks are to be tackled (Galton and Williamson 1992)
> >
> > (cited in Black 1998: 135)

Before moving on to consider self-assessment in the next section, it is important (in relation to the above list) to signal what Caroline Gipps has called 'learned helplessness' (Gipps 1994: 132). This is a condition describing the damage that can be done to pupils' self esteem as a result of feedback which reinforces in some pupils a *feeling* that they cannot learn. There is, as we might expect, a close correlation between positive self-esteem and high levels of attainment in school, and this is therefore more a problem of how to feed back to low attaining pupils (often referred to by teachers in a rather indiscriminate manner as 'the less able', risking damning individuals with a general label) than to those perceived by themselves and others as successful. It is for this reason that, to quote Paul Black once more, 'good formative assessment has therefore to be ipsative rather than normative, devoted to building self-esteem and belief in oneself in every pupil.' (Black 1998: 136). The size of the challenge to teachers is self evident when we remind ourselves of the research cited earlier in this chapter, showing that blanket praise for every small 'achievement' for such pupils is ineffective.

LINKING FEEDBACK AND PUPILS' SELF-ASSESSMENT

Perhaps the key point in our discussion of feedback is that to be effective it is best seen as a dialogue or conversation between teachers and pupils. Thus

Assessment: A view from the receiving end

Figure 8.6 Billy on the receiving end. This cartoon portrays the characteristics and some deficiencies of traditional 'marking'   Source: Lambert (1991)

effective classroom assessment is not a one-way street, something 'done to' pupils. Pupils have to be actively involved in the learning process; which means they have to be actively involved in the assessment process too.

Perhaps the key reason for this is that without dialogue and active involvement, the criteria by which achievement in the subject can be judged are not necessarily shared; indeed, they may not be understood by the pupils at all. In such cases some pupils become disempowered as learners; assessment is something done to them which usually shows they are failures (at least in relation to their peers). This is the point eloquently made by the well known cartoon starring Billy (Figure 8.6). At the very least Billy could do with understanding the marking criteria. The question is how best to develop such an understanding.

There is need to orchestrate a form of pupil involvement in assessment which is capable of empowering them. Part of the need is to change the pupils' understanding of assessment and what it is for. Involving pupils in self-assessment is a powerful way of achieving such goals, as fundamentally, it features assessment as something that is not 'done to' others; rather, it is something to be involved in. Some go further than this, claiming that 'self-assessment is intrinsic to learning' (Black 1998: 132). The box below uses a personal anecdote from one of the authors to illustrate how (purely intuitively at the time) this point was realised in practice in one secondary school department.

MAKING THE LINK: A PERSONAL ANECDOTE

These recollections take me back to the beginning of my second year as head of department.

My A-level results frankly had not been so good. And of course the Head was on to me like a shot: was it the syllabus? was it the students? . . . was it the teaching?

I looked at my present A-level students, especially those beginning their second year. They were bright, responsive, interested – every bit as much as last year's group – but were they going to reach their full potential?

To cut a long story short, the department decided that where we may have short-changed last year's students was in failing to help them make the link between the subject matter they were being taught and how to express what they had learnt in terms that would meet the requirements of the syllabus and examination.

This, however, was not taken as an invitation to *reduce* our teaching to question spotting and 'teaching to the test'. What we needed to do was to *enhance* our teaching:

(a)   to extend the teacher repertoire; for example increasing the amount of individualised coaching concerning specific aspects of the subject; and

(b)   to increase the amount of dialogue concerning achievement.

In practical terms this led to some changes. For example, in relation to 'test essays', which featured in the preparation of examination candidates in several departments of the school, we introduced a system which required the students to mark each other's. Fewer test essays were done: but each one was prepared by a class discussion on possible marking criteria relating to the question. The essay was then written during a following lesson, papers swapped and then marked for homework. A pair of students would be selected to take the lead in a critical discussion in the next lesson, based on their analysis of what had been read. Crucial in this new system, we thought, was that the *teacher also wrote the essay and swapped papers with a student*.

The quality of the discussions improved very quickly, moving from general to subject-specific analysis of both questions and alternative answers. They began to show students their own potential to influence outcomes. The students became more active participants in a learning process.

Examination results also improved. The department is convinced that the process outlined here played a prominent role. (But we cannot prove it.)

Perhaps our focus hitherto on student 'empowerment' through engaging in self-assessment fails adequately to express the potential of such forms of pupil involvement in promoting personal development (in addition to narrower academic attainment). Of course, such diverse 'aspects of achievement' (Hargreaves 1984) are closely related, and as Black reminds us, a 'pupil's development as a learner is closely bound up with personal development as a whole' (Black 1998: 133). The personal anecdote above suggests that improved formative assessment through open and honest involvement in self-assessment can build levels of motivation and self-esteem. This not only supported improved performance (including in the public examination), but it helped pupils become more effective learners, more able to analyse their own and others' work.

The very term 'self-assessment' implies a kind of approach to classrooms that has been out of favour in some quarters in recent years: broadly, a progressive, 'learner-centred' (Stiggins 1994) approach. Such an approach is more inclined to be sensitive to, and understand, the importance of pupils' feelings about learning. How people feel about themselves as learners is a key determinant on how much progress or how much success they can anticipate (or feel they 'deserve'). Sylva's research on early primary children (Sylva 1994) indicated that such feelings are both strong and laid down early: it is worth recording her summary of two main types of children that she found emerge

---

The influence of school: mastery and helpless children

Mastery children

- are motivated by the desire to learn
- will tackle difficult tasks in flexible and reflective ways
- are confident of success, believing that they can do it if they try
- believe that you can improve your intelligence
- if they see another hard-working child, they will say 'she must be interested'

Helpless children

- are motivated by a desire to be seen to do well
- seem to accept that they will fail because they are not clever enough
- believe that if something seems too hard there is nothing they can do about it
- tend therefore to avoid challenge
- do not believe that they can improve their intelligence

Figure 8.7 Mastery and helpless pupil characteristics
Source: Sylva (1994); cited in Black (1998: 133–134)

from school (Figure 8.7). Whether a child acquires 'mastery' or 'helpless' characteristics is not apparently related to 'ability'. Encouraging open and honest self-assessment can at least support pupils to avoid 'helplessness' by reducing the tendency under pressure to explain any difficulties (or successes) in terms of luck, mood, effort, teacher, health, family circumstances etc. Put in these terms, raising the level of pupil involvement in self-assessment is part of creating the whole classroom ecology which enables pupils to work with confidence – not always succeeding, often making mistakes, but always learning: what one mathematics teacher described as becoming 'more conscious in relation to their work' (Black and Atkin 1996: 110). We further a discussion on the relationship between teaching, assessment and learning in Chapter 9 on pp. 147–160.

So to summarise: pupils should be trained in self-assessment so that they can better understand learning goals and appreciate their own potential as learners. From the teacher's perspective the intention is to:

- break the pattern of passive learning;
- make learning goals ('the overarching picture') explicit to the pupils; and
- establish a positive action cycle with pupils and teacher working together. For example, the following three stage sequence can be practised:

1   to clarify the desired goal;
2   to establish the present position in relation to this goal; and
3   to find ways to close the gap.

What we have emphasised strongly is that opportunities for pupils to express their understanding have to be built into the teaching. The intention here is to initiate interaction and allow the teacher to build up knowledge of the learners – and, crucially, also to allow the pupil inside the teacher's head.

CONCLUSION

This chapter has covered a lot of ground. It would be possible, and perhaps highly desirable to summarise the main points; this would be a worthwhile task for you, the reader, to undertake. You would collect quite a lengthy list of key ideas, many of which are challenging, not least because they sometimes fly in the face of your personal experience as a student yourself, and also possibly as a student teacher observing assessment practice in your school. You may come up with statements like:

- Instruction and FA are indivisible – you cannot simply bolt on FA and expect teaching to remain unchanged.
- Dialogue between pupils and teachers is essential; it should be thoughtful and reflective, designed to explore understanding.
- Critically examine questioning – of individuals, pairs, groups and the whole class – do I only ask 'closed' questions? Do I find my pupils attempting to guess the 'right' answer? How long can I tolerate silence after posing a big question? Are my questions answered only by the usual few pupils? Do I find myself levelling down questions to ensure a response?
- Frequent short tests may be better than infrequent long ones in order to gain assessment evidence – but to what extent does my assessment strategy turn into a 'serial summative' data chase, rather than a truly formative experience for me and my pupils?
- How can I use feedback and involve pupils in self-assessment in a way that progressively builds confidence and self-esteem? Where does the use of praise fit into this and how do I use it judiciously?
- How do I accommodate the feelings of pupils, colleagues and parents into the approach to assessment that I wish to adopt?

This is not an exhaustive list of possible summary points or questions. The real purpose of this conclusion is not so much to reiterate such items, but to emphasise the main purpose of the chapter, which was to root the principal arms of effective classroom assessment practice (providing effective feedback and involving students in the assessment process) in a secure theoretical framework. What we hope is clear from this are three propositions, with which we can finally conclude the chapter:

- No matter how sophisticated the assessment regime, always keep asking the simple, basic questions: Why are we doing this and what for? What consequences do we expect? How will we ensure that the assessment will have consequential validity?
- Teachers need to possess an understanding of how children learn in order to use assessment to aid pupils' learning. As Ruth Sutton writes, 'Information and investigations about theories of learning and motivation may seem a long way from assessment but they are entirely pertinent and can be a very productive place to start' (Sutton 1995: 157).
- We have argued for a balanced approach to teaching, learning and assessment. We would expect diversity of teaching approaches in a secondary school as the particular priorities and emphases of different subjects vary. So too with assessment practice.

Beware any expert who posits all-embracing theories and solutions for you! Armed with some theoretical understanding (e.g. of constructivism), some principles (e.g. find out what the pupils know already and build it into the teaching programme) and one or two templates (e.g. how to handle examination preparation as a component of FA), it is up to teachers individually, or preferably in teams, to work out the details of implementation. This may involve a deal of trial and error.

FOR FURTHER THINKING

1. What are your underlying beliefs about learning? How do these influence your attitudes towards the assessment of pupils?
   To get you started, where do you place yourself in relation to the following polarised 'positions'?

   Is learning about:

   - delivery, coverage and knowledge transmission; or
   - interaction, construction, scaffolding and dialogue?

   Do you emphasise:

   - deep learning; or
   - surface learning?

Do you believe people have:

- a fixed intelligence quotient (IQ); or
- have untapped potential?

2.   From your observations of classrooms in your department or school, what appear to be the underlying beliefs about learning held by the teachers? How do these appear to influence their feelings towards formative assessment?

FOR FURTHER READING

H. Torrance and J. Pryor (1998) *Investigating Formative Assessment*. This is a readable, but comparatively unusual book in that it discusses in some detail some research into case studies of formative assessment practice. It is a very useful source for those wishing to delve deeper into practical and theoretical issues relating to formative assessment.

G. Stobart and C. Gipps (1997) *Assessment: a Teacher's Guide to the Issues*. This is a well known and practically oriented book (now in its third edition). Chapter 2 in particular, 'Assessment for learning', takes up the theme with which we introduced this chapter within a very broad overview of assessment as a whole.

9 Formative Assessment: Implications for Teaching and Learning

This chapter takes stock in relation to what we have learnt about class-room assessment so far, examining the practical implications of imple-menting formative classroom assessment (FA) for both pupils and teachers. One prominent aspect of FA, 'marking' is considered in some detail. A particular theme discussed in the chapter is the question of equity in educational assessment. It is perhaps an article of faith that educational assessment should be conducted in ways that are fair to all individuals and groups. Exactly what this means, particularly in terms of its implications for assessment practice is, like so much else in the consid-eration of classroom processes, not necessarily self-evident. It requires conscious and critical mental effort both to understand why unfairness can creep in and in identifying ways to avoid unfairness taking hold. It is important to achieve both these things in order to prevent teachers' judgements of individuals, and even whole groups of pupils, becoming skewed or biased.

GOOD CLASSROOM ASSESSMENT: HOW IT INFLUENCES LEARNING AND TEACHING STYLES

As is clear from our discussion so far, the distinctive feature of good class-room assessment is that it is used formatively. It is formative assessment (FA), which means that the information gathered is used to enhance the learning potential of the pupils. This is done by modifying the teaching in order to make it more effective – principally by incorporating feedback strategies at all stages of the planning, preparation and organisation of lessons, and involving students in thinking about their learning by engaging them in various forms of self-assessment.

We have reported some of the research evidence suggesting that good formative assessment *can* produce substantial learning gain (Black and Wiliam 1998a). This shows us that it is worth doing, even though it receives only a minute fraction of the material investment and support enjoyed by the external assessment industry, and in many ways has to be undertaken against the tidal flow of external tests and examinations discussed in Chapters 3–6 of this

MAIN CATEGORY	PRINCIPAL METHODS	COMMENTS
Classroom observations	■ Anecdotal comments. Teachers use an exercise book to record comments on individuals, one page per student. ■ Interviews with students or small groups. ■ Departmental checklists; based upon comment banks.	Enormous quantities of material concerning individual students get carried around, often in the teacher's head. Some kind of recording format – informal, or a more formalised 'profile' – makes this process more systematic and, by recording date and occasion, can provide the teacher with *evidence* for reporting purposes.
Objective tests	■ True/false tests. ■ Completion tests. ■ Matching tests. ■ Multiple-choice tests. ■ Short answer tests.	Easy to administer, easy to mark, but difficult to devise. Often over-emphasise the recall of facts. Even the most carefully designed multiple-choice tests, which can test for understanding, are difficult to use other than in an end-of-course setting. Often enjoyed by students and effective within their limitations, which need to be acknowledged.
Essays	■ Timed essays. ■ Resource-based essays. ■ Extended writing for specified audience.	Easy to administer, more difficult to mark. Carefully constructed questions can assess a range of skills and attributes ranging from recall to synthesis and evaluation. Considerable scope exists for involving students in *redrafting* arguments and ideas, enhancing essays as a formative assessment mechanism.
Structured questions	■ Stimulus response questions. This can cover a huge variety of questions and responses; often involves students in *description*, *transformation* and *analysis* of data. It is also possible, by asking appropriate questions, to assess students' powers of *evaluation* of the method of data presentation, or of the situation described by the data.	A very flexible format. For example, students can be asked to respond in or out of a specified role; the question can be self-contained (students can be asked to relate the data to a well-known case study; questions can be designed to *differentiate* by outcome or via an incline or steps of difficulty.

Figure 9.1 A summary of assessment methods available to teachers

Source: Lambert (1990)

MAIN CATEGORY	PRINCIPAL METHODS	COMMENTS
Enquiries	■ Using *secondary* sources: a 'teacher-planned enquiry'. ■ Using primary sources: an enquiry involving the collection of some data directly from the 'field', or an experiment.	Enquiry implies selecting and using *evidence* in order to identify, describe, analyse and draw conclusions concerning a particular issue or problem. Students need to be involved in a sequence of activities, over a considerable time period, and are often working individually. This, in turn, has involved teachers in devising support strategies, often with a focus on 'study skills'.
Self-assessment	■ Checklists. ■ Evaluation sheets. ■ Tutorial meetings, individually or in small groups. ■ Closely related to *peer-group* assessment.	Anyone who has attempted to assess him- or herself will know: (a) how difficult this process is, and (b) how rewarding it can be. It needs practice and it can lead to a deepening understanding of an individual's own strengths and how to counter weaknesses. Difficult to standardise and verify, though one of the benefits is to deepen a shared understanding of access criteria.
Oral assessment	■ Discussion work: students interact within a group. ■ Presentation: students prepare and present a verbal report to an audience.	Very motivating to some students (often, but not always, those who are less happy with the written form). Apart from the fact that these methods are very time consuming, the main challenge is to devise suitable and agreed *procedures* and *criteria*. In theory, oral techniques could be applied to *any* of the previous assessment techniques.

Figure 9.1 continued

book, and which seems to dominate the public debate about assessment in education.

Readers of the previous two chapters will also have correctly gained the impression that formative assessment is much more an integral part of teaching and learning than something that can be separated from it. This implies that the assessment process is, at least in part, subjective and highly context bound – 'a qualitative art calling for the judgement of the connoisseur' (Black 1998: 110). This is one reason why teachers often display mixed feelings towards it, for what is advocated with FA is worlds apart from the quantitative, objective paradigm of testing which tends to dominate outside the classroom, and which has had such a large influence on most of our lives (for teachers are successful products of the external examinations industry). It is also a reason why we have resisted any thought of going through or even listing 'FA methods'; after all, *any* technique, including those used in objective testing procedures, can be *used* formatively – though clearly some (e.g. open ended enquiries or projects) are more amenable to providing useful (usable) information than others (e.g. multiple choice tests). However, it may be helpful to focus more sharply on actual assessment practices – the 'technology' of FA – and we do so in this and the following chapter.

Focus on learning and teaching

Rather than concentrate on assessment methods as ends in themselves, as we have summarised in Figure 9.1, it is important to maintain our gaze on *how* using assessment formatively can impact on learning. Figure 9.2 attempts to do this. The ideal position which we describe here is by no means value free or neutral. It represents a viewpoint on learning which cannot be presumed to be universally shared. However, if we accept the general position set out in Figure 9.2, then the implications for teachers are far reaching. For some, far reaching implications merely embody a challenge which a confident and ambitious profession can work to address – and the rest of this chapter aims to identify signposts to aid this process. In general terms the challenge identified here is for teachers to focus more on learning (and less on teaching!); it is worth recording the remark cited in Black (1998), which may point to why (as we discussed in Chapter 7) good classroom assessment is so hard to find:

> Since assessment information is sure to reveal heterogeneity in learning needs, [subsequent] action has to include some form of differentiated teaching. One reason why this path is not followed was suggested by Perrenoud [1991: 89] 'There is a desire in everyone not the know about things about which one can do nothing'.
>
> (Black 1998: 116)

Whilst it would be foolish to underestimate the organisational challenges associated with adopting full-blooded formative classroom assessment (which, of course, includes responding to what we find out about the pupils we teach), we aim to show where practical steps can be taken by teachers to ensure that FA can be used effectively to enhance learning. The natural desire to ignore what may seem impossible to implement (in this case, differentiated, learner-centred teaching), may result from the perception that insuperable problems are to do *only* with organisational and time management issues. Such a perception is possibly inevitable if FA is seen as something to be added to existing teaching practices. But a more radical rethink of the relationship between teaching, learning and assessment enables us to understand these things as part of the same set of processes, easing considerably the lament that FA is 'OK in theory, but impractical'. At the same time, the focus on pedagogy (by

Ways in which good formative assessment can influence learning

- **Raising levels of motivation to learn**
  - by building a sense of success (though a demotivating sense of failure can also be constructed, especially if mistakes are simply corrected by the teacher-assessor and not used as a potential learning point);
  - by building a sense of independence and value as a learner: 'Teacher feedback not only aids the learning process, it also affects how children view themselves: children's academic self-esteem is determined largely through feedback from teachers' (Tunstall and Gipps 1995: 2).

- **Deciding what to learn**
  - by helping identify what is important to learn – partly by teachers helping pupils keep in sight the 'big picture';
  - by discriminating through teacher feedback between strengths and weaknesses.

- **Learning how to learn**
  - by encouraging an active or participatory approach to learning;
  - by showing that there are various ways to learn and choices can be made;
  - by inculcating self awareness and monitoring of progress against goals;
  - by developing confidence to apply learning to new contexts.

- **Evaluating learning**
  - practising how to apply criteria to assist making judgements about the effectiveness of learning;
  - using judgements to consolidate and/or prepare for next steps.

Figure 9.2 The possible impact of effective classroom assessment on pupils' learning
Source: adapted from Broadfoot (1996) and Crooks (1988)

which we imply the triangle of teaching, learning and assessment relationships) enables teachers to recapture, as they may have to from time to time, the notion that the art and science of teaching *matters*: it is unhelpful, as well as inaccurate, to suggest that teachers 'can do nothing' in terms of practising differentiated, learner-centered teaching.

Figure 9.2 clearly shows some of the ways teaching needs consciously to be oriented to learning, which in a sense is all that good FA demands. It is possible to add all manner of detail to such a summary of influences: for example, under 'learning how to learn', readers can be referred to work on *learning styles* (Kolb 1985) and think of ways (with older pupils) of making these explicit. Alternatively, under 'raising levels of motivation', we can imagine how an awareness of Howard Gardner's theory of *multiple intelligences* (Gardner 1983; 1994) could be most useful in helping teachers build in all pupils a sense of self-efficacy as learners.

Perhaps the most significant consideration, however, is something even more fundamental than any of the matters identified in Figure 9.2. What conception do pupils hold of the subject matter they are being taught? What is maths (or geography, or art, or English etc.) for? What is it about? A related question flowing from these concerns is the pupils' conception of what characterises *learning* that subject (e.g. Dowgill 1996). For instance, and to put it crudely, do pupils conceive learning your subject as accumulating facts, or developing ideas (concepts) to be understood and related to their everyday experience? Or third, do they take the subject matter simply as the means to high grades? These 'approaches' to learning have been studied by researchers

---

Approaches to learning

Deep
- Intention is to understand
- Vigorous interaction with the content
- Mental effort relating learning to previous knowledge and everyday experience
- Attempts to relate conclusions to available evidence
- Critical evaluation of arguments and/or claims

Surface
- Intention is to complete the task
- Attempts to memorise the material in preparation for formal assessment
- Task not taken on board personally and seen as externally imposed
- Learning treated as an accumulation of bits with little integration
- Limited awareness of overall purpose, strategies or the 'big picture'

Strategic
- Intention is to obtain the highest grades possible
- Effort tailored to maximise efficiency (and subsequent grades)
- Ensures all conditions for efficient working are in place
- Great awareness of the needs of the examination including marking schemes

---

Figure 9.3 Approaches to learning

and have been roughly characterised as surface, deep and strategic respectively: Figure 9.3 expands on this somewhat.

It may be possible to put names of pupils (or other people you know!) against each of the approaches summarised in Figure 9.3. But it is important to note that it is only the pupil's *dominant* approach we notice – in a sense, their natural proclivity; it would be a mistake to assume that the categories are mutually exclusive. We ought to avoid stereotyping people: in reality we are all capable of all three approaches to learning, possibly simultaneously between subjects. What we are arguing for here is that good subject teachers can help pupils decide what to learn and where to put their effort, show them how to learn in different ways to suit different purposes and how to evaluate their own learning. When such things are happening it could be thought of as a signifier of good teaching. To put this another way, good teachers employ formative assessment strategies to achieve learning gains for pupils. We examine how these ideas relate to actual practices associated with 'marking' later in this chapter (p. 160)

Another distinction sometimes made in relation to learning, derived from work in the USA, is that between 'mastery' and 'performance' learning. Mastery denotes when the aim of learning is seen to be achieving a measure of control or command of the material or series of tasks – and therefore is similar to what we have called deep learning. In contrast with this, and closer to strategic and surface approaches to learning, is when the pupils focus their attention on comparisons with others in the peer group, wanting to know 'how good' they are in relation to everyone else. This was a problem for Billy in Figure 8.6, and teachers can exacerbate this tendency, diverting the pupils' gaze away from their own progress (ipsative assessment), by the overuse or overemphasis of essentially norm referenced raw grades or marks.

Focus on teaching and learning

Although we have so far emphasised pupil learning in our discussion on the impact of FA, we have also inevitably examined teaching; how can we separate the two? We implied in the previous paragraphs emphasising learning, that good FA is in some ways synonymous with good teaching; or at least, we could not imagine one without the other. And crucially, we have continually had to conclude that good FA requires a teaching response: if we accept (and how could we deny it) that learners have different needs and dispositions, then teaching also needs to be differentiated. So let us now concentrate more fully on teachers and teaching.

Many teachers agree that if they adopt varied teaching methods and approaches their lessons are likely to be more interesting to pupils as a group and are likely to satisfy more of their individual learning needs. But we want to take you further than this broadly common-sense position which, despite its appeal, still offers pupils something of a lottery. It does not require teachers to understand individual student responses and (to use Sadler's words cited in Chapter 7, p. 122) 'improve the student's competence by short-circuiting the randomness and inefficiency of trial-and-error learning' (Sadler 1989). Differentiating teaching means adopting and adapting methods and approaches in order to respond to what the teacher learns about individual pupil needs. In broad brush terms this means planning lessons that have the inbuilt flexibility to allow this to happen.

It is worth dwelling on this point, for just as pupils have 'preferred learning styles', so do teachers have 'preferred teaching styles', often based upon assumptions about the nature of their subject, knowledge creation and communication which shape their conceptions of teaching. In her discussion of teaching style, which is defined as the way the teacher organises the classroom (the combination of teacher behaviour and chosen teaching strategy), Leask remarks:

> One of our student teachers, who carried out an analysis to establish the level of her interaction with pupils during a lesson, found that over a twenty minute period she spent only about ninety seconds supporting the work of individual pupils. For most of the rest of the time she was addressing the class as a whole. What surprised her was

---

Teacher 'behaviours'

Educationists tend to suggest that good teachers relate to pupils in such ways that show themselves to be:

enthusiastic
stimulating
encouraging
task oriented and business like
warm
tolerant and open minded
polite and tactful
trusting
flexible and adaptable
democratic
expecting pupils to learn
not interested in seeking popularity
capable of overcoming stereotypical responses to pupils
able to see pupils as individuals
a good listener
responsible for promoting pupil learning

Figure 9.4 Teacher behaviours often considered to be effective

Source: various

The participation dimension			
	Closed	Framed	Negotiated
Content	Tightly controlled by the teacher. Not negotiable.	Teacher controls the topic, frames of reference and tasks; criteria made explicit.	Discussed at each point; joint decisions.
Focus	Authoritative knowledge and skills; simplified monolithic.	Stress on empirical testing; processes chosen by teacher; some legitimation of pupil ideas.	Search for justifications and principles; strong legitimation of pupil ideas.
Pupils' role	Acceptance; routine performance; little access to principles.	Join in teacher's thinking; make hypotheses, set up tests; operate teacher's frame.	Discuss goals and methods critically; share responsibility for frame and criteria.
Key concepts	'Authority': the proper procedures and the right answers.	'Access' to skills, processes, criteria.	'Relevance'; critical discussion of pupils' priorities.
Methods	Exposition; worksheets (closed); note giving; individual exercises; routine practical work. Teacher evaluates.	Exposition, with discussion eliciting suggestions; individual/group problem solving; lists of tasks given; discussion of outcomes, but teacher adjudicates.	Group and class discussion and decision making about goals and criteria. Pupils plan and carry out work, make presentations, evaluate success.

Figure 9.5 Pupil participation and teaching styles

Source: from Capel *et al.* (1999: 270)

that she had intended her lesson to be much more pupil centred and thought she had gone some way to achieving that.

(Leask 1999: 273)

Though it surprised the student teacher, this finding may not have surprised her tutor or mentor. As the findings of the National Commission on Education, reported in Chapter 7, showed (p. 111), the kind of 'performance gap' indicated here is not uncommon. It may be that our guiding assumptions about teacher-work are so powerful that we fall prey to them despite ourselves. For what governs teacher behaviour (see, for example, Figure 9.4) and choice of teaching strategy? Deep down, if the teacher's conception of teaching is dominated by notions of knowledge transmission, with the teacher given the

Mosston's continuum of teaching styles

The command style This style is often described as autocratic or teacher centred. It is appropriate in certain contexts, e.g. teaching safe use of equipment, learning particular routines in dance.

The practice style Whilst similar to the command style, there is a shift in decision making to pupils and there is more scope with this style for the teacher to work with individuals whilst the group are occupied with practice tasks such as writing for a purpose in English or practising skills in mathematics.

The reciprocal style The pupils work in pairs evaluating each other's performance. Each partner is actively involved – one as the 'doer' and one observing, as the 'teacher partner'. The teacher works with the 'teacher partner' to improve their evaluative and feedback skills. This style provides increased possibilities for 'interaction and communication among students' and can be applied when pupils are learning a foreign language or learning routines in gymnastics. Pupils learn to judge performance against criteria.

The self-check style This style is designed to develop the learner's ability to evaluate their own performance. The teacher sets the tasks and the pupils evaluate their performance against criteria and set new goals in collaboration with the teacher – for example, some mathematics programmes are organised to allow this type of personal development. All pupils start at the same level and move up when the teacher deems them ready.

The inclusion style In this style, differentiated tasks are included to ensure that all pupils gain some feeling of success and so develop positive self-concepts, e.g. if an angled bar is provided for high jump practice, all pupils can succeed as they choose the height over which to jump. They decide at what level to start.

Guided discovery Mosston sees this as one of the most difficult styles. The teacher plans the pupil's learning programme on the basis of the level of cognitive development of the learner. The teacher then guides the pupil to find the answer – reframing the question and task if necessary. Pupils with special educational needs are often taught in small groups and this approach might be used by the teacher to develop an individualised learning programme for each pupil.

Figure 9.6 Mosston's continuum of teaching styles
Source: from Capel et al. (1999: 272)

Divergent style The learners are encouraged to find alternative solutions to a problem, e.g. in approaching a design problem in art.

The individual programme: learner's design The knowledge and skills needed to participate in this method of learning depend on the building up of skills and self-knowledge in earlier learning experiences. A pupil designs and carries out a programme of work within a framework agreed and monitored by the teacher. Pupils carrying out open-ended investigations in science provide an example of this style.

Learners' initiated style This style is more pupil directed than the previous style where the teacher provided a framework. At this point on the continuum, the stimulus for learning comes primarily from the pupil not wholly from the teacher. The pupil actively initiates the learning experience. Giving homework which allows pupils freedom to work on their own areas of interest in their own way would fall into this category. The teacher acts in a supportive role.

Self-teaching style This style describes independent learning without external support. For example, it is the type of learning that adults undergo as they learn from their own experiences.

Figure 9.6 (continued)

responsibility to 'deliver' a fixed and predetermined body of content, then it is unlikely that the teacher will *believe in* the efficacy of planning lessons with sufficient inbuilt flexibility to allow individual or small group support. The spotlight falls largely on the teacher for it is he or she who is understood to be at the centre of the lesson. On the other hand, if the teacher sees him(her)self more as the orchestrator, conductor or facilitator of learning (or indeed, sometimes coach or motivator) the spotlight falls more readily on pupils or small groups of pupils because *this* is where the action is. Because the teacher *believes in* the importance of hearing, listening to and responding to the pupils' voices he or she fashions the lesson to ensure that this happens.

There have been several attempts by educationists to articulate teaching styles more thoroughly. This book is not the place to explore these in detail, but summary frameworks are provided in Figures 9.5 and 9.6 because in considering the teaching implications of good formative assessment these offer substantial help in analysing teaching – which, as the student teacher cited above found, is a prerequisite to the development of a full repertoire, one that encompasses formative assessment approaches. When you study the summary frameworks, the following questions may assist you.

FOR FURTHER THINKING

[Refer to Figures 9.5 and 9.6.]

1.   Both frameworks are to be read in the form of a continuum. They are
      not to be read too rigidly. Also, do not assume that you can place a
      teacher or even a particular lesson precisely and immutably within the
      framework(s): style can and does vary! But which framework do you
      prefer? Why?
2.   Reflect back on a lesson you have recently observed. Apply your
      preferred framework to judge the *amount* and the *nature* of pupil
      involvement in the lesson (possibly at different stages during the
      lesson). Does the framework of teaching styles you have chosen help
      you identify alternative teacher behaviours or teaching strategies that
      were available during this lesson?
3.   Use the frameworks of teaching styles to consider the implications for
      you of incorporating good formative assessment into your teaching.

Mosston and Ashworth developed their framework (Figure 9.6) in the
context of teaching physical education, though it is applicable to most
curriculum areas. They identified in their model three phases during which
teachers (and indeed learners) need to make choices and take decisions: the
pre-impact (preparation), impact (execution or performance) and post-impact
(evaluation) phases. In the terms of our discussion on the role and place of
FA, we would emphasise the possibly counter-intuitive point that such phases
are *non-linear*: the evaluation 'phase', which incorporates assessment processes
and is ongoing throughout the lesson, should feed into the preparation 'phase',
for example. None the less, such distinctions are useful, not least in reminding
us that teaching has a crucial (though arguably undervalued by some practitioners) *executive* component which involves planning, monitoring and
evaluation. Serious engagement with these executive processes shows, in relation to the Mosston and Ashworth continuum, that

> A number of the [teaching] styles require the teacher to teach the
> pupils the style of learning they are expected to be undertaking.
> Developing such awareness on the part of the pupils can be seen as
> one of the learning objectives.
>
> (Leask 1999: 271)

To spell this out more fully, and turning more directly to the role and place
of FA in teaching, we can summarise the specific ways in which many pupils
need teacher assistance in order to become confident, well motivated and
independent lifelong learners (see summary below).

SUMMARY: HELPING PUPILS LEARN: ISSUES REQUIRING 'EXECUTIVE TEACHER THOUGHT AND ACTION'

On the basis of what they learn from listening to and interacting with the pupils, teachers can evaluate their teaching and if necessary incorporate changes. Any change needs to be soundly based on careful analysis of pupils' needs. The kinds of issues that teachers may need to address with individual pupils in the classroom include:

- understanding what the learning task requires in terms of effort and outcome;
- acquiring, developing and extending a range of learning strategies;
- encouraging a flexible and positive attitude to alternative learning strategies;
- increasing awareness of personal strengths and weaknesses;
- self-assessment of success;
- self-monitoring of progress;
- not being afraid of difficulty and struggle (resisting working only in the comfort zone);
- adopting a positive attitude to making mistakes; and
- increasing learning autonomy and responsibility.

To incorporate guidance to assist pupils with these kinds of issues requires conscious and disciplined planning. During the planning process teachers may (for example) ask themselves:

- How can I *model* aspects of the above (e.g. 'adopting a positive attitude to making mistakes') in my day-to-day teaching?
- How can my lesson incorporate discussion of 'alternative learning strategies'?
- When is it appropriate to allow pupils to struggle on their own? (and refuse them help?)
- Do I provide enough subject-specific feedback to individuals about their strengths and weaknesses? How do I provide space in my lesson to do this?

What the Summary contains is an agenda concerning the kind of relationship teachers can create with their pupils resulting from their own executive thought and action. Apart from the planning and preparation this implies, probably the most time-consuming activity teachers undertake outside the classroom is marking. This too requires careful executive thought and action, for marking is often central to the teacher–pupil relationship. We therefore consider it in detail in the next section.

Margin mark	Meaning	Mark in the writing
np.	New paragraph needed	⎡ around first word of new paragraph
run on	No new paragraph needed	⟨ between paragraphs
⋏	something is missed out	⋏ where something should be put in
⋏.	= full stop missing	
Sp.	Spelling mistake	Underline word. Print correct spelling in margin if needed. Maximum of four on each occasion.
″⋏ ″⋏	Quotation marks needed	
lc	Change from capitals to lower case (small letters)	circle the letters to be changed
?	Doesn't make sense	
X	Wrong	
✓	Good point	
✓✓	Very good point	

Figure 9.7 Some marking conventions

MARKING: WHY DO WE DO IT AND WHO IS IT FOR?

Marking is something all teachers do. In some ways it defines teachers – it is what they do, often accompanied by the condition familiar to all teachers as they prepare for the week, characterised by one head teacher we know as 'Sunday tummy'. But what exactly is it? Literally, it is the critical reading of pupils' work involving the annotation ('marking') of the script. Usually the annotation is in abbreviated form, often using symbols (e.g. Figure 9.7), but sometimes non–existent apart from a big tick at the end (possibly to indicate that the work has been read, or at least seen) and a grade or score according to some kind of simple rating scale (e.g. A–E; 1–10; per cent). Official orthodoxy, such as expressed by the Chief Inspector for Schools in his 1998 annual report, is critical of marking which offers only grades, or grades with comments so brief (e.g. 'good work' or 'not enough detail') to be of little use in helping pupils raise their performance or (better still) understand their achievement. This section explores marking in relation to our broader discussion of formative classroom assessment (FA).

At best marking can be the main vehicle on which to carry effective FA. It can be undertaken in such a way that the open and supportive classroom becomes a reality, in which precise and individually tailored feedback is assimilated by the pupils who themselves are involved in the assessment and monitoring process. However, marking can become a deeply disliked professional chore, subject to repeated procrastination as it is relegated below other out of class processes such as planning, preparation and administration – and perhaps inevitably therefore, sometimes being undertaken superficially (see box below for an account of the pressures of marking).

RUTH REMEMBERS HER EARLY MARKING (1)

Looking back on my years in the classroom, I'm not happy about the way I approached marking as a secondary teacher. I was clear that marking should give my pupils feedback about their work so they could improve it next time, but I was overwhelmed by the sheer quantity of it, not always clear what I was looking for, and often distracted by the cosmetics of presentation rather than the knowledge or understanding which took a little longer to spot. In my first year of teaching I had four examination classes. . . . I also had several other classes of younger pupils, all of whose books had to be marked with reasonable frequency, but I got bogged down by it, and fell behind, so that work might be marked weeks after it was completed, when any feedback was no longer of interest to the children or of great relevance to their learning. Not infrequently, late in the evening, half-way through a pile of books or essays which never seemed to diminish, I asked myself what was the point of it all. I knew that I had to recognise that the work had been read, but specific feedback demanded more than that. Without more careful scrutiny of what they'd done, I had little to say to them when work was returned, they took less notice, and my dissatisfaction with the whole process grew. By the time the nightly routine of marking had been completed I was usually too tired to put enough energy into planning, or creative ideas, or the essential [executive] details which can so affect a teacher's day.

Source: Sutton (1995: 64–65)

At worst, badly done marking can be damaging, not only because it gets in the way and distorts the teacher's executive decision making, but also because it can transmit unhelpful messages about what is valued about the handed in work and how a pupil can improve in the subject. For example,

> Too often marking seems aimless, bland and mysterious, largely because it is almost entirely norm-referenced: work is judged merely on superficial criteria such as presentation and quantity, against the norm of that class or year group.
>
> (Lambert and Balderstone 1999: 94)

This quote and Ruth's memories once more take us back to Billy (Figure 8.6, p. 140) and the difficulty he had understanding what his marks meant. He had two possible reference points: himself and his peers. In neither case did he have enough to form an understanding of his achievement and how to respond the next time. Despite receiving 'good marks', it was a somewhat dispiriting experience trying to decode the teacher's message. And in truth, perhaps the message the teacher wanted to communicate was far from clear in the first place (see box below). There is little doubt in our minds that clear learning objectives, expressed as achievable outcomes, underpin effective marking.

A STUDENT TEACHER: MARKING FOR THE FIRST TIME

In line with departmental policy, I took the books in. I carried them home to mark. I had a green pen (I vowed never to use red!). I was ready. But where to start?

The first book I opened revealed rather grubby pages and work which did not seem finished. Were they all like this? I quickly skimmed through the whole pile. This gave me my 'standard'. Most books were at or near the standard – they received seven out of ten. A few (including the first one I picked up) were below standard – they got six. A few were above standard and got eight.

I later refined and widened this crude three point scale (disguised as marks out of ten) by extending the scale from five to nine out of ten. It took me some time to realise that I had invented (as I guess many teachers do) a norm referenced system of levels. Frankly, I could have placed at a level most of the pupils, most of the time, quite accurately without really reading their work.

What I needed was guidance to enable me to transform my day-to-day 'marking' into something that was both more effective and efficient.

As we saw in the opening chapter of this book, *ranking* pupils and *judging* their work (assigning a value to it) are two quite different activities. What the student teacher had appreciated by the time she came to write down her thoughts recorded above, is that her norm referenced marking scheme was nothing more than an exercise in ranking her pupils. All she had to do was to decide an arbitrary 'standard' gleaned from an overview of the pupils' work and then place the pupils accordingly; in fact, it was not even as sophisticated as true ranking because inevitably most pupils were 'placed' equal with others.

If assessment requires a judgement to be made concerning the merits of the work, then the student teacher's marking barely counts as assessment. In order to assign a value to the work, in preference to merely placing it at a level in relation to the average, or norm, the marker is greatly assisted if he or she has *criteria*. Assessment criteria link directly with learning objectives. The latter specify what are the intended learning outcomes of the task, while the former guide the marker with clear signposts identifying what to look for of significance in the work. When the marker is clear about the expected outcomes of the task, it is then possible to express these to the pupils in terms that they will understand, sometimes by showing them, or demonstrating, success.

Clear objectives or criteria, sometimes expressed in terms of learning outcomes, also enable the marker to *focus* the marking. As Ruth candidly admitted, the marking business can become overwhelming especially if, in the absence of clear purpose, teachers imagine they have to mark everything (they want to be seen to be thorough). But 'thorough' may not be the same as 'smart' (like not being able to see the wood for the trees). Some departments have invested time and effort developing smart or 'intelligent' marking which claims to analyse pupils' work rather than blitz it indiscriminately with red ink and corrections. It 'targets' just a small number of key ideas, or perhaps a common misconception (plus, possibly, some spelling mistakes). This has much to commend it, and pupils can be encouraged to handle this approach successfully, for example, by understanding that they will be expected to learn *no more than* three spellings when the work is returned − but they will be tested on these next lesson.

But targeted marking, unless the focus is clearly articulated in advance can also mislead, perhaps in its mission not to upset or demoralise the pupil, for it could be mistaken for not really caring about detail. Thus, the executive processes which underpin the practical activity of teaching are once more to the fore. Deciding the assessment focus is best done in advance, probably with departmental colleagues, so that appropriate preparations can be made, including preparing the pupils. It is for this reason that the assessment focus should be identified as part of the curriculum plan or scheme of work, so that it forms part of a rolling programme related to the bigger picture expressed by the overarching goals and purposes of the subject.

Any discussion on criteria in relation to marking and formative assessment needs to address the issue of 'effort'. Many schools have invented effort grades defined by broad criteria and have done so with the best of intentions, usually to balance the stark message contained in the 'achievement' grade, and to reward industry and application. Some teachers we know mark only with effort grades. Our analysis leads us to conclude, however, that marking with effort grades is at best dubious and at worst (as in the latter case when *all* the pupil has to go on is an effort grade), an abrogation of professional duty by the teacher. As effort grades seem to be more prominent with low attaining pupils than the academically more gifted, it can be seen to be even more careless, for it is these pupils (as we found in Chapter 7) who stand to gain most from individualised, subject-specific feedback.

The greatest question mark over effort grading concerns the criteria: how do we know what kind of 'effort' a pupil has made? On what grounds do we judge this – and is there a natural tendency to overvalue quantity and presentation as some kind of surrogate measure of effort? The scope for bias (see next section) is also considerable. But it is in any case difficult to see how good effort marks can in the long term 'compensate' someone who consistently shows low levels of knowledge, understanding or skill. It would be interesting to research the relationship between self-esteem and various kinds of annotations, grades and feedback marked on pupils' work. In the meantime, effort *marks or grades* are, in our view, best avoided.

Although our student teacher's and Ruth's memories of marking help us discuss the *purpose* of marking and hint at how to raise its effectiveness and efficiency, neither passage directly addressed the question of whom the marking is for. Perhaps this is because the answer to this question is so obvious. But a brief further reflection from Ruth (below) may help muddy the water!

RUTH REMEMBERS HER EARLY MARKING (2)

Little of this dissatisfaction [about marking] could have been deduced from my 'mark-book', a large buff coloured commercially printed creation, containing hundreds of pink lines dividing large pages into thousands of little boxes, into which I carefully inserted the codes, grades and symbols derived from the rather cursory assessment process. At a glance everything appeared to be in order: there was something in every box, but what did it all mean? Not much actually.

Source: Sutton (1995: 65)

For whom is marking done? Well the pupils of course. But what Ruth is telling us here is that marking often succumbs to a kind of 'accountability trap'. To the student teacher perhaps it seems that although marking is done on the pupils it is mainly for the purpose of producing records for the benefit of the PGCE tutor who is shortly to assess their competence. For the staffroom cynic, replace 'PGCE tutor' with 'Head' or 'OFSTED inspector'. Somehow, in the search for evidence, the pupil is marginalised as the presumed bureaucratic needs of senior colleagues (and parents) supplant the softer person-to-person communication of assessment. So long as numbers or grades accumulate in the mark-book, this line of argument seems to suggest, we can demonstrate our competence! This is a mirage.

Probably such attitudes have always underestimated the perspicacity of tutors, Heads or OFSTED inspectors. Neat and full mark-books, as Ruth realised, mean little in themselves, and these days the various quality agencies will certainly look for evidence that records have been *used* effectively. It is important to realise here that we are not arguing against the need to keep accurate assessment records. Indeed, on the contrary, we are arguing that they should be taken more seriously rather than less. Records are vital, and arguably, the keeping and handling of records could be seen to be as much as 50 per cent of the day-to-day assessment, or marking, process. However, the classic form of the teacher's mark-book needs to be reconsidered; if it cannot be redesigned completely from scratch, the existing records can be supplemented either by the use of a 'day book' or by the use of file cards (see Figure 9.8).

The fundamental issue in reconsidering the form that assessment records should take is the need to accommodate their inevitably multipurpose nature, from the bureaucratic to the educational:

- they do need to be able to demonstrate that work has been set and marked by you;
- they need to show *what* work has been completed successfully (and less successfully) by pupils – its content coverage, the context of skills work etc.;
- they should provide the basis for a detailed summative report to be compiled for the parent or next teacher;
- they should provide, if possible, subject-specific analysis of next steps *for individual pupils* – feeding forward to the next topic – based upon the particular chosen assessment focus;
- they can also provide subject-specific next steps *for the teacher* when he or she comes to plan the next topic or module, or when the present topic or module is reviewed next year.

Such requirements imply some kind of combination of more traditional boxes and columns with a more open-ended format which can record written qualitative judgements. Laying down precisely the form of such records is beyond the scope of this book, and in any case would vary enormously, and quite legitimately, from school to school (and, perhaps, subject to subject). Sutton (1995) advances one suggestion taken from a middle school, designed to incorporate information that the school deemed essential: as Figure 9.8 shows, this included noting the *context* of assessments, their particular *focus* and the need to use assessments to *feedforward*, both with pupils and in planning the curriculum.

This is a medium-term record, designed to achieve *Context, Focus* and *Feedforward*

Pupil's name	Specific assessment focus – criteria and methods			Next steps
	1.	2.	3.	
(up to 30 lines here)				

Topic: Brief Description_____

Date: _____   _____

Evaluation: (Notes to guide the effective management of the topic next time around)

Figure 9.8 Pro-forma for recording assessment information

Perhaps a tip from psychologists is useful at this point. When describing, or analysing pupils, concentrate on the behaviour, actions or outcomes, not the 'person'. The teacher is, of course, pupil centred, but just as a doctor is concerned with the whole person but must nevertheless examine as objectively as possible the symptoms, the teacher needs to analyse what can be observed or learnt from the pupil – and then find a way to engage the pupil with what he or she has learnt. We want to move away from succumbing to the risk of damning people with generalities. To say that 'Chris is no good at maths' or that 'Jess is just a trouble-maker in my lessons' (and we have heard much worse damning generalities than these!), does not actually help rectify matters.

Linking marking with formative assessment, as we have tried to do in this section, implies the development of some demanding skills on the part of teachers. Perhaps the best place for beginning teachers to start is in practising succinct but meaningful written feedback to pupils on their written work. Comments need to be precise and subject-specific, positive whilst avoiding blanket or meaningless praise and focused on next steps. Figure 9.9 shows simple distinctions in the way marking can be approached: we advocate a balanced pathway through these polarised positions, perhaps varying between students depending on what the teacher perceives to be the individual student

Approaches to marking

Student teachers, when embarking on marking pupils' work for the first time, are often surprised at how strongly the process sometimes steers them towards a focus on what is lacking in the work, encouraging a 'stick' rather than a 'carrot' approach.

This table opens up this issue. Discussing the implications of the contrasts shown will quickly demonstrate the dangers of concentrating on one approach to the exclusion of others.

'Carrot'	'Stick'
Type of marking	
Positive	Negative
Enthusiastic	Cool/distant
Constructive	Destructive
Eager	Harsh
Generous	Severe
Affirmative	Critical
Encouraging	Analytical
Marking style	
Gives credit	Finds fault
Looks for intrinsic merit	Compares to the 'model answer'
Marks from 'bottom up'	Marks from 'top down'
Comments	
You have . . .	You have not . . .
A good start that can be developed by	Develop this point
Good use of . . .	Poor use of . . .
Well done for . . .	It is a pity you have not . . .
Interesting point	What does this mean?
Re-write this point to gain the marks . . .	This does not make sense
Make more use of . . .	Explain!
The strengths in this are . . .	The weaknesses here are . . .
Ask me if you do not know why this is a brilliant sentence	Not good enough – see me!

Figure 9.9 Approaches to marking

Feedback on pupils' written work

These are some areas which may help teachers focus their comments on written work to enable pupils to identify their next steps and how to improve.

- How the answer was structured or sequenced
- How convincingly an argument was constructed
- Was the actual question understood and responded to?
- Did the answer keep to the point?
- Level of detail/description/analysis: e.g. how many variables were taken account of? any alternatives mentioned?
- How appropriate was the use of language – vocabulary, genre/register, style?
- Was the work imaginative?
- Were good links made? (How clear is the pupil's 'concept map'?)
- How effectively were examples, or case studies, used?
- Did the work demonstrate knowledge? (or did it hide its light under a bushel?)
- Spelling, punctuation and grammar – what (few) targets can be identified to improve accuracy?
- Presentation – how can the appearance of the work be improved? (and be more enjoyable to read!)

Figure 9.10 Suggestions for feedback on pupils' written work

need. Teachers may vary their approach with the same student from time to time, because 'what works' may not be immediately obvious.

Some student teachers have found that selecting from a small number of comment 'stems' have helped them: for example, 'You can improve this work by . . .', or 'Next time try to . . .'. Figure 9.9 also provides further examples of these. We should emphasise, however, what we are *not* suggesting here: we are *not* implying that each piece is given a thorough all-embracing critique. The real skill is knowing what single point to raise with the pupil. One specific target or next step stands some chance of being assimilated and acted upon, whereas scattering targets like confetti is as unhelpful as offering none at all. Figure 9.10 makes some suggestions of broad areas relating to written work which could help focus initial comments; but note, these are not subject specific (see For Further Thinking (p. 169), question 2).

Marking written work is of course only one opportunity to judge the learning outcomes of individual students, and we can finish this section by reminding ourselves that much can be learnt about pupils' capacities, likes and dislikes, confusions, difficulties or inspirations simply by talking to them. Indeed, this also helps broaden the evidence base teachers assemble in their quest to get to know the pupils as learners. Many primary school teachers, though probably fewer secondary school teachers, have long known that marking work *alongside the pupil* can be immensely valuable, because the work becomes the subject of conversation: such conversation is 'authentic', concerning work that was recently committed to paper, and producing feedback that is direct and instant. Often, when marked homework is handed back, it is two, three or more weeks since the pupil last gave it attention: authentic conversation is difficult in these circumstances. Perhaps secondary pupils should experience marking alongside the teacher at least once a year in each subject. They should also experience marking each other's work and marking their own work on the basis of criteria which they have discussed with the teacher beforehand. They should occasionally experience short, specific 'coaching' sessions from the teacher, perhaps in small groups. And the teacher's records should attempt to keep track of all this.

The implication of what we are proposing here is clear: lesson time needs to be devoted to assessment. Lessons therefore need to be planned to include flexible assessment time. Putting this another way, to use Ruth Sutton's words: 'we may marginally reduce the quantity of teaching in the interests of [raising] the quality of learning' (Sutton 1995: 69).

In many lessons, for example when pupils are 'on task', the time the teacher needs to engineer flexible assessment is there for the taking. What we think Sutton refers to is reducing the amount of whole class teaching; that is, she advocates sacrificing 'direct instruction' in favour of more individualised or small group interaction, including the teacher simply listening to the pupils at work. What we suggest here is that the teacher becomes conscious of moving role, from classroom 'cocktail waiter' ('serving' the pupils on demand) to professional coach, adviser or mentor, when most pupils may have to become independent of the teacher (and hands up will be ignored for a time), for he or she is busy with an individual or small group.

FOR FURTHER THINKING

1. How can marking in your school be successfully differentiated, and what benefits would this bring in relation to developing formative assessment?
2. With a group of subject specialist colleagues, identify a list of what might be termed 'big concepts' in your subject, ones which may be revisited often even in different content or topic areas of the teaching programme. (There may be literature in your subject area which helps you do this – for example, in geography, Leat (1998).) To what extent are these helpful in enabling you to focus your marking and identify next steps for the learner?

3.   In what ways can the pupils themselves be more involved in marking processes? What preparations need to be made if pupils are to be regularly involved in marking each other's work?

WHAT CAN TEACHERS DO TO ENSURE MAXIMUM FAIRNESS?

It is perhaps an article of faith that educational assessment should be conducted in ways that are fair to all individuals and groups. However, to understand what this means, let alone undertake actions to ensure that such a good intention is seen through in practice, takes considerable conscious mental effort. We have seen earlier in this book that bias and equity are complex problems resulting in strenuous efforts, for example on the part of external examinations agencies, to mitigate various sources of unfairness in the resulting test scores. But it is worth noting (again) the conclusion drawn by the authors of a large scale study of fairness in educational assessment:

> By now it should be clear that there is no such thing as a fair test, nor could there be: the situation is too complex and the notion too simplistic. However, by paying attention to what we know about factors in assessment and their administration and scoring, we can begin to work towards tests that are more fair to all groups likely to be taking them, and this is particularly important for assessment used for summative and accountability purposes.
>
> (Gipps and Murphy 1994: 273–274)

The final point in this quote is significant. It is implied that tackling these difficult issues may not be quite so important in the context of classroom assessment as it is in the field of external assessment. This is for a number of reasons. First, external, summative assessments have high stakes attached to them, whereas classroom FA is of low stake, more a form of conversation between teacher and pupil getting to know each other. Following from this, FA is usually less formal than assessment undertaken for summative purposes, enabling more 'negotiation' to take place; FA is always provisional to a certain extent. Third, because of the low stakes and informality associated with FA, together with its main purpose to be put to use in the classroom, any action taken on the basis of the teacher's judgement of a pupil can easily be changed if it were found that the judgement was misleading or wrong. Conversely, an experienced teacher may be able to infer from the slightest evidence that a pupil has grasped a certain skill or concept and quite correctly move on (subject to accepting the possibility that things might change): that is to say, there is no need to endure all sorts of elaborate procedures to ensure reliable and fair results, as has to be done in the external examinations industry for example (see Chapters 2 and 4 of this book).

On the other hand, the same informality and 'private' nature of FA, identified above as sources of reassurance against possible threats to equity, could also be seen as dangers. Formative assessment is almost by definition subjective. Unless the teacher is aware of possible *between groups* and *individual* bias in the way pupils respond to questions, there is the possibility that the use of FA will serve to confirm, strengthen or exacerbate certain assumptions or judgements made about pupils which may not be fair. Figure 9.11 provides a brief summary of the possible ways in which questions may be unfair to different pupils or groups of pupils. In addition to being alert to such dangers, teachers undertaking classroom assessments must also be aware of the potential for bias to reside in themselves (not just in the questions or in the characteristics of the pupils). That is, in the way they interpret how the pupils have responded. As Black explains,

> There is evidence of teachers behaving differently towards boys and girls, towards pupils from different social classes, and towards good looking and plain-looking pupils. In each of these cases, some teachers would rate a particular piece of work more highly if it came from one type of pupil rather than the other.
>
> (Black 1998: 115)

Of course it could be argued that one positive outcome of good FA is to reduce such bias, for deep knowledge of individuals counteracts stereotypical or superficial judgements. The problem for the teacher is to remain as open as possible and avoid the temptation to *pre*judge. A provocative (but not scientific) experiment to undertake with a group of subject specialists can easily illustrate the problem (see box below).

AN EXPERIMENT IN MARKING FOR A GROUP OF TRAINEE TEACHERS

- Run this experiment with a group of colleagues 'cold' – do not prepare the group.
- Photocopy in sufficient numbers an essay (or if time a range of essays).
- Write a name, chosen from the list below, on the top of each copy.
- Distribute the essay(s) and give the group five minutes to mark it on a 1–10 scale.
- Ask the group to feed back their marks for you to tabulate and display (even at this stage the group does not know that they have been marking the same essay).

The question for discussion is: Did the name on the essay influence the marking outcome? It may be possible to identify presumed gender, class and ethnicity as possible influences.

Boys	Girls
Chris	Toni
Gary	Sharon
Tim	Gemma
Darren	Bianca
William	Anne
Elvis	Tammy
Tariq	Fathom
Shane	Mel

(A fuller version of this activity can be found in Lambert (1999: 310–313)).

What we may conclude from such an experiment, which often (though not invariably, depending on the essay chosen) shows some names get better marks than others, is that using marking criteria linked to certain learning objectives helps teachers avoid prejudgements – but that the temptation to make judgements based upon such thin 'evidence' as a name is indeed surprisingly powerful.

Thus in the kinds of classrooms we have been advocating in this chapter teachers have to be aware of, and be prepared to act systemmatically to avoid, the myriad ways in which human relationships can be managed unfairly: boys demanding (and receiving) more attention than girls; compliant pupils displaying industry and effort being rewarded with good achievement marks (whether deserved or not); different expectations of pupils contaminating the teacher's response to them. In relation to this last point, there is a history of differential expectations in the UK which helps provide perspective to the depth of this problem. For example, Cohen writes of a long standing and deep seated prejudice against girls' achievement:

> Thus if little girls were quicker and generally more advanced than boys of the same age, this was not because they were cleverer. On the contrary, it was because boys were thoughtful and deep that they were slow and appeared dull: 'gold sparkles less than tinsel'.
>
> By the closing decades of the 19th century, conspicuous dullness, the sign of the upperclass boy's incommensurable potential, placed him at the apex of evolution, and distinguished him not just from all girls but from bright and expressive lower-class boys.
>
> (Cohen 1998: 25)

Possible sources of unfairness in assessment

- The context may favour a particular group. For example, the context of mechanical devices or engines almost certainly favours most boys; the majority of girls seem to prefer contexts involving people and human experience.
- The task design may also have bias, most boys being happier with abstract questions than girls who usually prefer questions with more direct personal implications.
- In general, boys seem to score better than girls on multiple choice tests, while girls do better on essay type questions. One reason for this could be that boys are more likely to guess when they are unsure of an answer, whereas girls hold fire.
- Coursework for external examinations is said to favour girls more than boys, possibly because it benefits from more careful or thorough completion.
- Some questions are only intelligible in certain cultural or social contexts – teachers may have to be careful not to assume that western, suburban, white, middle class 'norms' are equally understood by all pupils in socially and culturally diverse classrooms.
- Some questions may test the pupil's ability to decode the teacher's use of English rather than encourage the pupil to show what he or she knows, understands and can do.

Note that points such as these suggest a range of 'between groups' differences. We have tried to express these carefully, being aware that within group differences actually may be as great if not greater than those between groups. That is to say (for example), it would be crude and absurd to suggest that *all* boys do better in multiple choice tests than *all* girls!

Figure 9.11 The possible ways in which questions can be unfair to different pupils or groups of pupils (see also Chapter 2)

Source: adapted from Black (1998: 50).

It is interesting that the rather belated concern in the late 1990s about 'boys' underachievement' is even now usually expressed not in absolute terms but to do with 'falling behind' girls (at least in terms of GCSE results).

The quotation above leads us to an even more difficult issue, namely to do with 'ability' (also discussed briefly in Chapter 8, p. 143). To what extent are the informal assessments made by teachers influenced by opinions about a pupil's 'ability' rather than strictly on evidence of achievement? To what extent, therefore, are teachers (and perhaps pupils and parents) still in the shadow of the post-war British fixation with 'IQ' (a person's 'intelligence quotient')? The problem with using 'ability' or fixed 'intelligence' too readily to judge achievement is that it assumes that pupils' varied response to teaching is virtually predetermined. If this assumption prevails then teachers can only conclude that they can do little or nothing to cause the pupils to improve. Thus, pupils' potential is predetermined too. Labelling children too rigidly according to their 'ability' is perhaps the most damaging unfairness of all, and runs counter to the goals of formative classroom assessment.

FOR FURTHER THINKING

As we have seen (p. 170) Gipps and Murphy (1994) assert that there is no such thing as a 'fair test'. In effect we have been arguing in this section that there is also no such thing as 'fair teaching' (i.e. fair classroom assessment), and for the same reason: the complexities are too great. However, like Gipps and Murphy, this should not stop us from self-consciously striving to be as fair as possible. There are little tests that we can give ourselves to keep us on our toes in this respect. For example, for a class you teach:

- From memory, list the names of every pupil in the class down the left hand side of a piece of A4.
- Now check against the class list. Who was missing? Is there anything significant about the order in which the names tumbled out of your head?
- Now try to write one sentence against each name about the *individual as a learner in your subject*.
- For how many names has this proved too difficult? In what ways is this significant?

This food-for-thought task was stimulated by the telling remark that all classrooms contain pupils made up of 'the good, the bad and the missing' (Sutton 1995) – not physically missing, but missing from the teacher's consciousness.

CONCLUSION: DIVERSITY IS THE KEY

This chapter has discussed in detail the *implications* of adopting a meaningful formative assessment regime. Whilst it is in some ways insidious to suggest we can simmer the whole discussion down to a few headlines or bullet points, we do feel that fundamentally it is that simple. Though the theoretical and practical issues associated with teaching and learning styles, day-to-day marking processes and the crucial questions concerning the equity of our procedures and approaches are indeed complex, at the heart of the matter lies one rather obvious conclusion: that *diversity* is the key operational touchstone to guide effective classroom assessment.

Obvious maybe, but until recently *uniformity* seemed to be the quality that characterised so many secondary schools in Britain. One reason for this may have been that although it may be simple to accept diversity in principle, the implications of doing so are, as we have seen, multifaceted and require a flexible response from the level of the individual teacher to the level of the whole system.

If we accept pupil diversity as our starting point – diverse abilities and capacities of various kinds, diverse approaches to learning, diverse conceptions of what the learning process entails, diverse ways of expression and communication and diverse ways in which we teachers may inadvertently disadvantage a person or whole group – then what we must also accept is that our teaching repertoire should be as wide as we can possibly extend it. Teachers with extensive repertoires can make choices about how to approach a topic, and furthermore have alternatives for when the chosen strategy fails (as it sometimes does). Choices can be made on the basis of fitness for purpose: What am I trying to achieve? How can I best get there?

Such a simple (but challenging) notion is becoming widely accepted. Take, for example, the US National Forum on Assessment (NFA) which includes in its *Criteria for Evaluation of Student Assessment Systems*:

- to ensure fairness, students should have multiple opportunities to meet standards and should be able to meet them in different ways;

> (NFA 1992: 32, cited in Stobart and Gipps 1997: 59)

Nobody expects *equality of outcome* to result from extending variety to teaching learning and assessment practices, but it is thought to be the way to ensure genuine *equality of access* to the curriculum and support pupils to reach their potential. For some, this may require lifting their expectations of themselves.

What we conclude is that maximising opportunities to learn for all pupils is the clear implication of integrating formative assessment into classroom teaching. To achieve such a result, however, requires careful executive thought and action on the part of teachers in order to raise the validity of the assessment process. Validity in this context is taken to mean 'consequential validity' (similar to 'unitary validity' introduced in Chapter 2), *the* key concept of Chapters 7–9 of this book. Paul Black summarises this term as a measure of 'whether the inferences and actions based on a test result can be justified' (Black 1998: 54). Earlier in this book (p. 132) we took a slightly broader view, implying that the validity of undertaking an assessment could be determined by *whether* consequences of educational value flowed from it. Combining these definitions provides a very powerful concept, akin to 'fitness for purpose', which can be used to drive incisive, critical reflection on our evolving classroom practice.

FOR FURTHER THINKING

Read this statement:

> The close interaction between assessment practices and learning
> practices means that the validity of assessments is linked to models of
> learning used in pedagogy.
>
> (Black 1998: 55)

1. Using direct observations of your own teaching practice, or of teachers
    you have observed at work, identify examples of two contrasting class-
    room assessment practices:

    (a) One that has in your view a high level of validity in the terms
         set out in the quotation
    (b) One that has a relatively low level of validity in these terms.

2. Keep a tally of the kinds of assessment opportunities you manage to
    plan and implement during your block teaching practice. Attempt an
    evaluation of each one in terms of its consequential validity and fitness
    for purpose.

FOR FURTHER READING

P. Black (1998) *Testing: Friend or Foe? Theory and Practice in Assessment and
Testing*. This is a rich resource which forms an invaluable reference to dip
into regularly, particularly for many of the complex conceptual issues
involved in any serious discussion of assessment. As the title suggests it overtly
tries to link theory and practice. It takes a balanced and undogmatic stance.

M. James (1998) *Using Assessment for School Improvement*. This book is
written from the perspective of using assessment to support learning in the
context of what has become known as 'school improvement'. It certainly
helps raise questions about what we might understand by 'improvement':
of what? for whom?

C. Gipps and P. Murphy (1994) *A Fair Test? Assessment, Achievement and
Equity*. This is still an excellent, full discussion of the tricky and difficult to
resolve issues around bias in assessment. It has a comprehensive review of
relevant literature on the subject.

For readers interested in following up some of the ideas mentioned earlier
in this chapter concerning learning, here are two good sources: P. Honey
and A. Mumford (1992) *The Manual of Learning Styles* and D. Kolb (1985)
Learning Style Inventory.

10 Teacher Assessment: A Case Study

ASSESSMENT IN EDUCATION AND EDUCATIONAL ASSESSMENT: ACROSS THE TWO CULTURES

The concluding chapters of this book are designed to synthesise the preceding discussions into a coherent whole. Even to attempt such a thing is of course a major challenge. We proceed by introducing in Chapter 10 a case study of National Curriculum 'Teacher Assessment' for one subject at Key Stage 3. In so doing we explore approaches by which the assessment apparatus of 'level descriptions' designed for summative purposes, can be used to support formative assessment practice. As we have stressed throughout the book, this is not to say that so-called 'teacher assessment' is necessarily formative simply because it is carried out by teachers, but we will show how it could become so. Thus, to borrow the terminology used by the Assessment Reform Group (1999), we suggest that the adoption of certain kinds of classroom processes may enable teachers to assess for learning, *whilst using the structures which have been devised for the assessment* of learning.

Chapter 11 concludes by acknowledging the self-evident importance of assessment in education, but also by emphasising that relatively little of it is in fact educational. We therefore advocate sustained grass-roots efforts by teachers to shape and direct assessment practice with clear educational goals, noting Caroline Gipps' (1994) criteria for developing 'educational assessment'. The key point of these chapters is arguably the key point of the whole book, that there are two very distinct 'cultures' of assessment in education: on the one hand there is external sum-mative assessment, and on the other there is classroom-based formative assessment. The former dominates the public discourse, consumes significant resources and is highly influential in comparison with the latter which has tended to be marginalised and not fully understood, partly as a result of confusion over the competing purposes of assessment in education.

SUMMATIVE PURPOSE AND FORMATIVE PRACTICE

In this chapter we discuss in some detail how Teacher Assessment (TA) in one National Curriculum subject (geography) can be configured in such a way that the two assessment cultures identified in this book can be served. This should be read like a case study which will have applications to other subject areas, although of course there will be particular aspects to the story which will vary, sometimes substantially, between subjects.

TEACHER ASSESSMENT IN GEOGRAPHY (KS3)

Geography is a foundation subject in the National Curriculum. Teachers of geography are required to report a National Curriculum Level for every pupil at the end of Year 9 (the end of Key Stage 3). No external tests are used to determine levels. Thus, teachers undertake this statutory duty by a process of Teacher Assessment. Teacher Assessment (TA) is a term which is relatively new, as it does not pre-date the introduction of the National Curriculum in England and Wales. The Task Group on Assessment and Testing (TGAT), which was convened in 1987 in order to advise the government on a national assessment system with which to underpin the new curriculum under the 1988 Education Reform Act (see Chapter 2), introduced TA as a technical term. It is vital to understand that TA does not refer to the assessment of teachers, but to assessments undertaken *by* teachers – originally, to complement external National Curriculum test scores. As we have seen, there was confusion about the main purpose it was meant to serve; as direct classroom assessment it had great formative potential but this was crowded out by its need to contribute to the summative reporting of National Curriculum Levels.

A term was needed which would describe the part played in National Curriculum assessment not defined by external tests (the so-called 'standard assessment tasks' or 'SATs'). The model chosen by TGAT was an ambitious and some would say enlightened one involving a *combination* of externally set and marked tests and tasks with classroom judgements made directly by teachers. It is the latter that the Task Group referred to as TA. The TGAT overtly recognised the distinctive formative and summative functions of assessment, but proposed a single national assessment system which would fulfil both purposes. TA was in many ways the key to the successful implementation of the proposed system (which was accepted by the government of the day), being the vehicle for carrying forward a number of cherished principles clearly spelt out by the group. For example:

> The assessment process itself should not determine what is to be taught and learned. It should be the servant, not the master, of the curriculum. Yet it should not simply be a bolt-on addition at the end. Rather, it should be an integral part of the education process,

continually providing both 'feedback' and 'feedforward'. It therefore needs to be incorporated systematically into teaching strategies and practices at all levels. Since the results of assessment can serve a number of different purposes, these purposes have to be kept in mind when the arrangements for assessment are designed.

(DES/WO, 1988: para 4)

This is not to say that the proposal was for a simple division between formative assessment (undertaken by TA) and summative assessment (undertaken by SATs). The final sentence above is a telling one, implying that any assessment can be used in different ways. We certainly agree that assessment does not become formative just because it is carried out by teachers: it depends on the teacher's intentions and how he or she will use the assessment. The idea that the TGAT seemed to suggest was that assessments used primarily for summative purposes may also, if designed carefully enough, be used formatively (though it is harder to see such crossover working in the other direction).

We do not have the space here to provide a detailed history of National Curriculum assessment and geography. Suffice it to say that the TGAT proposals were never fully implemented. They were complex and sophisticated and caused severe technical problems, especially for the SAT developers. We will outline some of these problems as they affected geography in our case study below, but as we have already observed in this book, it has been argued (Daugherty 1995) that the fundamental flaw in the TGAT proposals was indeed the confusion of purpose. In short, a single assessment system was being asked to do too much, fufil too many diverse needs. There is perhaps a lesson here for the gathering enthusiasm for 'value added' procedures and processes in schools and colleges (see Chapter 4): we should be wary of relying too heavily on a single mechanism and be aware of its differential impact between, for example, the level of individual students and institutions. In the case of the National Curriculum assessment, the single system was originally asked to fulfil needs so different that failure was perhaps inevitable. On the other hand, this does not necessarily mean that processes designed for summative purposes have no formative potential.

The present case study takes as its starting point the simple 'fact of life' that teachers need to engage with both. They must use summative assessment structures (in this case the National Curriculum level descriptions) and for educational reasons they must also engage in formative assessment. How do we square this circle?

To begin with we need to know something about the subject in question, geography. Figure 10.1 provides a basic summary of geography as a subject in the National Curriculum, and Figure 10.2 reproduces in full the level descriptions appropriate to the vast majority of KS3 pupils (i.e. levels 3 to 7). From these details we can gain an impression of the subject which is, like most others, broad and multifaceted, but with several particular features; in the case of geography these include a concern with understanding environmental issues

---

Geography in the National Curriculum
What kind of subject is geography?

- Geography consists of a single attainment target, 'geography'.
- Though widely considered to be one of the 'humanities' geography has links with many subjects across the curriculum including science (especially physical geography) and the arts (especially human geography).
- The level descriptions for geography (see Figure 10.2) contain the following strands describing progress and achievement:

  - ability to undertake geographical enquiry (enquiry skills);
  - knowledge and understanding of places;
  - knowledge and understanding of patterns and processes;
  - knowledge and understanding of environmental relationships and issues.

- Geography is often considered to be a 'content rich' subject, implying a heavy emphasis on knowledge: people and places, or as it is sometimes stated 'capes and bays'.
- As the level descriptions suggest, though knowledge is important it is no more so than the understanding of processes and the application principles.
- The skills base of geography is wide, including the development of intellectual skills subsumed under 'enquiry'.

Figure 10.1 A summary sketch of geography in the National Curriculum

(which are usually controversial and require analysis of values dimensions), the development of enquiry skills and the acquisition of certain kinds of knowledge (e.g. of places) which contributes to pupils' cultural literacy.

It is worth noting, because it is directly relevant to the present discussion, that the first version of the National Curriculum, introduced in schools in 1991, had to be revised radically partly as a result of assessment problems. One of the principles laid down by TGAT was that assessment had to be criteria referenced and that consequently the subjects, including geography, were articulated in terms of 'attainment targets' (of which there were originally five in 1991, reduced to one in the 1995 revision). These were specified in detail by so-called 'statements of attainment' (SoA) which tried to define the levels of attainment. In the case of geography, which the government of the day wished to express and emphasise as 'content rich' (see Lambert 1996), most SoA were written in terms of knowledge acquisition. For example, at level 6, pupils would need to show that they could 'Compare the general features of the USA, USSR and Japan' (DES 1991). This was just one of 184 such SoA. We have chosen this one (but could have chosen many others) because it shows rather clearly the technical problems which contributed to the need for urgent revision to the curriculum in 1995. Incidentally, it also shows rather well the danger of expressing educational achievement in knowledge acquisition terms: no sooner was this specification published (1991) than the 'USSR' disintegrated! The technical problems can be expressed as questions:

- What makes this SoA level 6? Why couldn't this statement be level 4, or level 8? We can presumably compare countries at *any* of these levels! But what would distinguish, say, a level 4 description from one at level 6?
- What exactly are 'general features'? Do we need additional criteria to help pin down and specify this?

We discussed criteria referencing in a number of locations in this book, and have shown that although attractive in many ways this approach to assessment probably cannot exist in a 'pure form'. There is a 'Holy Grail' quality to assessment criteria: we can never specify them exactly enough to be absolutely water tight about their meaning. In the case of the 1991 geography National Curriculum nearly 200 statements of attainment (to all intents and purposes, assessment criteria) could not convincingly express progress and advancing attainment through the levels. Attempts to produce external tests that could assess pupils' attainment against them failed. In the meantime, teachers were led to believe they needed to assemble evidence on them all, for every child they taught, for the purposes of teacher assessment. This was impossible and it became increasingly clear that even to try was meaningless: it had the effect of disaggregating achievement into little separate pieces – a particularly damaging effect in geography, a subject whose position on the formal curriculum is often justified in terms of its ability to bridge and synthesise across the disparate 'arts–science' divide.

The 1995 revision of the National Curriculum geography abolished SoA, reduced the content load and produced eight level descriptions (with an additional one to describe outstanding achievement), five of which are shown in Figure 10.2. Any thought of external summative testing was dropped and so it was left to Teacher Assessment alone to provide a summative level for each pupil. The School Curriculum and Assessment Authority (SCAA, later to become QCA) produced exemplification materials (SCAA 1996) which proved popular and helpful to teachers, using the analysis of children's work to indicate standards at different levels. The methodology teachers were encouraged to adopt was to take each pupil's work in the round and make a 'best fit' judgement against the level descriptions. That is to say, it was accepted that the level descriptions were:

- general; and
- could not be used in a hard and fast manner.

Attainment target for geography

Level 3

Pupils show their knowledge, skills and understanding in studies at a local scale. They describe and compare the physical and human features of different localities and offer explanations for the locations of some of those features. They are aware that different places may have both similar and different characteristics. They offer reasons for some of their observations and for their views and judgements about places and environments. They recognise how people seek to improve and sustain environments. They use skills and sources of evidence to respond to a range of geographical questions, and begin to use appropriate vocabulary to communicate their findings.

Level 4

Pupils show their knowledge, skills and understanding in studies of a range of places and environments at more than one scale and in different parts of the world. They begin to recognise and describe geographical patterns and to appreciate the importance of wider geographical location in understanding places. They recognise and describe physical and human processes. They begin to understand how these can change the features of places, and how these changes affect the lives and activities of people living there. They understand how people can both improve and damage the environment. They explain their own views and the views that other people hold about an environmental change. Drawing on their knowledge and understanding, they suggest suitable geographical questions, and use a range of geographical skills from the key stage 2 or 3 programme of study to help them investigate places and environments. They use primary and secondary sources of evidence in their investigations and communicate their findings using appropriate vocabulary.

Level 5

Pupils show their knowledge, skills and understanding in studies of a range of places and environments at more than one scale and in different parts of the world. They describe and begin to explain geographical patterns and physical and human processes. They describe how these processes can lead to similarities and differences in the environments of different places and in the lives of people who live there. They recognise some of the links and relationships that make places dependent on each other. They suggest explanations for the ways in which human activities cause changes to the environment and the different views people hold about them. They recognise how people try to manage environments sustainably. They explain their own views and begin to suggest relevant geographical questions and issues. Drawing on their knowledge and understanding, they select and use appropriate skills and ways of presenting information from the key stage 2 or 3 programme of study to help them investigate places

Figure 10.2 Level descriptions for geography at KS3 (levels 3–7)

and environments. They select information and sources of evidence, suggest plausible conclusions to their investigations and present their findings both graphically and in writing.

Level 6

Pupils show their knowledge, skills and understanding in studies of a wide range of places and environments at various scales, from local to global, and in different parts of the world. They describe and explain a range of physical and human processes and recognise that these processes interact to produce the distinctive characteristics of places. They describe ways in which physical and human processes operating at different scales create geographical patterns and lead to changes in places. They appreciate the many links and relationships that make places dependent on each other. They recognise how conflicting demands on the environment may arise and describe and compare different approaches to managing environments. They appreciate that different values and attitudes, including their own, result in different approaches that have different effects on people and places. Drawing on their knowledge and understanding, they suggest relevant geographical questions and issues and appropriate sequences of investigation. They select a range of skills and sources of evidence from the key stage 3 programme of study and use them effectively in their investigations. They present their findings in a coherent way and reach conclusions that are consistent with the evidence.

Level 7

Pupils show their knowledge, skills and understanding in studies of a wide range of places and environments at various scales, from local to global, and in different parts of the world. They describe interactions within and between physical and human processes, and show how these interactions create geographical patterns and help change places and environments. They understand that many factors, including people's values and attitudes, influence the decisions made about places and environments, and use this understanding to explain the resulting changes. They appreciate that the environment in a place and the lives of the people who live there are affected by actions and events in other places. They recognise that human actions, including their own, may have unintended environmental consequences and that change sometimes leads to conflict. They appreciate that considerations of sustainable development affect the planning and management of environments and resources. With growing independence, they draw on their knowledge and understanding to identify geographical questions and issues and establish their own sequence of investigation. They select and use accurately a wide range of skills from the key stage 3 programme of study. They evaluate critically sources of evidence, present well-argued summaries of their investigations and begin to reach substantiated conclusions.

Figure 10.2 (continued)

In other words, it would not be possible (let alone desirable) to 'prove' that child X was at level 4 or that child Y was at level 7. To try would be to fall into the SoA trap again – and chase 'evidence' for disaggregated bits of the level descriptions. The methodology was to keep the level descriptions *whole* and examine the child's attainment *as a whole*, using a range of assessment approaches from the formal to the informal. For this reason, it was understood that marking individual pieces of work using the level descriptions was ill-advised, for it was, according to the methodology, theoretically impossible: a single piece of work could not possibly 'cover' the four main strands of geographical attainment (see Figure 10.1) present in each level description.

All the same, some teachers have tried to mark work with levels. Probably the reason for this is the natural urge to use National Curriculum assessment transparently, in order to encourage pupils to gain a better understanding of what the levels are and how they express progress in geography. However, they are a far too blunt an instrument to be used in this way. If we accept the original TGAT hypothesis that ten levels could adequately cover the range of attainment across all aptitudes and abilities between the ages of 5 and 16 years, we can see that one level represents at least two years' progress for the individual pupil (on average). Thus, it is possible that a pupil could remain at (say) level 4 for the whole of Year 7 and 8, and possibly longer. This would not be especially motivating. Friendlier and more sensitive mechanisms must be found for assessing pupils' work formatively (see Chapter 9 on 'marking').

We are not saying that level descriptions do not have a formative potential, however. In essence, the formative capacity of the level descriptions lies in their potential to clarify, first among teachers of geography and second among pupils, certain criteria for describing progess in geography. If they can provide a shared basis for

- articulating feedback and feedforward between teachers and pupils; and
- promoting self-assessment among pupils

then, as we have seen in Chapters 7–9, they could become a powerful ally in a quest to develop a formative assessment strategy.

The realisation that in order for level descriptions to perform their summative role teachers *need* to generate such a shared understanding of what they mean and how they can be intepreted, simply serves to strengthen the case being made here. To expect the standards to be defined by others or imposed by a central agency is, as we have seen, akin to the search for the Holy Grail. What is needed is some kind of mechanism so that teachers (at least those in the same geography department, but ultimately between schools as well) are able to examine the standards expressed by the level descriptions in relation to the work produced by the pupils they teach. They will argue about the work, how it should be interpreted and what range of evidence is required to make dependable level judgements. Guidance (such as SCAA 1996) can help, but there is no short cut to this process. It is important to understand

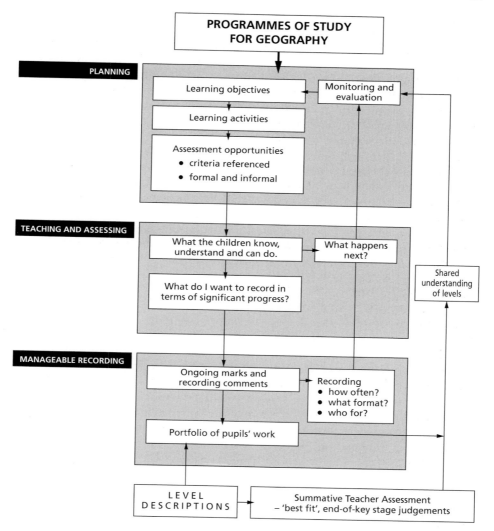

Figure 10.3 The place of teacher assessment in KS3 geography
Source: Butt *et al.* (1995); see also Hopkins *et al.* (2000).

that it is a similar process to that which underpins external examination moderation procedures: looking at the evidence within the framework of general criteria and agreeing a judgement concerning its value. Stobart and Gipps argue that such activity should now form an essential part of every teacher's professional development:

> The teacher must remain central to assessment, which itself is grounded in a 'local' context which allows flexibility of approach.

Rigour can be maintained by reporting against national standards and using external moderation.

(Stobart and Gipps 1997: 110)

What we are arguing is that the processes underpinning such professional judgement not only serve the needs of summative teacher assessment (TA), but are also essential in providing the basis for subject-specific and effective formative assessment. Figure 10.3 shows how the Geographical Association (GA) articulated this idea – at least in part – to its members soon after the 1995 revised National Curriculum was introduced. This simplified model shows a feedback loop which takes intelligence concerning the strengths and weaknesses contained in pupils' work back to influence lesson planning: assessment directly influencing teaching programme. As we shall see below, albeit only implicit in the GA's model, this intelligence also provides the basis for surefooted, subject-specific intervention with the pupils themselves.

The assessment mechanism recommended to serve such diverse needs was described as the departmental or 'standards portfolio'.

PRODUCING KS3 'STANDARDS PORTFOLIOS'

This section explains the concept of standards portfolios and how they have been used as part of the initial training of teachers. It rests heavily on the instructions given to secondary geography PGCE students midway through their first period of practical teaching experience. In advance of introducing the task whereby each student teacher produces a portfolio, sessions are held on the principles of formative assessment and in particular on the practice of marking pupils' work. The task itself, from its inception to its conclusion in the form of a 'moderation' meeting, is staged over a period of approximately half a term. It encourages school-based collaboration between the student teachers and their subject mentors in selecting pupils' work. Indeed, school subject mentors are invited to the moderation of standards portfolios as this is a unique opportunity to look at standards from a large number of partner schools across the region. In essence the task is to compile a folder of photocopied work chosen from different pupils and illustrating a balanced range of topics and tasks. The folder, taken as a whole, aims to illustrate through the selection of pupils' work the standards at two particular levels. Student teachers are advised to concentrate on either levels 3 and 5, or levels 5 and 7 (see Figure 10.4); in either case, when applying the 'best fit' methodology, student teachers have to deal with five level descriptions in order fully to make their judgements. In addition student teachers are given a further guidance sheet (Figure 10.5).

Selecting pupils' work to include in a standards portfolio is a tricky task, but one that appears to be highly valued by student teachers and their subject mentors, because it extends and deepens their ability to analyse pupils' work and progress. Another outcome of the moderation meeting is much authentic

Your standards portfolio: steps to follow

You decide (in your tutor group) two levels on which to concentrate – 3/5 or 5/7.

Your analysis of the levels will enable you to identify a 'shopping list' of indicators to help you judge pupils appropriately. Each level contains reference to four strands of geography – and the shopping list should include evidence of attainment for all of these:

- ability to undertake geographical enquiry (enquiry skills);
- knowledge and understanding of places;
- knowledge and understanding of patterns and processes; and
- knowledge and understanding of environmental relationships and issues.

Assemble a range of pupils' work that in your considered view exemplifies *each* of your chosen standards (level 3 and 5; or 5 and 7) with reference to the four strands.

You need to consider the following practical points:

- How is a portfolio presented? (a ring binder is suitable).
- Do you select real work or photocopies of it for inclusion in the portfolio?
- How much work needs to be selected – how voluminous is a portfolio?
- What is a 'piece of work'? What kinds of work can a portfolio *not* show?
- How many different pupils should be used?

There are further technical points to consider:

- How do you show the *context* of the work? (when it was done, what help was given, what resources were available (etc.)) because all this affects the assessment of it.
- How do you show how the work was assessed? – how you justify your valuation of it. Clear, analytical annotation of the work seems essential.

Figure 10.4 Standards portfolios: instructions to PGCE students

---

Assembling a standards portfolio of pupils' work
Further guidance

- A piece of 'work' is a completed task of some kind; it may be a single homework or a more lengthy task representing several lessons' work.
- Work from three or four pupils may suffice; but it is the work, not the pupils, that the portfolio exhibits.
- Once pieces have been put into a portfolio, they are non-returnable to the pupils; photocopying can get over this problem – each portfolio must not become too voluminous, so the copying should not be prohibitive. To get pupils to complete a 'best draft' is also a possibility.
- The portfolio is meant to be indicative, not a document of 'proof'. It needs to be digestible and its contents easily accessed. It must not become too large therefore and experience indicates that about six to eight 'pieces of work' is appropriate.
- When selected each piece of work needs detailed (but not copious) annotation in clear handwriting (green or red pen – whichever colour you choose, use it consistently), focused on *what the work shows* and *what it fails to show* in terms of elements of the level description.
- Each piece of work needs a completed context sheet (see Figure 10.6). This helps other teachers 'read' the work and understand your assessment of it; increasing such transferability ultimately contributes to increasing *dependability* of assessments. It also forces the issue of how to advise the author of that work to improve.

Figure 10.5 Standards portfolio: further guidance given to PGCE students

debate about the utility of various kinds of annotation ('marking') of pupils' work, and what counts as precise and subject specific feedback. Several sudent teachers also see the potential of adapting the portfolio concept in various ways, for example, by asking the pupils themselves to make selections of their own work according to carefully adapted criteria based on the level descriptions.

As we saw in Chapter 8, research shows that formative assessment is successful when it involves new ways to enhance feedback – requiring significant changes in classroom practice, encouraging active involvement of pupils, especially in self-assessment. As we also saw, this is no 'quick fix'. It is not easy to achieve, especially in the broader context of pressure – from senior management, parents and the pupils themselves – to concentrate effort solely on summative 'results'. The research shows that there are also traps awaiting the unwary; enthusiastic teachers who may introduce formative processes a little carelessly may, for example:

Annotation of children's work samples

- Subject ....   Date ....
- Topic/Unit ....   PoS ref: ....

- Context (description of learning activity; degree of support)

- Who chose this piece of work? ....

- What does this piece show?
  (why has it been selected?)

- What (if anything) does this piece fail to demonstrate?

- Next steps:

Figure 10.6 Standards portfolio 'context sheet'

- provide too much generous unfocused praise which can be unhelpful to pupils; and
- set and mark too many teachers' tests which encourage surface learning.

In addition, it has been found that

- classrooms, even in the same department, are often 'black boxes' with little sharing of practice; and that
- the quantity and presentation of work tends to be overemphasised.

Furthermore,

- marks and grades are sometimes grossly overemphasised to the detriment of encouraging pupils to analyse strengths and weaknesses; this also
- encourages in pupils the comparison of marks (not personal improvement).

Meanwhile,

- teachers' feedback is often 'social and managerial' at the expense of learning functions; and
- while teachers can often predict external examination results accurately – this may simply indicate that they understand the *tests* but possess less understanding of *learning needs*. Sometimes this seems to have resulted from
- too much focus on the collection of marks which outweighs the analysis of pupils' learning needs.

We believe that assembling and maintaining standards portfolios can help counter some of these potential pitfalls.

FOR FURTHER THINKING

Take each of the bullet pointed 'traps' for the unwary, which signpost some of the difficulties encountered in introducing effective formative assessment.

In relation to the assembly and maintenance of a standards portfolio, discuss how they may be countered.

In what ways do standards portfolios support

1. summative assessment, and
2. formative assessment?

11 Issues in Assessment: Summary Discussion

This chapter sets out to provide the synthesis and summary promised on page 175. Though generic and largely conducted on the level of principle, the chapter draws from the case study presented in Chapter 10.

ASSESSMENT IN EDUCATION AND EDUCATIONAL STANDARDS

Assessment in education is required to serve many diverse purposes. Some of these can be regarded as mutually incompatible: for example, a simple, reliable assessment system designed to select pupils for Higher Education cannot easily also serve the purpose of providing valid diagnosis of individual learning difficulties. We have broadly distinguished in this book two 'cultures' of assessment to a large extent based upon differences of function: first, the external, overwhelmingly summative assessment 'industry' and second, the classroom-based assessment undertaken by teachers, which has formative potential. We have argued throughout that both are necessary. However, they:

- fulfil entirely different purposes;
- are valued unequally by the system; and
- co-exist in conditions of tension.

This book argues that all teachers need to understand such conditions of co-existence of the two cultures, for they are in a position to mediate the system in a fair and effective way for the maximum benefit of their pupils. They need to appreciate fully the impact and implications of assessment undertaken to fulfil different purposes, because such professional knowledge provides the basis for keeping the system as a whole in healthy balance.

External summative assessment is driven by the bureaucratic needs of the system, which requires that students are graded for various reasons, including selection. It is also used to provide data for those who judge the 'effectiveness' of teachers, schools and the system at large, at least in part, by the use of output measures. It therefore carries a high stake to it and, partly as a result of this, is characterised by elaborate processes to safeguard the reliability of the scores obtained. Furthermore, it is dominated (at least in the UK) by external agencies, again designed to safeguard the 'gold standard' of the public examination. The publication of examination results in league tables from the early 1990s served to raise the stakes still further and heightened in the minds of teachers, pupils and the public at large the association of standards with Key Stage tests and public examinations. It has long been recognised that such pressure can result in teaching (and learning) 'to the test', a process that can, if taken to extremes, be damaging – for example by encouraging surface learning at the expense of deep learning (Davis 1998, 1999). The notion of 'high stakes' operates at two levels at least: for the *individual* a high-stakes examination can be motivating, but when the stakes are raised at the *institutional* level pressures can be transferred 'down the line' in a way that can distort the curriculum experience (see for example, Stobart and Gipps 1997). The box below takes these points further in relation to the issue of raising standards in education.

RAISING STANDARDS

Anyone with a serious interest in education – teachers, pupils, parents, politicians, employers – is interested in raising standards. To this extent the phrase 'raising standards' is uncontroversial.

However, when we try to specify what the phrase means, and then how to measure standards, we move very quickly from calm and shallow waters into the deeper and more treacherous open sea.

In recent years, successive British governments have been unable to resist the temptation *to use external summative tests in an attempt to raise standards*. This can be considered especially problematic.

Davis (1999), for example, uses the term 'connectedness' to distinguish between deeper and more surface learning: 'I cannot be intelligently literate and numerate unless I have linked relevant knowledge and concepts in my mind' (p. 6). He goes on to argue that,

> written tests cannot properly assess the extent of candidates'
> 'connected' knowledge. They fail to discriminate between two
> categories of pupils:
> 1.   those who have 'learned up' particular sets of facts or specific
>   skills but who can only use them efficiently in examination
>   contexts, and
> 2.   those who are developing a richer, more connected knowledge,
>   in the light of which they can obtain satisfactory test scores.
>
> (*ibid.*: 7)

Thus, improving tests scores recorded for a school, an LEA or across the whole country, though clearly reflecting improved pupil performance in the tests, may provide misleading messages about standards – depending of course on what we think standards are. For example, unless we take steps to find out about the pupils as learners we may fail to help them develop 'a richer more connected knowledge'. Over-reliance on external summative assessment, or teaching to the test, is therefore a risky strategy to adopt to raise standards – again, depending on what we value as 'high standards'. To use Davis' words again:

> the description 'raising standards' . . . is not a synonym for improving examination performance. A competitive industrial economy needs employees who can both communicate and listen, make flexible and intelligent use of their knowledge and skills, work effectively with others and who are suitably motivated. These qualities cannot be tested by examinations. Indeed the pressure to improve test performance may reduce the likelihood of children developing these traits.
>
> (*ibid.*: 2)

As the box shows, the seemingly ubiquitous standards debate is shot through with values. What teachers value, in terms of the goals they adopt to help guide their executive thoughts and actions (see Chapter 9), really matters. Exactly how far it is possible to agree with Davis' analysis of the limitations of external examinations depends to a degree on the form and content of those examinations. But it also depends on the teachers' interventions, and how they interpret their role. Teachers are in a position to hold in check the potential of external tests to obliterate wider educational purposes, so long as they see their role as extending beyond preparing pupils only for the examinations.

Formative classroom assessment, on the other hand, has a lower profile than external examinations. It is motivated by the educational goal to improve learning (note the change of language here – learning, not standards). It happens in the classroom and is 'private' rather than 'public', being between the pupil and teacher (and sometimes parents). It is usually harder to summarise the 'results' of classroom assessment (it does not even have to result in a numerical score or grade) and is therefore difficult to use in a way to make 'odious comparisons' (Black 1998: 146). It has a low stake, therefore, and is less influenced by concerns of test reliability and comparisons of pupils than by the need to understand the learners as individuals, and to ensure that they also have growing awareness of themselves as learners. It takes place frequently during a teaching programme, using all kinds of evidence. Indeed, when operating properly it can be indistinguishable from teaching. It is, however, easier said than done, and, for reasons we discussed in Chapter 7, relatively hard to find in schools in a fully developed and effective form.

We have suggested on a number of occasions throughout this book that one of the reasons for the lack of development of formative assessment, with a focus on learning, is the priority given to high-stakes summative assessment in terms of funding, public accountability and political rhetoric. Preparing pupils by focusing on the examination or test has never in modern times been so prominent in the minds of teachers, pupils, parents and policy-makers. While this may result in a rise in examination scores in the short term, it also can have a substantial negative 'backwash effect' on the curriculum and pedagogy: as we noted in Chapter 8 more focused 'objectives led' teaching is arguably 'narrower' teaching too, and as we also discussed in Chapter 9, teaching to the test tends to encourage surface learning at the expense of deeper thinking. Teaching to the test, with all its emphasis on the threat of the final score, together with memorisation, repetitive practising of certain techniques, getting through the course and revision, militates against the inclination to use classroom space and time for softer, more individualised formative assessment.

And yet using lessons as formative assessment opportunities provides the teacher with evidence and information about how pupils are progressing, not only in relation to short-term lesson objectives but to broader, longer-term goals as well. Using formative assessment effectively can help teachers judge whether the teaching programme is sufficiently challenging, relevant and worthwhile, considerations that can easily fall off the agenda if the examination is allowed to become the sole motivation of teachers and pupils. We acknowledge that this is a difficult argument because there are those who would assert that good *examination results* are evidence enough of good teaching! This may well be the case, but it is not necessarily so. There are pupils who achieve good grades having overcome the obstacle of poor teaching; there are others who despite good grades still do not see themselves as knowledgeable and confident in the subject.

Assessment: of learning, and for learning. Another way of expressing the two main 'cultures' of assessment in education is to distinguish between the assessment *of* learning (external summative) and assessment *for* learning (formative classroom). As the Assessment Reform Group (ARG) maintains, the former dominates the latter, possibly to a damaging degree:

> A clear distinction should be made between assessment of learning for the purposes of grading and reporting, which has its own well-established procedures, and assessment for learning which call for different priorities, new procedures and a new commitment. In the recent past, policy priorities have arguably resulted in too much attention being given to finding reliable ways of comparing children, teachers and schools.
>
> (Assessment Reform Group [ARG] 1999: 2)

There is an important realisation lurking here, plain to see but one which seems to require enormous courage or ambition on the part of teachers *and pupils*, to act upon. If assessment for learning can be undertaken successfully, as the ARG urges, then surely we do not need to be too worried about the summative tests which assess the product of learning. Pupils who have been taught to be deeper, more confident thinkers, and who have learned more effectively, can surely achieve better test scores than otherwise they would have done. That is, 'raising standards' as measured by external tests is commensurate with, and does not work against, 'improving learning'. The ARG certainly think so, continuing,

> The important message now confronting the educational community is that assessment which is explicitly designed to promote learning is the single most powerful tool we have for both raising standards and empowering lifelong learners.
>
> (*ibid.*: 2)

The basis for making this statement is the research evidence to which we have referred frequently in this book. For instance, with reference to Black and Wiliam (1998a) the Group states that research has

> proved without a shadow of doubt that, when carried out effectively, informal classroom assessment with constructive feedback to the student will raise levels of achievement.
>
> (p. 1)

This is in stark contrast to another statement that '[t]here is no evidence that increasing the amount of testing will enhance learning.' (*ibid.*: 2).

It is unusual in the field of education that research can communicate such a clear, unambiguous message. We need to be careful, however, to ensure that we 'hear' this message accurately. Can assessment in education raise standards? Definitely, yes. Although testing may not always be able successfully to assess capacities such as the demonstration of connected knowledge (see box p. 192), certain standards *can* be assessed reliably by increasingly sophisticated examinations and testing procedures. But it is not *the testing process* that *raises* standards: remember the phrase we coined in Chapter 7 (p. 113) – 'weighing the baby does not make it grow'.

Of course, it is common sense for teachers to ensure that pupils know how to do tests and examinations: a certain amount of practice and coaching is sensible and most pupils can improve as a result. We can also agree with the other common-sense notion that a test helps some pupils improve because it can be motivating, though probably not to all pupils. But making good judgements about the qualities of pupils' work ('the assessment *of* learning'), useful in itself albeit providing only part of the picture, is not the same thing as *using* assessment to support future learning and thus raise achievement ('assessment *for* learning').

On the other hand, one of the consistent themes running through this book has been the idea that, although 'oppositional' in many respects, external summative testing and formative classroom assessment processes are the facts of life for most teachers. Teachers are involved with both. But rather than operate two apparently mutually exclusive or contradictory systems which is stressful and in some ways frustrating, it is helpful to acknowledge the different functions and strengths of each in order to maximise professional benefit. To restate this more directly as a question: are there ways in which expertise in summative testing processes can be harnessed to support or enhance formative classroom assessment processes? This is a question explicitly designed to test the notion whether assessment of and for learning are really mutually exclusive: they are different cultures (some would say representing different paradigms), but, we argue, from within the same universe.

We answer our question in the affirmative; although the purposes and assumptions of classroom assessment are quite different, experience of the world of external summative assessment can be useful. Even though the extraordinary growth in external testing in recent years has been accompanied by a tendency for schools also to increase the quantity of formal testing within schools, which in itself does nothing to enhance formative assessment skills, teachers in general have nevertheless become more proficient with what we might call the 'formal assessment technology' – in particular moderation procedures and the application of mark schemes. What this possibly implies is that teachers' judgements of standards are becoming more secure as they become more widely communicated and shared. This is a good thing in itself, supported not only by the awarding bodies through INSET but also by the government's main education quango, QCA. The preceding chapter explored how this experience can be deployed to support formative classroom assessment in the context of Teacher Assessment in one National Curriculum subject.

We do not ignore the strength of the potential negative curriculum backwash arising from the way National Curriculum tests and public examinations have been perceived. For example, there is some evidence to suggest that during the immediate aftermath of the National Curriculum, when all core and foundation subjects were to be externally tested as well as 'teacher assessed', many teachers resorted to imposing a formal testing regime of their own (see for example, Daugherty and Lambert 1994) in the belief that this was what was required. There may have been an assumption that teachers needed to introduce assessment systems and structures specifically to achieve the same levels as the external tests; that is to say, if the teacher-assessed levels were found to be out of line with the external tests they would be deemed 'false'. This thinking is of course wrong headed, just as we would be foolish to expect GCSE coursework (set and marked by the school) to reflect exactly the pupils' performance in the examination paper (set and marked by the examination board and written under examination conditions); if the mark distributions were the same, then why have coursework? We have coursework to increase the validity of the examination as a whole, by assessing things that the pencil and paper tests cannot do well. For this reason, it would be *expected* that coursework and examination scores would be different (Wood 1991; Lloyd 1999).

The fact that classroom and external assessments produce different 'results' is only a problem if the two need to be combined in some way to produce a single aggregate mark, one distorting, or even obliterating, the other. GCSE coursework should therefore not be confused with formative assessment, and neither, strictly speaking, should National Curriculum Teacher Assessment (though both may be used formatively as we discussed in Chapter 10). A key point to realise is that the moment classroom assessment is undertaken to serve summative purposes it loses much of its formative potential. This is a serious dilemma for teachers. The two assessment cultures can learn from each other in terms of techniques, but the identity of each needs to be respected.

Summary. What the general thrust of the above discussion suggests to us is that formative assessment should occupy a prominent place in day-to-day teaching and learning. This will involve informal assessment processes (see for example Figure 11.1) as well as occasionally more formal approaches such as some of those in Figure 9.1 on pp. 148–149)

As we have seen in Chapters 7–9, although most teachers know perfectly well what methods and techniques are available for teacher assessment, using them formatively has proved more difficult, requiring a leap of faith – or as we put it above, courage and ambition. We have argued that caution informing pedagogic and curriculum decisions is a form of negative backwash following the system–wide overemphasis on external summative testing. Testing in itself is not harmful. Indeed, as we discussed in Chapters 3–6, well–designed tests and examinations can be a force for welcome innovation and change. But too much of it, undertaken in the belief that doing more of it will itself raise standards, gets in the way of effective teaching. Formative assessment is embedded in the classroom as an essential component of effective teaching,

- Observing pupils at work, watching and listening to them
- Using a repertoire of whole class questioning strategies, including very open ones, in order to hear pupils' reasoning and speculations
- Setting tasks of various kinds including homework tasks which may be more open ended – writings, drawings, concept mapping and so on
- Organising set pieces in which pupils have to communicate their findings and conclusions – through games and simulations, debates, and other group exercises
- Occasional one-to-one subject-specific conversations with pupils about work and progress

Figure 11.1 Less formal methods used to gather assessment information

which is dedicated to building bridges and other support structures to help pupils direct their efforts and grow in their self-awareness and confidence as learners.

FOR FURTHER THINKING

1. Draw up two 'balance sheets' of pros and cons, one for formative classroom assessment and the other for external summative assessment, which summarise the main arguments about the relationship between assessment and raising standards in education.
2. Identify why, in the name of raising standards, recent and current policy has invested heavily in external summative assessment and relatively less so in formative classroom processes.
3. What in your view are the educational costs and benefits of a system heavily dependent on external summative assessment to maintain standards?

PROFESSIONAL PRACTICE AND 'EDUCATIONAL ASSESSMENT'

In our consideration of the National Curriculum, and what has become known as Teacher Assessment (TA), we noted a number of issues, not least the need for National Curriculum assessment to serve more than one purpose. What we presented in the previous section was in effect a particular case study, to show how despite conflicting demands being placed upon it, TA can be undertaken in an *educational* manner. However, this is possible only with conscious and deliberate effort, such is the powerful influence exerted by the external summative assessment regime which has now taken hold.

Macintosh (1986), even before the National Curriculum assessment system had been conceived, considered that direct assessments undertaken by teachers had fallen foul of 'the British obsession for preferring to do worse on those examinations which carry greater prestige rather than do better on those that are more useful' (cited in Stobart and Gipps 1997: 110). Our general point, illustrated by the case study, is *not* that external summative assessment is 'bad' and internal classroom assessment is 'good', because both are necessary for different reasons. The point is that the present balance struck between the two is unhealthy, and has shifted even more in recent years to negate the potential benefits of varied learning and assessment experiences. But our case study does, we believe, show how teachers can mitigate such effects.

We are now said to live in an information age in which all that is known is just a few seconds away from millions of computer screens. In education, one implication of this is that assessment *for* learning should take precedence over assessment *of* learning. The latter may still have a place (though we can debate the form and contents of such tests), but the former is likely to be more useful. As Stobart and Gipps (*ibid.*) suggest, the longer term implications of *this* include the notion that universal, external, objective assessment may begin to lose its credibility against the varied, flexible, subjective classroom-based assessments designed to support pupils 'learning how to learn'.

Some writers have argued that what is now needed is a reconceptualising of 'educational assessment' (Gipps 1994) as we have become more sophisticated, and ambitious, in our understanding of assessment issues. In one sense such a notion has informed this entire book, for we have chosen to divide the main contents into two more or less equal parts, dealing with external and classroom assessment respectively. Hopefully it is now clear why: the assumptions that underpin the practices discussed in Chapters 3–6 are quite different from those in Chapters 7–9. More specifically on this theme, Caroline Gipps has written that the 'most challenging task in developing a theory of educational assessment is that of *reconceptualising reliability*. Underlying this challenge is a shift in our world view' (*ibid.*: 167; our emphasis). We believe developing such a theory is very important, for without a better theorised 'assessment for learning', many teachers may find it difficult to move away from assuming that the dominant, and heavily theorised 'assessment of learning' is the 'right' one.

What is advocated here is something like a paradigm shift from a scientific, psychometric model of assessment to an educational model (as has been argued, in effect, throughout this book, but especially in Chapters 7–9). To quote Gipps at some length:

> Assessment is not an exact science, and we must stop presenting it as such. This is of course part of the post-modern condition – a suspension of belief in the absolute status of 'scientific' knowledge. The modernist stance suggests that it is possible to be a disinterested observer, while the post-modernist stance indicates that such detachment is not possible: we are social beings who construe the world according to our values and perceptions. The constructivist paradigm does not accept that reality is fixed and independent of the observer; rather reality is constructed by the observer, thus there are multiple constructions of reality. This paradigm would then deny the existence of such a thing as a 'true score'.
>
> (*ibid.*: 167)

In other words, in relation to developing National Curriculum Teacher Assessment, scores are heavily dependent on their context or circumstances, the marker and the motivation and perceptions of the pupils being assessed. This is not to adopt an extreme relativist position of 'anything goes'; rigour can be maintained by assessing against national criteria and the use of peer moderation (as was the case in assembling a standards portfolio described in Chapter 10). But it is to question the feasibility, or even desirability, of preserving traditionally rigid, objectivist assumptions of reliability. Relaxing on reliability enables us to raise the level of validity in the assessment process.

To put the point simply, an *educational* model of teacher assessment is unlikely to be achieved easily in a system in which summative assessment is allowed to dominate – whether this be external examinations or under an internal departmental regime dependent entirely on standardised end-of-module tests. Indeed, as we argued in Chapters 3–6, it is worth remembering that there is, in any case, a certain mythology about the reliability of external examinations. And with regard to validity, as Black summarises, it 'is very difficult to check and is widely neglected' by the awarding bodies (Black 1998: 54).

But can an alternative framework be identified? Such a framework would support the development of teacher assessment using constructivist principles like those Gipps outlines, and it would need to be robust enough that a school's reported assessments may 'mean something' beyond the confines of the particularity of a single school. Figure 11.2 summarises what Gipps considers to be 'alternative criteria of quality in educational assessment' (*ibid*.: 172). The thinking task, which follows, invites you to consider these criteria in detail – and in so doing provides you with an agenda for continued professional development in the field of assessment.

FOR FURTHER THINKING

Developing assessment policy and practice

1. Read the contents of Figure 11.2. Compare and contrast the terminology and definitions with those of validity and reliability introduced in Chapter 1.
2. In practical terms decide how your own assessment practice maximises 'curriculum fidelity' (rather like validity) and 'equity' (or fairness).
3. In practical terms decide how the department in which you work could ensure 'comparability', and 'dependability' in assessment (together these terms are like the traditional, but rather more rigid, notion of 'reliability').
4. Imagine a meeting with a number of colleagues from different schools which has been called to help 'moderate' (or standardise) end of key stage National Curriculum assessments. Decide how you would present a Level 5 portfolio of pupils' work to maximise its 'transferability'; what would you include in your 'context description'?

Teachers working towards developing their practice in a manner that accords to such criteria for educational assessment (Figure 11.2) will need to invest considerable mental effort to ensure an appropriate 'educational framework'. Assessments will need to be varied and flexible, yet comparable with those made of other pupils and those undertaken by other teachers. They need to be authentic, having maximum curriculum fidelity, and as a result teachers may need to resist the 'British obsession' (Macintosh 1986) with high status

Criterion	Comment
Curriculum fidelity	A similar idea to 'validity', but easier to specify as it relates strictly to the statutory National Curriculum. (e.g. have the teaching and assessment programmes included opportunities for pupils to engage in active and independent enquiry?)
Comparability	A similar, though less rigid, idea to 'reliability' achieved through: – consistency of approach by teachers – common understanding of assessment criteria The above can be maximised by: – training; using exemplars; moderation
Dependability and public credibility	A term which combines notions of validity and reliability (and recognises their relationship which is one of tension). Dependable assessment is that which **can demonstrate that steps have been taken** to: – maximise curriculum fidelity, and – optimise comparability Assessment that is dependable gains public credibility.
Transferability	Authentic assessment, having maximum curriculum fidelity, is unlikely to yield *scores* which are generalisable. On the other hand, it is possible to judge the 'transferability' of an assessment, if we have a detailed description of the context in which it took place. Those undertaking educational assessment should be prepared to offer such description.
Context description	This reflects the aim of good assessment to elicit quality performance from all pupils. This is achieved by providing multiple opportunities and various contexts and circumstances in which pupils can show what they can do.
Equity	Steps are taken to minimise sources of bias and unfairness.

Figure 11.2 An 'educational framework' for teacher assessment

Source: Gipps (1994)

scores and grades (apart from when it comes to selection and certification, which need not have a place until 18 years old – see next section). We therefore see the priority for the future to place much greater emphasis than hitherto on classroom assessment which is formative. The teacher's quest will not be to place an 'objective' label on each pupil but to understand how they are learning (or why they are not) in particular local contexts. This will be challenging, requiring subject specialists continually to keep under critical review notions of progress in their specialist areas, and thus drawing heavily both on their subject expertise and knowledge of pupils.

We believe that teachers have the right and a duty to work in these ways, notwithstanding the friction that exists between the professional desire to develop the skills of classroom assessment and demands of the wider external environment. But it is as well to be aware of the power of the external examination system to distort attempts by teachers to build their capacities in the classroom. The point has been made succinctly:

> the current focus on mass testing and reporting has placed too much emphasis on the purpose of evaluating schools, which in turn has narrowed assessment strategies.
>
> (Stobart and Gipps 1997: 111)

We shall finish this book with a brief concluding discussion on the mass examinations industry.

EDUCATIONAL ASSESSMENT: VALUE FOR MONEY?

There is now in England and Wales a large 'examinations industry' (see Chapters 3–6). This industry consumes a significant proportion of the annual education spend. As we have seen, it has enormous impact on schools, teachers and pupils. If it were reduced in size or cost, presumably more financial resources within education budgets (and from parents) could be directed to textbooks, ICT or the fabric of school buildings.

This may or may not be the case. What we wish to consider in this concluding section is the question of whether the system of external summative assessment that has now arisen provides value for money (see also Chapter 3). In 1994, Marks estimated that '[t]he total cost of national curriculum testing could . . . reach £1.7 billion' (Marks 1994: 300). The cost of GCSE examinations could, he seemed to argue, exceed even that figure if 'teacher time for the very time consuming activities of marking and supervision [of coursework]' (ibid.: 301) were fully costed. These are extraordinary figures which he used (they may be exaggerated) to argue the case for more cost effective 'simple pencil and paper tests' to replace what he considered to be 'more complex tests' represented by the early National Curriculum 'SATs' and GCSE. As he correctly states:

> The costs, especially the opportunity costs in terms of teacher time and teaching opportunities forgone, of different methods of assessment are very rarely considered in any systematic way.
>
> (*ibid.*: 299)

Unfortunately, though he raises some questions, and makes assumptions about assessment which urge a fuller consideration of cost, Marks does not fully develop the issues. In advocating simpler, cheaper and more 'cost effective' tests, he fails to take up any serious attempt to relate assessment to its *purpose*. As we have seen throughout this book, purpose is a key consideration. There are usually competing potential uses for assessment in education and if steps are not taken to specify the main purpose then difficulties can emerge, as when a single system is used to perform too many conflicting roles. As the chief executive of the QCA stated on the eve of the publication of the 1999 national test results for 7, 11 and 14 year olds:

> I am confident we have a high-quality product (the tests) that will serve its objectives well. . . . Longer term, given the huge level of investment, a more fundamental review should not be ducked. . . . Our national curriculum test system is ambitious and sophisticated. We must ensure that it inspires confidence and that the tests are fit for the purpose for which they are intended.
>
> (Tate 1999: 17)

The implication here is that the question of purpose of the national tests should be clarified, or at least kept under review. All pupils being tested at intervals throughout their schooling should not be treated as some kind of 'given'. Returning to the case for cheaper tests, careful consideration of what assessment is *for* opens up limitations in the position that Marks adopts. For example:

- It is not helpful, and is perhaps a little careless, to assume that teaching and assessment are different activities ('teaching opportunities forgone'). Chapters 7–9 of this book build a case that refutes such a position. Assessment undertaken primarily for formative purposes, for example, to help pupils understand themselves as learners, is organically part of teaching. Of course it is quite possible to meet teachers and educationists (and pupils) who would find such an approach to classroom processes hard to accept because their fundamental conceptions of teaching and learning do not allow it.
- It is perhaps an equally narrow interpretation of teaching and learning that concludes teacher time invested in marking and moderation is somehow unproductive and a 'cost' rather than an 'investment'. As we noted in Chapter 4, even 'assistant examiners' of GCSE or A-level undertake the arduous task partly because it informs their own teaching so effectively. There can be no doubt that acquiring a deeper understanding of how the processes and procedures of the external

examinations industry operate, and how pupils generally respond, can help teachers prepare pupils for the examination, and indeed persuade pupils of the necessity to utilise 'higher level' skills such as analysis and evaluation – skills which have value beyond the examination context.

- Finally, *do* 'national tests' have to be sat by every pupil? Tate defended the sophisticated criteria-based national tests on the grounds that they tell us something about *national standards*, and successive governments have also attached great store to this function. But if that is the main function of the tests, then decades of experience in the social sciences show that *sampling* the population would be far more cost effective than having the whole population undertake the tests. Politicians often use sample polls based upon a tiny proportion of the voting population to tell them reliably about public opinion: a pupil sample could be tested using all manner of 'complex tests' to provide reliable evidence about standards being achieved nationally – at a fraction of the cost of the present examinations industry.

We made a similar point in Chapter 6, that institution-wide, aggregate 'value added' measures, assembled for managerial or accountability reasons, may distort the benefit of value-added approaches to assessing achievement and potential for the individual pupil.

What such an approach would not allow for, of course, is the production of national league tables. School league tables may or may not serve an important function, for example placing schools more overtly in competition with each other or informing parental choice, but such developments can be kept apart from the quite different function of monitoring national standards. It is a good question to ask exactly what is the main function of school league tables, and can they be justified on educational grounds?

On the future of the public examinations infrastructure, Tate, the former chief executive of the QCA, recently wrote:

> There is no other country in the developed world which has so many exams or spends such a high proportion of its education budget on this activity. Nor do other countries have a system with such high stakes – politically and educationally. There are plenty of other ways in which schools can be held accountable.
>
> While the government will point to improving results as evidence of rising standards and as a justification for more of the same, the time has come to consider whether the costs outweigh the benefits, especially for the GCSE.
>
> GCSE is of doubtful value to those at the top end of the academic ability spectrum. . . . Nor is the exam serving well those at the other end of the ability range, who are branded as failures if they have not achieved C grades by the age of 16. . . .
>
> Schools have long argued that internal assessment is more effective and the external moderation would preserve national standards. Bright

students could begin advanced level courses a year earlier and slower learners could complete a full set of GCSE-standard modules by 17 or 18.

Far from removing a major academic motivator at the end of key stage 4, our proposals would increase motivation for young people at all levels of ability.

(Tate 1999: 19)

This book has maintained that the present balance between external and classroom assessment in Britain is unhealthy. Moves to undermine the grip of the external examinations industry would potentially yield great benefits. But such moves are unlikely to happen until fundamental reconsideration of a number of basic assumptions is undertaken.

The present examinations system is expensive – but 'saving money' is not the best platform on which to base any reform of the status quo. Classroom assessment, especially that which benefits from regular, professional, external moderation is itself expensive, because teachers need time to prepare and to meet.

Education systems less dependent upon external examinations (for example, Germany) have other, equally important contrasting features. Teachers are contracted to serve substantially less 'contact time' and consequently have more time and space in which to carry out internal assessments.

Teachers need to accept, indeed embrace, the need to be publicly accountable. It is possible that the external examinations industry in England and Wales has been able to achieve such a dominant position because for some reason teachers have not been 'trusted' by the public nor by politicians. Such a hypothesis is of course controversial, but deserves consideration: what do teachers have to do to regain that part of their public functions at present subcontracted to the examinations industry?

FOR FURTHER THINKING

Discuss with colleagues the case for and the case against retaining the GCSE as a national public examination for 16 year olds.

FOR FURTHER READING

C. Gipps (1994) *Beyond Testing: Towards a Theory of Educational Assessment*. This is a wide ranging book covering key issues such as validity, reliability and the ethics of assessment. It also introduces the 'criteria' for educational assessment referred to in this chapter.

A. Davis (1999) *Educational Assessment: a Critique of Current Policy*. This monograph provides a highly readable and provocative philosophical critique of assessment policy in England and Wales at the turn of the century. It highlights discussion on the values placed on what educational assessment is able to achieve.

References

Aaronovitch, D. (1999) 'We need old Gradgrind back in our schools – at least for now', *The Independent* 20 August.

Aldrich, R. (1996) *Education for the Nation*, London: Cassell.

Aldrich, R. and White, J. (1998) *The National Curriculum beyond 2000: the QCA and the Aims of Education*, London: Institute of Education, University of London.

Anthony, V. (1999) 'Why exams are failing' in *The Times* 1 December: 45.

Anthony, V. and Dunford, J. (1999) 'Loosen the straitjacket of exams', in *The Times Educational Supplement*, 10 September: 19.

AQA (1999) *General Certificate of Education Business Studies Specification 2001/2*, Guildford: Assessment and Qualifications Alliance.

Assessment Reform Group (1999) *Assessment for Learning. Beyond the Black Box*, Cambridge: University of Cambridge School of Education.

Barnes, D., Johnson, G., Jordan, S., Layton, D., Medway, P. and Yeomans, D. (1987) *Learning Styles in TVEI 14–16: Evaluation Report No 3*, MSC, Leeds University.

Biggs, J. (1998) 'Assessment and classroom learning: the role of summative assessment', in *Assessment in Education* 5(1): 103–110.

Bishop, J. H. (1995) 'Incentives to study and the organisation of secondary instruction', in W. E. Becker and W. J. Baumol (eds), *Assessing Educational Practices: the Contribution of Economics*, Boston: MIT Press.

Black, P. (1993) 'The shifting scenery of the National Curriculum' in P. O'Hear and J. White (eds), *Assessing the National Curriculum*, London: Paul Chapman Publishing.

Black, P. (1996) 'Revolutionary tales – from the frontiers of assessment', in *Assessment in Education* 3(1).

Black, P. (1998) *Testing: Friend or Foe? Theory and Practice of Assessment and Testing*, London: Falmer Press.

Black, P. and Atkin, J. (1996) *Changing the Subject: Innovations in Science, Mathematics and Technology Education*, London: Routledge for the OECD.

Black, P. and Wiliam, D. (1998a) 'Assessment and classroom learning', in *Assessment in Education* 5(1): 7–74.

Black, P. and Wiliam, D. (1998b) *Inside the Black Box*, University of London: Department of Education, Kings College.

Brant, J., Lines, D. and Unwin, L. (2000) 'Eight out of ten isn't good enough' in *Teacher Development: an International Journal of Teachers' Professional Development* 3(3).

Broadfoot, P. (1987) *Introducing Profiling: a Practical Manual*, London: Macmillan.

Broadfoot, P. (1996) *Education, Assessment and Society: a Sociological Analysis*, Buckingham: Open University Press.

Bruner, J. (1960) *The Process of Education*, Cambridge MA: Harvard University Press.

Butt, G., Lambert, D. and Telfer, S. (1995) *Assessment Works*, Sheffield: Geographical Association.

Capel, S., Leask, M. and Turner, T. (1999) *Learning to Teach in the Secondary School*, Second edition, London: Routledge.

Capey, J. (1995) *GNVQ Assessment Review*, London: NCVQ.

Centre for Curriculum and Assessment Studies, University of Bristol and the International Centre for Research on Assessment, University of London, (1995) *Evaluation of the Use of Set Assignments in GNVQ*, Report prepared for the MSC. London: Institute of Education.

Chase, C. (1986) 'Essay test scoring: interaction of relevant variables', in *Journal of Educational Measurement* 23: 33–42.

Chitty, C. (1996) *Generating a National Curriculum. Block 4: Organising and Control of Schooling*, Milton Keynes: The Open University.

Cohen, M. (1998) 'A habit of healthy idleness: boys' underachievement in historical perspective', in D. Epstein, J. Elwood, V. Hey and J. Maw (eds), *Failing Boys? Issues in Gender and Achievement*, pp. 19–34, Buckingham: Open University Press.

Crooks, T. (1988) 'The impact of classroom evaluation practices on students', in *Review of Educational Research*, 58(4): 438–481.

Daugherty, R. (1995) *National Curriculum Assessment: a Review of Policy 1987–1994* London: Falmer.

Daugherty, R. and Lambert, D. (1994) 'Teacher assessment and geography in the National Curriculum', in *Geography* 79(4): 339–349.

Davies, N. (1999a) 'Schools in crisis. Part 1' in the *Guardian* 14 September: 1 and 4–5.

Davies, N. (1999b) 'Schools in crisis. Part 2' in the *Guardian* 15 September: 1 and 4–5.

Davies, N. (1999c) 'Schools in crisis. Part 3' in the *Guardian* 16 September: 1 and 4–5.

Davis, A. (1998) *The Limits of Educational Assessment,* Oxford: Blackwell Publishers.

Davis, A. (1999) *Educational Assessment: a Critique of Current Policy,* Philosophy of Education Society of Great Britain.

de Luca, C. (1994) *The Impact of Examination Systems on Curriculum Development: an International Study*, United Nations Educational, Scientific and Cultural Organization.

Dearing, R. (1993) *The National Curriculum and its Assessment: Interim Report*, London: SCAA.

Dearing, R. (1996) *Review of Qualifications for 16–19 Year Olds*, London: SCAA.

DES (1988) *Advancing A-Levels, Report of the Committee Chaired by Professor Higginson*, London: HMSO.

DES (1991) *Geography in the National Curriculum*, London: HMSO.

DES/WO (1988) *National Curriculum Task Group on Assessment and Testing – a Report* London: DES.

DfEE (1997) *Qualifying for Success. A Consultative Paper on the Future of Post-16 Qualifications*, London: DfEE Publications.

DfEE (1998) *Teaching: High Status, High Standards. Requirements for Courses of Initial Teacher Training*, Department for Education and Employment Circular 4/98, London: DfEE Publications.

Dockrell, B. (1995a) 'Approaches to educational assessment', in C. Desforges (ed.), *An Introduction to Teaching: Psychological Perspectives*, pp. 291–306 Oxford: Blackwell.

Dockrell, B. (1995b) 'Assessment teaching and learning', in C. Desforges (ed.), *An Introduction to Teaching: Psychological Perspectives* pp. 307–324, Oxford: Blackwell.

DOE (1972) *Training for the Future*, London: HMSO.

Dowgill, P. (1996) 'Pupils' conceptions of geography and learning geography', unpublished PhD thesis, University of London Institute of Education.

Dwyer, C. (1994) *Development of the Knowledge Base for the Praxis 111: Classroom Performance Assessments Assessment Criteria,* Princeton, NJ: Education Testing Service.

Dwyer, C. (1998) 'Assessment and classroom learning: theory and practice', in *Assessment in Education* 5(1): 131–137.

Eckstein, M. A. and Noah, H. J. (1993) *Secondary School Examinations: International Perspectives on Policies and Practice,* New Haven: Yale University Press.

Evans, B. and Waites, B. (1981) *IQ and Mental Testing: An Unnatural Science and its Social History,* London: MacMillan.

FEDA, Institute of Education and the Nuffield Foundation (1997) *GNVQs 1993–7. A National Survey Report,* London: Further Education Development Agency.

Finegold, D., Keep, E., Miliband, D., Raffe, D., Spours, K. and Young, M. (1990) *A British Baccalaureate: Overcoming Divisions between Education and Training,* London: Institute for Public Policy Research.

Frith, D. and Macintosh, H. (1984) *A Teacher's Guide to Assessment,* Cheltenham: Stanley Thorne.

Galton, M. and Williamson, J. (1992) *Group Work in the Primary Classroom,* London: Routledge.

Gardner, H. (1983) *Frames of Mind: The Theory of Multiple Intelligences,* New York: Basic Books.

Gardner, H. (1994) 'The theory of multiple intelligences', in B. Moon and A. Shelton Mayes (eds), *Teaching and Learning in the Secondary School,* Milton Keynes: Open University Press.

Geddes, B. (1995) *The Development of Accountancy Education, Training and Research in England: A Study of the Relationship between Professional Education and Training, Academic Education and Research, and Professional Practice in English Chartered Accountancy,* unpublished PhD. thesis, University of Manchester.

Gibbs, G., Habeshaw, S. and Habeshaw, T. (1988) *Interesting Ways to Assess Your Students,* Bristol: Technical and Educational Services Limited.

Gipps, C. (1986) 'GCSE: some background' in *The GCSE: An Uncommon Examination,* Bedford Way Papers, No 29, University of London Institute of Education.

Gipps, C. (1993) 'The structure for assessment and recording', in P. O'Hear and J. White (eds), *Assessing the National Curriculum,* London: Paul Chapman Publishing.

Gipps, C. (1994) *Beyond Testing: Towards a Theory of Educational Assessment,* Brighton: Falmer Press.

Gipps, C., Brown, M., McCallum, B. and McAllister, S. (1995) *Institution or Evidence?,* Buckingham: Open University Press.

Gipps, C. and Murphy, P. (1994) *A Fair Test? Assessment, Achievement and Equity,* Buckingham: Open University Press.

Gipps, C. and Wood, R. (1981) 'The testing of reading in LEAs. The Bullock Report 7 years on', in *Educational Studies* 7(2).

Goldstein, H. (1993) 'Assessment and accountability' in *Parliamentary Brief* 2 (3), October.

Good, F. and Cresswell, M. (1988) *Grading the GCSE,* London: SEC.

Graham, D. with Tytler, D. (1993) *A Lesson for Us All,* London: Routledge.

Green, A., Wolf, A. and Leney, T. (1999) *Convergence and Divergence in European Education and Training Systems,* London: Bedford Way Papers Institute of Education, University of London.

Guskey, T. (ed.) (1994) *High Stakes Performance Assessment: Perspectives on Kentucky's Educational Reform,* Thousand Oaks, CA, Corwin Press and London, Sage.

Hanson, F. A. (1993) *Testing, Testing: Social Consequences of the Examined Life*, Berkeley and Los Angeles: University of California Press.

Hargreaves, D. (1984) *Improving Secondary Schools: Report of the Committee on the Curriculum and Organisation of Secondary Schools*, London: ILEA.

Harlen, W. and James, M. (1997) 'Assessment and learning: differences and relationships between formative and summative assessment', in *Assessment in Education* 4(3): 365–380.

Harlen, W., Malcolm, H. and Byrne, M. (1995) *Assessment and National Testing in Primary Schools*, Edinburgh: SCRE Research Project.

Hitchcock, G. (1986) *Profiles and Profiling: a Practical Introduction*, Harlow: Longman.

Hodgson, A. and Spours, K. (1997a) 'Modularization and the 14–19 qualifications system' in A. Hodgson and K. Spours (eds) *Dearing and Beyond. 14–19 Qualifications, Frameworks and Systems*, London: Kogan Page.

Hodgson, A. and Spours, K. (1997b) 'From the 1991 White Paper to the Dearing Report: a conceptual and historical framework for the 1990s', in A. Hodgson and K. Spours (eds), *Dearing and Beyond. 14–19 Qualifications, Frameworks and Systems*, London: Kogan Page.

Hodkinson, P. and Mattinson, K. (1994) 'A bridge too far? The problems facing GNVQ', in *The Curriculum Journal* 5(3).

Honey, P. and Mumford, A. (1992) *The Manual of Learning Styles*, Maidenhead: Peter Honey.

Hopkins, J., Butt, G. and Telfer, S. (2000) *Assessment in Practice*, Sheffield: GA.

Hoskin, K. and Geddes, B. (1997) (eds) *ICAEW Pass Rates Research*, London: ICAEW.

Hughes, S. and Fisher-Hoch, H. (1997) *Valid and Invalid Sources of Difficulty in Maths Exam Questions*, UCLES, Paper Presented at IAEA.

Hurd, S., Coates, G. and Anderton, A. (1997) *The GCE Examining System: A Quasi Market Analysis*, Division of Economics Working Paper 97.9 Staffordshire University.

International Studies in Educational Achievement (1988) *The IEA Study of Written Composition I: The International Writing Tasks and Scoring Scales*, T. Gorman, A. Purves and R. Degenhart (eds), Oxford: Pergamon Press.

James, M. (1998) *Using Assessment for School Improvement*, Oxford: Heinemann.

Joyce, B. and Weil, M. (1986) *Models of Teaching* (3rd edition), MA: Allyn and Bacon.

Kolb, D. (1985) *Learning Style Inventory*, Boston: McBer and Co.

Kulik, J.A. and Kulik, C. (1989) Meta-analysis in Education, in *International Journal of Educational Research*, 13: 221–340.

Lambert, D. (1990) *Geography Assessment*, Cambridge: Cambridge University Press.

Lambert, D. (1991) *Geography Assessment: Supplementary Pack*, Cambridge: Cambridge University Press.

Lambert, D. (1996) 'Assessing pupils' attainments and supporting learning', in Kent *et al.* (eds), *Geography in Education* pp. 260–287, CUP.

Lambert, D. (1999) 'Assessment and the Improvement of Pupils' Work', in S. Capel, M. Leask and T. Turner (eds), *Learning to Teach in the Secondary School*, Second edition, London: Routledge.

Lambert, D. and Balderstone, D. (1999) 'Sunday evening at the kitchen table', in *Teaching Geography* 24(2): 92–95.

Lambert, D. and Daugherty, R. (1993) Teacher assessment: a snapshot of practice, *Teaching Geography* 18(3).

Lawson, N. (1992) *View from No. 11: Memoirs of a Tory Radical*, London: Bantam.

Lawton, D. (1994) *The Tory Mind on Education 1979–94*, London: The Falmer Press.

Lawton, D. (1996) *Beyond the National Curriculum: Teacher Professionalism and Empowerment*, London: Hodder and Stoughton.

Le Grand, J. (1991) 'Quasi-markets and social policy', in *Economic Journal* 101(3): 1256–1267.

Leask, M. (1999) 'Teaching styles', in S. Capel, M. Leask and T. Turner (eds), *Learning to Teach in the Secondary School*, Second edition, pp. 266–275, London: Routledge.

Leat, D. (1998) *Thinking Through Geography*, Cambridge: Chris Kington Publishers.

Lines, D. (1999) *Values and the curriculum: Economics and business education at different stages in the develpment of young people.* Unpublished PhD thesis, London: ILUE.

Lloyd, J. (1999) *How Exams Really Work,* London: Cassell.

Macintosh, H. (1986) 'Sacred cows of coursework', in C. Gipps (ed.), *The GCSE : an Uncommon Exam*, Bedford Way Papers, No. 29, University of London Institute of Education.

Madaus, G. (1988) 'The influence of testing on the curriculum', in L. Tanner (ed.), *Critical Issues in the Curriculum, 87th Yearbook of NSSE Part 1*, pp. 88–121, Chicago, Il: University of Chicago Press.

Marks, J. (1994) 'Methods of assessment: value for money', in B. Moon and A. Shelton Mayes (eds), *Teaching and Learning in the Secondary School*, London: Routledge/OU.

McLung, M. S. (1978) 'Are competency testing programs fair? Legal?', in *Proceedings of the National Conference on Minimum Competency Testing*, Portland, Or: Clearing House for Applied Performance Testing.

Messick, S. (1989) 'Validity', in R. Linn (ed.), *Educational Measurement*, Washington DC: Oryx and the American Council on Education.

Moore, A. (1999) *Teaching Multicultured Students: culturism and anti-culturism in school classrooms*, London: Falmer.

Moore, A. (2000) *Teaching and Learning: Pedagogy, Curriculum and Culture*, London: Routledge.

Mosston, M. and Ashworth, S. (1994) *Teaching Physical Education* (4th Edition), Colombus, OH: Merrill Publishing.

Murphy, P. (1990) 'TGAT: a conflict of purpose', in T. Horton (ed.), *Assessment Debates*, Milton Keynes: Open University.

NCE (1993) *Learning to Succeed: a Radical Look at Education Today and a Strategy for the Future, Report of the National Commission on Education*, London: Heinemann.

NCVQ (1993) *GNVQ Mandatory Units for Business*, London: National Council for Vocational Qualifications.

NFA (1992) *Criteria for Evaluation of Student Assessment Systems, Education Measurement: Issues and Practice*, Spring, Washington DC: National Forum on Assessment.

Nuttall, D. L. (1984) 'Doomsday or a new dawn? The prospects of a common system of examination at 16+', in P. M. Broadfoot (ed.), *Selection, Certification and Control*, Basingstoke: Falmer.

Nuttall, D. (1989) 'National assessment: will reality match aspirations?', paper delivered to the conference *Testing Times*, Macmillan Education, 8 March.

Perrenoud, P. (1991) 'Towards a pragmatic approach to formative evaluation', in P. Weston (ed.), *Assessment of Pupils' Achievement: Motivation and School Success*, Amsterdam: Swets and Zeitlinger, pp. 79-101.

Pollard, A., Broadfoot, P., Groll, P., Osborne, M. and Abbot, D. (1994) *Changing English Primary Schools? The Impact of the Educational Reform Act at Key Stage One*, London: Cassell.

Index